THE
COMPLETE IDIOT'S GUIDE® TO

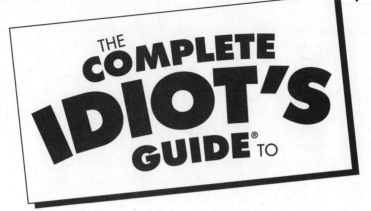

Career Advancement

by Marc Dorio

ALPHA

A member of Penguin Group (USA) Inc.

To my beautiful wife, Pat, whose love and support is beyond infinite.

ALPHA BOOKS

Published by the Penguin Group

Penguin Group (USA) Inc., 375 Hudson Street, New York, New York 10014, USA

Penguin Group (Canada), 90 Eglinton Avenue East, Suite 700, Toronto, Ontario M4P 2Y3, Canada (a division of Pearson Penguin Canada Inc.)

Penguin Books Ltd., 80 Strand, London WC2R 0RL, England

Penguin Ireland, 25 St. Stephen's Green, Dublin 2, Ireland (a division of Penguin Books Ltd.)

Penguin Group (Australia), 250 Camberwell Road, Camberwell, Victoria 3124, Australia (a division of Pearson Australia Group Pty. Ltd.)

Penguin Books India Pvt. Ltd., 11 Community Centre, Panchsheel Park, New Delhi—110 017, India

Penguin Group (NZ), 67 Apollo Drive, Rosedale, North Shore, Auckland 1311, New Zealand (a division of Pearson New Zealand Ltd.)

Penguin Books (South Africa) (Pty.) Ltd., 24 Sturdee Avenue, Rosebank, Johannesburg 2196, South Africa

Penguin Books Ltd., Registered Offices: 80 Strand, London WC2R 0RL, England

International Standard Book Number: 978-1-59257-832-0
Library of Congress Catalog Card Number: 2008931268

11 10 09   8 7 6 5 4 3 2 1

Interpretation of the printing code: The rightmost number of the first series of numbers is the year of the book's printing; the rightmost number of the second series of numbers is the number of the book's printing. For example, a printing code of 09-1 shows that the first printing occurred in 2009.

Printed in the United States of America

Note: This publication contains the opinions and ideas of its author. It is intended to provide helpful and informative material on the subject matter covered. It is sold with the understanding that the author and publisher are not engaged in rendering professional services in the book. If the reader requires personal assistance or advice, a competent professional should be consulted.

The author and publisher specifically disclaim any responsibility for any liability, loss, or risk, personal or otherwise, which is incurred as a consequence, directly or indirectly, of the use and application of any of the contents of this book.

Most Alpha books are available at special quantity discounts for bulk purchases for sales promotions, premiums, fundraising, or educational use. Special books, or book excerpts, can also be created to fit specific needs.

For details, write: Special Markets, Alpha Books, 375 Hudson Street, New York, NY 10014.

Publisher: *Marie Butler-Knight*
Editorial Director: *Mike Sanders*
Senior Managing Editor: *Billy Fields*
Executive Editor: *Randy Ladenheim-Gil*
Senior Development Editor: *Phil Kitchel*
Production Editor: *Megan Douglass*
Copy Editor: *Michael Dietsch*

Cartoonist: *Shannon Wheeler*
Cover Designer: *Bill Thomas*
Book Designer: *Trina Wurst*
Indexer: *Celia McCoy*
Layout: *Chad Dressler*
Proofreader: *Mary Hunt*

Contents at a Glance

Contents

Foreword

If there is any one attribute that is common among us, no matter what job we have, it is that we never learn about the topic of work the way we learn about English, math, history, or even something as mundane as making a bookshelf in woodshop. Take a moment to think about it. Did you have a class on work ethic, how to be a successful employee, or how work and away-from-work life should balance? How about making the decision to look for a job, how to understand your work environment, or plan your work future? Unless you are much different than the vast majority of people I have had the opportunity to work with over my career in human resources, your answer will be, no.

Over the years, in many of the workshops I've conducted, I've asked people to take a moment to reflect upon the possible differences between their in-work and away-from-work life, including attitudes, approaches, and general behavior, and time. When they calculate the hours they spend either at work or preparing for work, compared to total number of hours they are awake over the course of a week, they are amazed. Work consumes our time and life. Yet we rarely receive the type of education and ongoing information we need to make the good decisions that guide us through the ins and outs of work, until it's too late.

You may have seen the television commercial that depicts a carefree person driving a car who is suddenly the victim of a crash. A resonant voice in the background tells viewers that this is not the time to begin thinking about car insurance coverage. Not unlike career planning, the absolute worst time to think about a career is at the "point of impact," when things are bad, and we are least able to sort through the emotions and piles of information about what to do next. The age of the "gold watch" is over, the labor market is constantly shifting, and our skills to manage through it all are sorely lacking.

For those brave enough to spend time trying to manage certain aspects of their careers, the likelihood is they will search for information using the Internet. Go onto your favorite search engine and insert the phrase, "how to manage your career," and be prepared to wade through 1.5 million responses.

In this book, Marc Dorio skillfully translates into words his vast experience coaching and advising people who work at all organizational levels. He logically and thoughtfully lays out both the concepts and techniques needed to gain greater insight and control of your career. The simple rules, wisdom, and self-assessments serve as the basic career planning education we all so desperately need, but rarely receive. This book will undoubtedly become a trusted resource and constant reference guide as you take the first, and ongoing steps to manage your career and that all-consuming part of life we nonchalantly refer to as work.

David L. Waldman
Vice President, Human Resources and Administration
Robert Wood Johnson Foundation
Princeton, NJ

Introduction

Every book is written with a specific point of view; this book is no exception. There are a number of really good books in print about planning and managing a career. Most of them, however, view career planning from the narrow perspective of serial job changes. That is, you reach a point where you know you can and should do better, so you find another job with another company that offers the opportunity you seek and move on.

This approach is pretty much the result of the end of the notion of working for one company for life. However, when this idea was in its prime, companies hadn't begun to diversify very widely as they have more recently. Conglomerates hadn't become what they are today. And the job and career opportunities now offered by many of them didn't exist.

Today, the company you work for could be one of many owned by an enlightened conglomerate. Each may be operated separately, but they all exist to provide value to each other and to the central company. The most progressive of them cooperate willingly with each other to provide you with the advancement opportunities that you used to have to get by quitting one company and moving to another. Today it's possible to move to another company and stay within a general corporate framework. It took a while before many companies recognized this, but when they looked at the cost of replacing good talent, it finally struck home. A whack on the side of the head often provides the insight unavailable from even the brightest managers.

This means that moving up doesn't necessarily mean moving out. Now, there are other options to consider. You can often transfer to another company or division within the conglomerate family where the opportunity you want exists. You can get the next-rung job or you can move to a company where your career aspirations may not be blocked as they might be at present. In other words, you have far more opportunities to enhance your career directly or indirectly by moving over to another family company where your path may not be blocked.

Needless to say, if a move up or a move over isn't possible, you can still move out to a different company. I have written this book from the perspective of these three paths: up, over, or out. The suggestions and plans I include are appropriate whichever alternative you choose. It's the broadening of perspective that makes this book different from all the others.

This is not a job-search book, although a lot of what is included will definitely help you in your job search. There are excellent books on job-search methods and techniques—they pick up where this book leaves off. This book will help you lay the groundwork and create your plan. Once you have read it and understand the concepts, you will be in a far better position to begin your actual search.

I want to stress up front that I am not giving you a rigid career plan to follow. I am giving you all the tools you need and that guidance to use them. Your career plan will never be the same as someone else's, even someone in your field. This book, then, is about career tactics and strategies.

From your perspective, a strategy is your big picture. To use a term currently in vogue, your strategy should result in your personal "brand," the picture you want your present employer to see if you are looking to move up or over, or for another employer to see when considering you for possible employment. It's not enough to just do great things, you have to let others know what you have done and what you can do. There's a really a fine line here between a respected personal brand and being an overbearing braggart. I address this issue throughout the book.

Tactics are the specific activities you perform in service of your strategy. If your strategy is to gain a reputation as the marketing manager companies might want to hire, a typical tactic might be to write articles for the magazines prospective employers might read. I discuss tactics in detail throughout the book, so I won't belabor the point here.

This book is organized serially. If you are starting from scratch, begin with Chapter 1 and read each chapter in turn and your plan should unfold as you go along. On the other hand, if you already have a career plan and it has been less valuable than you thought it might, just dip into the chapters that you feel will help you fill in the blanks.

I have avoided the use of a lot of checklists. They are included where I feel they will be of immediate practical value, but I have avoided using them widely simply because they tend to paint too rigid a picture of career activity. I don't want you to think of yourself in terms of some rating scale. I want you to picture yourself in more flexible terms. If you were a "9" yesterday on some rating scale, you may be a "7" today. There is an implied precision to numbers, but there is also a tyranny in their use. I want you to picture yourself as an ever evolving person.

Lastly, I want you to understand that career planning is not something you do once and then follow one path to retirement. Career planning requires regular maintenance. Like the engine in your car, you have to change the spark plugs once in a while. Throughout the chapters ahead, I alert you to when it's time for a check-up and what to do when you discover that your plugs may not be firing as they should.

Think of this book as your career toolbox. You may need every tool the first time you look under the hood. But after that you pick and choose the tools you need as they are needed.

Don't forget that some tools need to be sharpened occasionally!

def•i•ni•tion

Here you'll find explanations of more specialized jargon you might not be familiar with.

Right Move

These boxes give you some quick tips to speed your career planning.

Case in Point

Quotes and anecdotes from people who've been there.

Career News

Here's where I have posted current information on what's happening in the world of work.

Career Alert

In these boxes you'll be alerted to potential problems and given tips on how to deal with them.

Acknowledgments

I would like to acknowledge my friend and colleague Bert Holtje, who conceived the idea for this book, and my many clients who daily so generously share their career journeys with me.

Trademarks

All terms mentioned in this book that are known to be or are suspected of being trademarks or service marks have been appropriately capitalized. Alpha Books and Penguin Group (USA) Inc. cannot attest to the accuracy of this information. Use of a term in this book should not be regarded as affecting the validity of any trademark or service mark.

Part 1

Why Make a Move and Why Make It Now?

There are many reasons to consider changing jobs, but unless your decision is based on sound career planning, you could make mistakes. The chapters in this part introduce you to the up, over, or out approach to career planning, and each chapter focuses on proven career-planning techniques. You have more options than you might imagine, and the chapters in this part outline them.

Of special interest to those who are concerned about the employment environment, there are techniques for assessing the signals an employer might be sending and how they relate to individual career planning. Further, there are techniques described for evaluating a personal situation as it relates to general employment conditions. You may be doing a great job, but when certain conditions are in place, your career may not be as stable as you thought it was. Learn why and what you can do to correct the situation.

How to Test Your Readiness

In This Chapter

- ◆ Set up your short- and long-term career plans

- ◆ Pay attention to your inner career coach's voice

- ◆ Answer five questions that will put you on the right track right away

- ◆ Your choice: move up, over, or out

People change jobs for a variety of reasons. Some do it to advance their careers and others are motivated by the prospect of making more money. It's common for people to move on when they are bored, unchallenged, and even when they find that they simply can't get along with some co-workers. Being passed over for promotion, feeling overworked, or knowing that people in other companies are being paid more to do the same work are also reasons I hear regularly. These are all valid reasons to move on. But in some cases the stated reasons often mask other, *un*stated reasons. One of my goals in writing this book is to help you discover the real reasons why you may want to move on, why a move may be necessary, and why standing pat may be the best approach after all.

This book is more about self-discovery than anything else. But to discover who you are and what you want from life and work, you need to understand where you stand right now. So as we go from chapter to chapter together, you will be painting a picture of yourself against a background of your life as it is now and as you would like it to be. That's what career management is all about, and it's a lifelong process.

Two-and-a-Half Cheers for Career Planning

Traditionally, career planning implies that you have significant control over your working life. I hope that this doesn't come as a shock, but you do … and you don't. Without any planning at all, you are totally at the whim of others and the conditions that impact all of us. With some planning, on the other hand, you gain a significant measure of control over your career. The plain truth is that you have considerable control over your career in the short term, but less control over it in the long term. Does this mean that you should forget long-term planning? Absolutely not. You achieve your long-term goals by adjusting the plans you make to achieve your short-term career steps.

Case in Point

A client of mine had set her long-term sights on a senior-level marketing management job in a high-tech field. She had developed a careful plan and achieved her early goals when the bottom fell out of the field she had chosen. She wasn't out of work when she and I first met, but she knew she might be soon. "What should I do?" she asked.

My advice was that she keep her long-term goals clearly in mind, but investigate other means of reaching them, given the downturn in her field. Her solution was to find a job with a conglomerate where she could use her sales skills in a different field. She did. When the slump in her chosen field subsided a few years later, her employer transferred her to a company it owned in the field where she had been and wanted to return to. In short, an end-run around the problem kept her on course. It takes careful planning, but that's half the fun of life and work—isn't it?

Looking Behind the Curtain

In the film classic, *The Wizard of Oz*, Dorothy is warned not to look behind the curtain that hides the source of a booming and ominous voice. She does, of course, and sees that the voice belongs to someone much different. Your first step is to look behind your own curtain. You have been telling yourself lots of things as you moved along your career path. But are you really being honest with yourself? Seeing life through tinted glasses is not a personality fault. We all do it. However, when we discover that we have been generating booming voices that turn out to be less threatening, life gets real again. So let's get real.

I'm not going to answer the five questions that follow. Only you can do that, and your first assignment is to commit these questions to memory and answer them throughout your reading of this book. If it helps, copy them and read them to yourself as you start each new chapter.

Warning: By the time you finish reading this book you may answer some or even all of them quite differently than you do right now. This is a good sign! Life isn't cut in stone and neither are you. Now, the questions!

♦ **What bugs you most about the state of your career?** Try to answer this question both in terms of what's actually happening to you and how that varies from what you wish was really happening.

♦ **When you talk about your career, how do you sound to others?** This kind of self-analysis isn't easy. You may find it easier to ask a trusted friend for his or her comments on how you sound. You're looking for words like enthusiastic, disappointed, discouraged, excited. Forget any deep analysis, just look for the high and low markers that punctuate your comments.

♦ **What do you see yourself doing a year from now? Five years from now?** Answer in terms of both your hopes and actual plans.

♦ **How do you rate your career satisfaction so far?** The easiest way to do this is by creating a scale and giving your level a number. Use a range that has an actual midpoint. This means picking an odd-numbered scale. I'd suggest 1 to 9, with one being "awful," five being "okay," and 9 being "great." Don't be surprised as the number you select now changes from chapter to chapter. You will be learning a lot that will encourage you to look at your career from a different perspective.

♦ **What is preventing you from making a career move right now?** Include the obvious, such as no jobs open in your field, and the not-so-obvious, such as that it scares the daylights out of you to take a chance on a move. Be honest. There are no right or wrong answers, only answers that will help you plan and manage your career better and more efficiently.

I suggest that you write your answers to these questions and store them somewhere. Keep the answers simple and direct and date each entry. When you finish reading this book you should be able to chart your progress in career awareness simply by reading your answers sequentially. A few of my clients have logged their answers in their computers, others on paper notebooks. However you do it, just do it!

Were there any surprises? Keep in mind that your answers represent where you stand now, what you are presently feeling, and how you feel about your career future. In short, these answers are your baseline, from which you can not only judge what you will learn in the pages ahead, but how you can judge the changes you might make and plan in your life's work.

Unless you're a lot different from most people, you probably discovered some interesting things about yourself. In answer to the question about being bugged, one person said, "I discovered that nothing serious was bugging me about my career. It was me actually bugging myself that was the problem." This was quite an insight and helped the person considerably by forcing her to focus on external events rather than ruminating about things that simply were not under her control.

Another person told me that the only thing holding him back from making a change was comments his colleagues had made to him. It seems that his co-workers tended to denigrate each other when they discussed career growth, and no one in his immediate group wanted to offend the others. So they avoided making career plans that might result in social pressure. Once he got over this, he was on his way to a better job.

> **Right Move** _____
>
> There is no right or wrong time to consider a career move. Apart from actually being out of work, your career planning should proceed as planned regardless of whether the economy booms or busts. Needless to say, good times and bad times have different effects, but don't fall prey to the doomsayers who will tell you that you should never make a move in a slow economy. You just have to do it with more care.

If all this is new to you, you are probably energized by what you see about yourself. If you have been doing career management already, you probably see ways to tweak your plan. You now have some momentum and you have discovered new paths to explore. Again, to quote a resident of Oz, "If you don't know where you're going, any road will do." But, this is your life and any road just won't do!

First Things First

Much of what follows in the pages of this book involves making serious commitments and possibly making some serious career decisions that will have major effects on your life. So before we get into the heavy stuff, let's look at the major sources of job dissatisfaction and see whether minor surgery can solve the problems before we head for the OR.

You like your job, but you feel your recent employment review doesn't paint a good picture of you. First of all, many performance reviews (in my humble estimation) do more harm than good. Sure, some are done very well, but most employee reviews are done by people whose work isn't in human resources. It's time-consuming and tedious, like asking the head of the shipping department to review and report on the work of the manufacturing department. Sure, many people take the assignment seriously, but when they don't, you can suffer—or even find yourself promoted to jobs you are not yet qualified to handle.

Case in Point

A client who was seeking guidance in a career change had received a poor performance review after having received good to excellent reviews for the past five years. The poor review had actually shattered his confidence and he felt that his future with his present employer had been cut off at the legs.

Questioning revealed that the executive who had done the review was new to the company. In trying to be as thorough as possible, he had asked for comments among my client's co-workers. Unfortunately, one of the people questioned had been having a running feud with my client and saw this as an opportunity to get even. (Yes, it does happen!) I suggested to my client that he talk with the reviewing exec and urge him to dig into this situation, which he did. The truth emerged, the poor review was amended and everything ended up fine.

The point is this: you can challenge performance reviews. However, make sure that you have facts to buttress your case.

Things are changing at the job and you're not happy with the changes. Change is inevitable, but not all change is good or bad. The questions you have to ask in terms of your career plans are these: are the changes good or bad for you, and are the changes good or bad for the company? It's natural to view change that disrupts you and the work you do for the company as a problem. But before you take any giant steps, make sure that the changes are good for both of you in the long run. Adapting to changes mandated from above is seldom easy, especially when you may not be happy with them initially. So think about the long term. Also keep in mind that the changes you see today may only be the first of others to come.

Give the changes a chance. Don't hesitate to talk with your boss about them if you feel that they are not really in the best interest of the company. However, do it in a way that shows you have the company's well-being in mind as well as your own. Nobody likes a whiner, especially one who doesn't offer alternative solutions to the problems the changes are designed to address.

You work with and for idiots. Your boss doesn't know what he's doing, your assistant is always late, and the guy in the mailroom always delivers your mail to someone three floors down with a name that isn't even close to yours. Welcome to the real world. Nobody's perfect. But suppose you decided that you had enough and took another job only to discover that the idiots at your new job are even worse. It could happen.

My point is this: don't sweat the small stuff, or even some of the big stuff as long as it doesn't happen all the time and as long as there are ways you can have some say in the solution.

Personal responsibilities are making it difficult for you to work at your peak. A few years ago, this could have been a serious problem for quite a few people. Today, however, flextime, work-at-home possibilities, job-sharing, and even telecommuting can often solve very difficult problems for both you and your employer. In fact, more than a few companies are being run with these plans exclusively. I've heard of some companies that drastically reduced their expenses by using these systems and selling off their expensive real estate. Check it out. It's a cliché, but this is one of the waves of the future.

Deciding Which Is the Best Move for You

Basically, there are three alternatives available to all who work as employees. They are …

- You can move up.
- You can move over.
- You can move out.

If you move up, you pretty much have decided that your long-term career is with your present employer. You should keep in mind, then, that growth for you lies in rising to greater and greater responsibility within the company. You can of course, choose to stay at a comfortable level and take care of any growing financial needs by doing other work outside the company. This is not an unusual plan and many people go this route. However, as you get older and older in the same job, you will feel the pressure of younger people who might feel blocked when you occupy a spot that they aspire to in their climb on the corporate ladder.

If you move over, you're on the same bus, but you have taken a different seat. In general, moving over often does mean moving up. More than a few of my clients have moved from lesser jobs in one division to higher-level jobs in other divisions or subsidiaries of their company. You must have, of course, appropriately transferable skills. This approach has the important benefit that most often these moves count in terms of retirement points, and seniority perks. On the downside, they often involve actual physical moves. Your family may have planted roots that resist an uprooting.

If you move out, obviously, you can pull up stakes and start with another company. Fresh starts, while sometimes emotionally wrenching, can often be the best thing to do. Getting out of a comfortable environment does force you to do a lot of refocusing, and what you see you just may like a lot better.

Career Alert

Unstable economic times can be scary, but they often provide the stimulus most of us need to get out of a rut. Keep in mind that if you feel your job might be on the block for reasons other than your performance, you might be offered significant incentives to take a hike. Depending on your level of employment, these incentives could involve nice lump sums plus the continuation of your insurance for many months after separation. So, don't jump ship too soon. If you quit, you get nothing, but if you're smart, you will use the time you think you have left to start looking for another job on the QT.

The Least You Need to Know

♦ You do have considerable control over the success of your career. But you need to listen to yourself carefully as well as to others who are in direct positions to help you.

♦ Not all the signs you see are as dire as you might expect. Office gossip, unless verified, should never be fully trusted.

♦ Honest answers to the five simple questions in this chapter can jump start your career right now.

♦ Whether you get the itch to move, or the nudge from your current employer, you can move over, up, or out. Fired, or fired up—the choice can be yours to make.

2

Move Up, Over, or Out?

In This Chapter

- ◆ Discovering the three paths to career growth

- ◆ Determining how you fit in with your employer's long-term plans

- ◆ Steps to take when you want to remain with your present employer

- ◆ Steps to take when you want to move up, over, or out

Let me lay it on the line—lifetime job security simply doesn't exist. You may work for a company now that makes sincere promises and honest commitments to its employees. But these commitments are seldom part of the package that another company buys when it takes over the company that employs you. I wish I had better news. Despite how unnerving all this may seem, there are far greater opportunities to achieve stability as well as growth today than there have even been.

You Are the Boss

Whether you run a drill press or handle corporate press relations, you are on the payroll because you are a player on a team that produces revenue. When the cost to produce that revenue exceeds profits, things are sure to change. Sadly, these changes often result in events that affect your career. You may produce more parts on the drill press than anyone else, or place more editorials in the business press than your co-workers, but you will share and bear the brunt of corporate anxiety when goals aren't met. You may even share them when goals are met and even exceeded. The motto of the Boy Scouts should be the motto of everyone who is employed by someone else—be prepared!

Please keep in mind that I am not advocating policy—I am reporting on what exists and how you can learn to live with it. Or more to the point, how you can learn how to turn all this to your advantage. I do think, however, that regardless of the disruptions we are all much better off today than we were when everyone's goal was 30 years and a gold watch.

What we are seeing today may seem heartless, especially to those who remember when people worked at one job forever. However, the corporate drive for greater and greater profits at the heart of these policies has fostered change that has important benefits for employees today at all levels. For one thing, it has created an environment in which employees see themselves more as productive individuals rather than just as cogs in a wheel. That knowledge alone is emotionally liberating. As comforting as it may have been to work for a very paternalistic company, there was always the nagging feeling that you had handed over the control of your destiny to someone else. Sure, all kinds of things can still have negative effects on your career. But now you have a much larger measure of control over your life. And that's what this book is all about.

You Have Options You've Probably Never Considered

There is never one perfect time to make a career change. You have to consider family commitments, the state of the economy, and I'm sure you can add a few that I have never thought of. However the shifts we have seen in business ownership and management over the past 20 or so years have made it possible for you to do things when you want to do them, and not always when you are forced to do them.

As I write this, the economy is slowing down again, and many will tell you that this is the time to sit tight and not make a change until things get better. Baloney! If the time is right for you, then now is the time. It may take longer, or it may take more effort to get what you want. But the sit-and-wait thing is just an excuse.

> ### Right Move
>
> A theme of this book is career *management.* Management is an ongoing process. When you are not under any pressure to move, you are more likely to look in nooks and crannies you would not consider if you had just been handed your walking papers. This exploratory process can produce ideas and places to work that you may not have ever considered otherwise. A word to your "headhunter" is often enough for him or her to look in different areas for you. When neither of you is under the gun, some very creative things can happen.

Fortunately, the way most companies are run today has created opportunities for career-minded people that never existed before. When you worked in that big, warm, and fuzzy organization, you had only one path to walk, and it was rigidly mapped and occasionally strewn with roadblocks over which you had no control. People who had jobs you could do better, but had seniority, could block a promotion that you deserved. And more than a few big companies moved people like checkers, with little understanding of the effect of their decisions on individuals or the corporation. It was warm and fuzzy, but it was a trap.

Now, you have real options and real opportunities:

- ◆ You can move up.
- ◆ You can move over.
- ◆ You can move out.

Moving Up

Moving up today usually means moving just a step at a time up the corporate ladder, and not necessarily going the distance for the gold watch. It's an option you should take when it's available and appropriate, and one you can also make happen in some cases. I'd like to add, however, that you should only take it when you are sure that you can fulfill the expectations. The Peter Principle—rising beyond one's capabilities—can be disastrous. Know when you are ready for the responsibility and everything should be fine. I will go into this in detail in later chapters.

Are You Ready?

Whether you are planning a long or short stay with your current employer, moving up is important for many reasons. Apart from the money and perks, any growth you can show on your resume plays well for your career. Stuck in rank for more than a few years doesn't send the best vibes. However, you must be ready for the move; you must be able to handle the new responsibility.

> **Right Move** _____
>
> Once you establish yourself successfully in your current job, it makes sense to level with your boss that you do want to continue to grow within the corporation. Remember, your boss wants to move up, too. Just make sure that you show that your enthusiasm for growth will not endanger your effectiveness on your current team. If you sense that your boss might be threatened by such a direct approach, talk with someone in human resources. Make sure that the HR person knows you're a team player and are not trying to undermine anyone.

What Are You Looking For?

Far too many people I've coached have not clearly defined what they want in an upward move. More than likely you can get a raise—if you deserve it—at your current level if you push for it. But the desire to move up should be defined by more than money. Here are some of the ways to speed up your growth with your current employer.

Becoming the Go-To Person

Work is about mastery as well as money. Working at a job that you have mastered and now do almost by rote is deadening. Stick with it and you will be seen as having leveled off and, possibly, unpromotable. One way to get the attention of those who may not be listening to your pleas for a new assignment is to take on a project that is clearly outside of the scope of your current job. There usually are more than a few projects floating around any office that others have avoided. Take on a dreaded job and prove yourself capable.

Expanding the Scope of Your Work

Many of my current assignments are from major pharmaceutical companies whose employees want to move up but are pigeon holed by career-defining advanced degrees. Moving from research to management with an M.D. or a Ph.D. may seem unusual, but it really isn't. It's a common career path these days. Don't let conventional blinkers keep you from exploring every possibility.

Prepare Your Second-in-Command

All too often I see advancement blocked because the company sees an employee as indispensable. They feel that no one else can do his or her job as well. Training your number-two to take over for you is a gutsy move, but when you make it clear to all—your boss and your number-two—what you are doing and what you want, you will have created the image of a self-confident person who has the company's best interests at heart.

Find a Mentor

Try to establish a relationship with someone higher up in the organization who can act as an unofficial counselor to you. That person probably should not be someone who would not be responsible for any promotions you may get. In other words that person should be knowledgeable and well connected, but essentially neutral. Look for someone who avoids the office gossip scene.

Moving Over

Management is a profession as well as a skill. A well-trained and experienced manager should be able to manage an accounting department as well as an advertising department. Think about it: most presidents of universities started as lecturers in the field in which they did their college work. I know of a historian who became president of a major university. I know of another who studied foreign policy who became vice president of a medical school. Unless you are planning to stay with a certain skill specialty, you should consider the possibilities of lateral moves within your company that could lead to better access to growth than your present job.

The toughest part of this move is convincing top management that you can do it. Generally speaking, most corporate executives wear blinkers when it comes to suggestions like this. But just because it is more difficult doesn't mean it can't be done. You just have to build a good case for your pitch and then make sure that you do what you say you can do when given the opportunities.

What Are You Looking For?

First of all, you are telling your boss that you want to continue and expand your career within the company. You are saying that you like the company enough to take a big chance by tackling a move over. You get a lot of points for this kind of gutsy move.

But you better be sure you can pull it off. Just getting the title isn't going to mean much if you don't win over the people in the department you will manage, especially if they thought one of them should have gotten the job. There are ways, however, of doing this with a minimum of pain and discomfort for all. More on this later.

Baby Steps or Giant Steps?

If you have the option, a gradual approach is far less wrenching for all involved. However, if the job is thrust upon you, dig in and do it! Most large corporations have a policy of hiring from within if possible before recruiting from the outside. Check the listings of jobs that are open in other departments and other companies owned by your employer. See if any of them appeal to you, and see if you have the skills and experience needed to be considered for them.

> **Right Move**
>
> Think about creating your own job within the company. A few years ago one of my clients found that a number of projects had been avoided by others in her company. She suggested that she be relieved from her regular responsibilities and be given the opportunity to tackle these jobs. The company agreed, she took on the projects, and within a few years had created her own department. You could say that she actually grew a new job within the company and ended up owning it.

Lobbying on Your Own Behalf

In some ways the idea of moving over to a totally different job within your present organization is like moving up within your current specialty. The main difference is that you have to convince people that you have the flexibility to adapt quickly to a different environment. This means taking a more proactive approach. Doing your present job has given you visibility in a limited sphere of the company. Try to show how the work you did in your current job relates to work you'd like to undertake in another department. Make specific cases and have facts and figures to buttress your case.

Take Some Courses

This is the era of continuing adult education. High schools, community colleges, and universities all offer adults some form of continuing education. I recently looked into the course offerings of schools in the Boston, New York, and Washington areas and discovered literally thousands of courses that could be taken by anyone seeking to grow in their present fields, and to shift from one field to another. Many companies offer to pick up the tab, or at least part of the tab, when these courses lead to skill and professional development that relates to their employment.

Do Volunteer Work

Doing volunteer work outside of your job helps the people the organization serves and you as a caring human being. It also can give you credits in fields in which you would like to work professionally. There is no shortage of opportunities to help others, whether you work on a social service team or knock on doors for a get-out-the-vote campaign. Many larger companies have organized groups within the corporate structure to work with outside community service organizations. Check these first. They can save you some time, and they can also spotlight you as a person who is willing to do more than the usual with your life.

Moving Out

Moving up or over in the company that now employs you has its hazards, but it's nowhere near as scary as casting off and setting sail in a totally different ship. Look at it this way, though: the chances are that you just might find a better work environment than you now have. Nowadays most people will work for at least six employers during their career, so changing companies no longer carries the stigma that it used to. And you'll never know how good or bad your current work environment really is until you jump into another. When you know it's time to go, do it—but do it carefully.

This is not a job-finding type of career book. There are plenty of good books on this subject, and I've listed some of the best in the appendix. This book is about everything else you need to do to manage your career. And moving out is one of those things.

Here are some of the major factors that point to a move out:

◆ You've done a great job, your performance reviews have been good, and you are told how much your work is appreciated. Yet you are not promoted. Your requests for promotion and greater responsibility are denied.

◆ You have a clear picture of your lifetime career goals and it just doesn't seem as though these goals can be met by your present employer, no matter how well you do your job.

◆ You thought advancement might just take time, but time doesn't seem to be important to your employer.

◆ You are bored with your current job. It might have been a challenge when you first took it, but it no longer excites you and you don't see any potential for that to change.

◆ Your company seems content to do business as usual. Although the company may be successful and provides solid financial rewards to all, the owner or managers may see this as a comfort zone for themselves, even though it isn't for you.

◆ You have had feelers from other companies or recruiters about considering another job. Anyone who does an outstanding job for his employer is always fair game for companies looking for employees. Unsolicited offers and feelers from headhunters are a good sign that your value is seen by others who might be in a position to cure the itch you now have about your current employer.

◆ You discover that you are being marginalized, despite the glowing comments about the quality of your work. This, too, often means that there is something in the wind over which you have no control, like a distant relative of one of the stockholders who is now on the payroll. This is not all that common, but it does happen.

The chapters that follow are all about you. Whether you move up, over, or out, all of the information that follows will help you manage your career moves.

The Least You Need to Know

◆ You have more direct control over your career and work life than you think. Whether times are good or bad, you can do more to build a successful and rewarding career than you might have been able to even a few short years ago.

◆ You have three ways to take direct control over your career. You can move over or up with your present employer, or you can move out to more fertile ground.

◆ Being called a job-hopper is no longer a pejorative. In fact, it's often seen as a sign of someone anxious and willing to move up and take greater and greater responsibility.

◆ Management training programs within major corporations that used to attract the best and the brightest are very much out of style. Most companies realize that people are going to move from job to job. Welcome to the mobile world of employment.

Chapter 3

It's Not Just a Feeling

In This Chapter

- Feelings are important career clues
- Decide which feelings need immediate attention
- Addressing both gut feelings and niggling feelings
- Knowing when positive feelings don't mean everything is okay
- Sharpening your decision-making skills

We all experience our own feelings, and we observe them in others. Yet there is no precise way to define or measure them. Responding to the same event, my number 8 on a scale of 1 to 9 to describe a feeling might be a 5 for you. This doesn't mean that we shouldn't trust our feelings when making career decisions, but it does mean that using feelings alone is a risky way of making life decisions.

Feelings (Almost) Never Lie

Feelings can be best described as our reactions to events in our heads as well as events that exist in the world around us. What we feel and how strongly we feel depends to a large extent on what we have experienced in the past. From your perspective as a person managing a lifetime career, feelings generally come more from vague signs and signals rather than those that produce an immediate duck-and-cover response. Seeing your boss whispering to the co-worker with whom you are competing for a promotion may evoke immediate negative feelings. However, they may just be exchanging jokes better whispered than told out loud. So trust your feelings, but get reality checks, too.

You weren't asked to attend a meeting to which you are usually invited. Everyone's filing into the meeting room and you're sitting at your desk. What went wrong? Why weren't you on the list? Does this mean that you have been downgraded to the B list? Does it mean that you are going to be fired? Maybe you should call your headhunter immediately? Could it be that you won't be able to pay the mortgage and maybe you will lose the house? And what about the bright future that the kindergarten teacher painted for little Tommy the other day? Harvard is out of the question now, isn't it?

If you are like most people—and I really mean most people—you have thoughts like this from time to time. That entire scenario runs though your head in less than a minute—then the door opens and your boss says, "What are you sitting there for? You know we can't start without you." It turns out that the intern who typed up the meeting list just missed your name. Whew! You vow never to let your feelings take over like that again. But they do, don't they?

Feelings can set all sorts of thoughts and emotions into action. And that's why feelings, as important as they are, should be part of a decision, but seldom used to make snap decisions.

How to Read Your Feelings

Feelings are real. Where you get in trouble is in the way you interpret them and the way you respond to them. Feelings are signposts. Some tell of danger, some tell of good fortune. Whether they are valid or not is a matter for you to determine.

That Niggling Feeling Is Real

Feelings come and feelings go, but a niggling feeling is one that doesn't set off major alarms. It's just there, and you are aware of it from time to time. The best way to deal with this type of feeling is to make a note of the situations and people who arouse it. Keep a running record and sooner or later, you will see a pattern emerge. When it does, you will be in a much better position to determine whether it's worth pursuing, or whether you should simply put it out of your mind.

Typically, niggling feelings center on issues of anonymity and irrelevance. Your boss won't look you in the eye. Your co-workers tend to gather without you. Or if you are included in the group, you feel as though you are being ignored. The truth is that this does happen all the time and more often than not the feeling you experience is situation specific. For example, the exclusion may be the result of your being seen as not especially interested in the topic being discussed, not that you are being intentionally ignored for some sinister reason. Your running record of the situations in which a niggling feeling occurs will expose this. Then, you just have to tell yourself that it has nothing to do with you and go about your business.

Gut Feelings Are Real, Too

Gut feelings are the duck-and-cover feelings you get when there is immediate danger. They serve a purpose—they get you out of the way of an oncoming car—but you seldom experience them in day-to-day business situations. However, immediate and intense feelings can often trigger the niggling feelings I just described.

You might hear people talking about responding to gut feelings as just using common sense. When your gut tells you to jump to avoid an oncoming car, that's common sense. When your gut tells you to quit on the spot because your boss chewed you out for something, that's not common sense.

Career Alert

Gut feelings trigger reflexive responses. That is, you tend to respond to them as you did to a similar situation in the past. What may have served you well in the past may be totally inappropriate in another situation. So pay attention to your gut feelings, but don't jump to disastrous conclusions.

Negative Feelings in the Office

Your boss walks by, doesn't acknowledge your presence, and proceeds to talk to someone else. You spent months on a project that, while acknowledged by your boss, seems to be useless in the overall scheme of things. In other words, you perceive that you are nearly anonymous to those who should know you are there, and you get the impression that all your efforts go for naught. They do create unsettled feelings, but here's how to evaluate them.

You're Being Ignored

Being ignored is not pleasant. However, until you're sure it's intentional, don't let it get to you. The only way to put an end to this feeling is to find out why it is happening. It's not easy or advisable to take the direct approach and ask the person who is ignoring you. However, you can usually uncover the source of the problem just by closely watching the person who is ignoring you in other situations. More than likely it's just the way he or she interacts with all people. If it isn't, you may have to bite the bullet—or ask someone who is closer to the person than you to see if there is a real problem.

Your Work Isn't Appreciated

Everyone needs to know that their work is appreciated and that it does have an impact on the business. Immediate gratification for a job well done seldom is part of the feedback most employees get. You may be told that your report is acceptable, but until it is implemented, which may take some time, you may never hear just how valuable your efforts were. However, being given make-work projects is not a good sign. In this case, you are probably well advised to directly ask why. Sometimes, a bite-the-bullet approach is needed.

Right Move _____

Look at the others around you doing similar work. Ask yourself, "What are they doing that I am not doing, and what are they doing differently?" Take your cues from their behavior and make the changes in the way you work. This may be all it takes to get back on the "A" list with your boss.

Evaluate Yourself

Some companies perform formal performance evaluations; some provide their employees with some form of self-test. Both are usually reviewed by the employee's direct supervisor and someone in the HR department. These reviews are usually pretty straightforward and measure the observable stuff. You can get good marks on these just by doing the job you were hired to do. However, there's more to any job, and it's what you do beyond the basics that usually stands out.

Right Move _____

This is the first of several self-evaluations you will do as you read this book. Take them seriously. Tell yourself the truth. Remember, there are no right or wrong answers. As Shakespeare wrote, "To thine own self be true."

Does Your Job Description Match Your Job?

Would your job description have to be revised to actually reflect what you do every day? We'll address this subject again later in this book. For now, however, think about how your answer might be reflecting on your feelings. If there are any discrepancies, they could be responsible for some of the niggling feelings you may be having.

Your boss may be seeing you in a light that you don't see yourself. Perception is reality, and here is one place where the gap should be closed quickly. For now, just make sure that your boss sees you as he or she should in terms of your actual job description.

Are You Achieving Your Goals?

Some goals are set in stone—that is, copied and in everyone's files. Other may have been set verbally. The documented goals are the easiest to address. You can haul out the documents, review them, and make improvements when needed. However, if you and your boss have set goals verbally, the chances are that he or she and even you have a different idea of them with the passage of time.

For this reason, I usually suggest that my clients submit regular progress reports to their bosses, whether they're required or not. Mid-course corrections are easy to make, but by the end of a complex project, you and your boss may each see the project differently from the way it was envisioned originally. Make sure that you and your boss still see the project in the same light.

Where Have You Fallen Down?

Some assignments are easy to put off. They may not seem important to you, but they may loom large in the eyes of others. Even though you doubled sales last year and developed a new product that is about to end Microsoft's hold on the market, you may have forgotten all about the boss's project involving selecting a new wallpaper for the waiting room. And that's what's bugging her, and that's what giving you anxiety when she seems to avoid you. I think you know what to do here without any professional help!

Not All Feelings Are Negative

Why did I leave positive feelings to last in this chapter? Simply because the comedian's golden rule applies to just about any human activity: "Always leave 'em laughing." Not that all this is funny, but it's positive and life confirming.

Both negative and positive feelings provide information that you can and should in your regular career management. Think of it as course-correcting feedback, similar to the information a navigator gets when he "shoots" the sun at regular intervals. The more often the information is obtained, the less dramatic the course corrections need to be. Take an occasional sighting and you may be way off course.

Good feelings tend to confirm that what you are doing is right, and negative feelings can signal the need for a course correction. The most important thing to keep in mind about feelings is that they vary in intensity, and charting the intensity of regular occurring feelings is what gives you a good handle on the trajectory of your career.

Get to the Source of Your Feelings

Feelings are signals. Good feelings tend to tell us that we are on course; bad feelings can signal that a change in course is necessary. However, feelings themselves are just signals. It is important to understand what is causing these feelings. When you know what is causing a feeling, you're usually in a position to do something about it. But there is a slippery slope in this. You must be sure that you have reached the source. Many explorers claimed to have found the source of the Nile River, but most were wrong, as was discovered when views from the air permitted a panoramic view of the river. This is what you need to do—seek a wide and panoramic view of the events that lead up to your feelings, both positive and negative.

 Right Move _____

As important as it is to understand what is causing your feelings, both positive and negative, it is just as important not to lose sight of the big picture. Feelings provide guide posts; you provide the energy that propels your career. Psychologists will tell you not to obsess with trivial details. In plain language, don't sweat the small stuff!

Trust Your Judgment

Sound judgment is based on what you already know about something, and your best guess about the things you don't know. Your "best guess" is what is most often called judgment or intuition. Intuition has a bad name because many so-called intuitive decisions don't work out too well, but you can fine-tune your use of your intuition.

Recognition-primed decision making is a fancy term for the way most people make so-called snap decisions. Let's say you're meeting with a potential employer and that person asks you for an immediate decision: do you want the job or not? You're faced with an immediate decision. You're there because you want to move on—but what are all the implications of taking this particular job? The list can be long, but for the sake of this example let's shorten it considerably.

If you say yes, you have closed out other options. If you say no, you may not get another offer, or another offer as good as this one. What do you do?

You're saying yes or no to yourself on a number of issues. You can make those individual decisions easier if you anticipate the major events you will encounter in the interview and be prepared to make on-the-spot decisions. There are two ways to do this. You can quickly review and reject all the alternatives and choose the last one standing. Or you can try to pick the best one from the lot, which means dumping all the alternatives at once.

Either is practical, and the choice is pretty much up to you. Either way, you will have to look closely at the feelings you have for the different alternatives. But the key point is that you should try to anticipate the choices you may have to make and be prepared to stick with your decision.

> ### Career News
>
> All the branches of the military, most of the major fire and police departments, and a good share of the first responder corps in the United States teach some form of recognition-primed decision making. It gets complex for them because lives often hang in the balance. But when your career hangs in the balance, it can pay to learn more about this technique. Several good sources of information and training are listed in the appendix.

Everyone's work lifestyle is different. Some people like to play it fast and loose, make decisions on the fly, and then pick up the pieces later. Others like life to be more orderly and predictable. No one style is best for everyone and you should determine which is for you and stick with it. Trying to be a fireball when you are a cautious and deliberate person is no way to live and manage a career.

One way to get a handle on your style and make the most of it is to learn a meditation technique. There is nothing sinister, religious, or mystical about a basic daily meditation routine. Fifteen minutes a day of quiet contemplation often helps people understand their feelings and to make the most of them. Actual meditation techniques are beyond the scope of this book; however, I have listed several references in the appendix for you to check out.

The Least You Need to Know

- Feelings are signals, and how you interpret and respond to them is critical.

- Intuition and judgment come from both positive and negative past experiences.

- Keeping a simple log of recurring feelings is the fastest way to get at the reasons for them.

- Simple meditation techniques can work for everyone.

Chapter 4

What Is Your Boss Telling You?

In This Chapter

- ◆ Spotting the critical signals
- ◆ What the signals really mean
- ◆ When to react and when to stand pat
- ◆ Sending your own signals

What your boss tells you about your performance is important. However, what he or she doesn't say may be even more important. You need both direct and indirect feedback as you plan your next move. The trick is in knowing how, where, and when to gather the information and how to use it to determine whether up, over, or out is the right move for you. Keep the motto of the Coast Guard in mind: Semper Paratus—Always Prepared.

Feedback Comes in Many Forms

Career-sensitive information may come your way at any time and from a variety of workplace situations. It can range from the most formal, such as your annual performance review, and even from the most casual of comments made by colleagues. It's important to stay focused, and to try to detect all the critical career signals you need to make your up, over or out decision.

There are eight critical occasions where you can gather the information you need to manage and advance your career. Try to use as many sources as possible before you make any serious decisions. In other words, don't jump to conclusions, whether the information warms your heart or scares the daylights out of you. The eight occasions make up the rest of this chapter.

Career Alert

Don't ignore comments casually made by colleagues—gossip. However, you should always evaluate gossip relative to reality and the intentions of the person doing the gossiping. Gossip that relates to you directly is seldom a real cause for concern. In other words, don't sweat the small stuff. However, the office grapevine is often quite accurate when it passes tidbits that relate to you in a more indirect way. Rumors of high-level turmoil that could affect your career are often surprisingly accurate. In general, the more volatile the situation, the more accurate the gossip can be. A CEO on the verge of leaving, the presence of "suits" where they are seldom seen, and reports of hostile takeovers are probably a lot more important than a vague feeling that someone might not like you.

Your Performance Review

This nerve-wracking event is usually the best time to get a formal read on where you stand with your employer. A well-done review can let you know how your job performance is rated by those who have the most to say about your future with the company. It can highlight areas where you might need improvement, and it can also spotlight your strengths. For those in an active "up, over, or out" mode, it can provide most of the critical information needed to make the best decisions.

However, not all performance reviews are done well.

Prepare Carefully

You may have already discovered that the quality of your performance review can range from hurried, perfunctory, and late to methodical, thorough, and timely. It all depends on your boss's management style, communication skills, and level of interest in the review process. Or it just might be a matter of a busy or overwhelmed boss with little or no time to focus on what he or she might consider to be a nuisance task. Whatever your current situation, you can make a difference in making your performance review worthwhile. By applying just a few well-chosen and well-executed strategies, you have the power to transform even the most perfunctory review into a noteworthy and productive experience.

Before the meeting, prepare by collecting documentation that demonstrates the level of your job performance and highlights your accomplishments since the last review. The difference between the current and the last review will be a critical factor. Documentation might include a complimentary e-mail from a customer, or even an "attaboy" from another department head thanking you for your assistance with a difficult project. You also might have facts and figures on your sales, your quality record, or how your suggestions resulted in a process improvement. All of this can be very effective in helping your cause.

Right Move _____

Be sure to collect job performance data throughout the year and keep it in one place in your computer or even in a file folder. If you don't do this, you may forget or have an unclear recollection when review time rolls around. One of my clients even makes and stores notes on a little memory stick that he has attached to his keychain.

Polish Your Act

Do a mock review and self-evaluation by filling out a blank review form. Use your company's review ranking system and substantiate your ranking with specific examples of where you met or exceeded a particular performance element—such as "teamwork" or "job knowledge." Create a performance-improvement plan that shows the steps you have already taken to close a performance gap.

Practice your performance review meeting with a friend or trusted co-worker. Your spouse may not be the best judge since he or she has more at stake than might a friend or co-worker. Anticipate your boss's feedback and questions and prepare your responses accordingly. This "dry run" will increase your effectiveness dramatically.

Right Move _____

When you are aware of a shortcoming, and you think it might be brought up in your review, take the initiative and mention it before the boss does. However, be sure that you can explain exactly how you are taking steps to correct the problem. The best defense is a good offense!

Listen to *Everything* Said

During the actual meeting, listen carefully to what is said—and what is not being said. Ask open-ended questions such as, "Could you tell me more about that?" This can often help you uncover what is not being said. Other helpful questions include, "So, in other words, you feel I need more customer contact?" The answers to questions like this are often critical in deciding whether to stay or move on.

> **Right Move** _____
>
> Most performance-review sessions allow for the person being reviewed to ask questions. Plan the questions you want to ask well in advance of the review session, mainly to make them seem spontaneous. Ask both factual and open-ended questions.

It also helps to ask for specific, work-related examples in order to understand the boss's assessment. The answers to these questions help move the assessment away from the personal and into the factual areas of your review. They also give you insight into the boss's perception of you and the signals your on-the-job behavior is sending to others. Based on what you hear, you can begin to put together a clearer picture of where you stand in terms of reality and how you might be perceived by your boss.

New Project Assignments

How and to whom your boss assigns projects can be an indication of your status within the department. For example, do the assignments you're given reflect your professional ability, or are they the ones often given to a newly hired junior person? Here is where things not said can often loom larger than things said.

People being groomed for greater responsibility are often given assignments that stretch their present capabilities. The goal is not only to get the work done, but also to test their ability at the above-and-beyond level. Performance under stress is a key issue in executive growth. So don't complain about getting tough assignments—think of them as tests you have to pass on your way up.

If you are given that super great important assignment, be sure to thank those who got you the assignment. But while you're at it, try to get a feel for just why you were chosen. It's as important to know whether you were chosen for your skills and ability as it is to know that you got the job because no one else wanted it. This is often an area where you will learn more about your status in the company than in most formal situations.

Some executives claim you can get more indirect, career-related information through a new project assignment than in just about any other situation. For example, how a new project is funded can give you an idea of whether the company is risk-averse or willing to take chances. Your own professional goals may be more in tune with a company that plays it safe or one that is willing to take chances. The information you uncover in this area can be key to both your short- and long-term career plans.

Right Move

If someone else is chosen for an important assignment that you wanted, try to determine why. What does the other person bring to the assignment in the way of skills, experience, and personal style that you don't bring? This is a tough thing to do, but remember, your goal is to know yourself.

It's More Than Just Money

A promotion is a sure sign that you are on the right track, in the fast lane, and destined for greater things—right?

Not necessarily. There's often more unsaid in a promotion than is said in the corporate press release. For example, who were your competitors for the job? Was the job offered to others who turned it down? Why did they turn it down? The list is long, but I think you get the idea.

Years ago a client of mine was given a significant promotion only to discover that he was the only one the directors felt could handle an especially difficult employee. As it turned out, he could and did handle the employee well, but knowing that he got the job for what he felt were less than desirable reasons sent the signal that this was not a company he wanted to stay with for long. However, he did use the promotion as a key point in his resumé—without discussing the reasons for it, of course.

Make the Most of Every Promotion

Most promotions carry with them the strong signals that you are valued by those who have some say about your future. Even though you may not be actively looking to move on, the best time to collect endorsements is when you are riding high.

It's not a good idea to just ask a person to write something for you, but you can get those attaboys by writing a thank-you note for a recent promotion. I have yet to meet a boss who wasn't flattered by such a letter and didn't respond with a follow-up letter that can go immediately into your file for future use. My client with the keychain memory stick converts the letters to PDF files and stores them with everything else.

Even Failing to Get a Promotion Has Benefits

Not getting the promotion isn't the end of the world, but it does tell you something, and you'd better find out what. It's reasonable to expect some answers when it was obvious that you deserved the promotion. Any discussions should be open, frank, and congenial. Make it clear that you are disappointed, but that you can understand the situation.

However, this is a point where what is not said will be more important than what is said. Again, from my files, a client who was passed over for promotion discovered that the person who got the coveted job was a distant relative of the person doing the hiring. Sound familiar? This was his signal to take the "out" option rather than to think of "up" or even "over." Decisions made on such criteria are not made in healthy business environments.

Money Talks—Your Salary and Bonus Review

Much of what I've already said about the performance review applies to this situation, too. However, you can learn some interesting and valuable lessons when the talk turns to money. The reasons given for raises and those offered for not giving them can provide significant clues to use when you're thinking about staying or leaving.

First of all, money is important both as an achievement marker and as a guide to your standing in your field. Second, everybody lies about money. Third, it's usually impossible to verify anything people tell you unless you see the check.

So what does this say to you? Know your worth to your company and know what other companies might be willing to pay you. Forget all the other stuff. But remember, the term *money* includes actual salary, bonuses, and benefits.

Career Alert _____

Salary increases and bonuses are always welcome. However, the lack of a raise or bonus doesn't always mean you should plan a move. Make sure you know why you got or didn't get the raise or bonus. And, make sure you have a clear picture of the financial status of the company that employs you. A raise denial by a company experiencing financial difficulty is not necessarily a sign that you have performed poorly. Get the complete picture before you jump to any conclusions.

If you work for a large organization with a number of people working at the same level as you, try to determine where you stand relative to them. This isn't easy information to get, as you probably know, but it's not difficult to read the faces of those who got raises and those who did not.

If you are denied a raise or bonus, you have a right to know why. Ask your boss first. And of course, you can always petition those above your boss or go to the human services department. Again, keep in mind that performance is no longer a guarantee that you will be paid better. Most people improve their careers—and their paychecks—by making moves.

It's tempting to use national statistics to evaluate your current salary. However, there can be very large differences in what people are paid to do similar jobs in different parts of the country. Also the closer your job is to the company's core field, the more you will be paid. An accountant for a financial institution is likely to be paid more than an accountant doing the same job for a metal stamping company. So be sure that you evaluate the financial signals your employer is sending relative to geography and industry.

Meetings That Matter

Formal meetings are generally good sources of clues about how your performance is being perceived. There are the broad clues: you're invited—or not invited—to meetings to which you should be invited. There are subtle clues: you are asked or not asked for your input during the meetings. And there are even more subtle clues, such as where you are asked to sit, and how those other than your boss respond to you.

However, keep in mind that everyone at any meeting wants to shine, so some of what appears to be shunning behavior might just be defensive on the part of the person you feel might be giving you the cold shoulder. Paranoia runs rampant in every meeting. Don't overreact to every slight.

Casual meetings, such as those that used to be referred to as "water cooler" meetings, are also good places to get feedback. Listen to what people generally say about other people before you take what they say too seriously. Some people are chronically

Right Move

If you have a close friend who attends the same meetings, ask for his or her views on what you thought might be either good or bad signs. When asking someone to do this, try to appear neutral, not looking for either bravos or boos. Friends want to help, and they often try to please when they feel they know that you are anxious about something.

optimistic and some seem to be in the dumps most of the time. Evaluate any information with these filters in place. And remember, what you hear in casual conversation is seldom important enough by itself to make any major decisions. Just plug it into the matrix of all the other information and impressions that is constantly in flux in any office.

Your Domain Can Be a Key Indicator

Of all the symbols that abound in the typical office, the myth of the corner office is the most pernicious. When people are promoted, a bigger and better office is seldom part of the deal. However, when you go from manager to VP, a bigger office is usually involved. So it's not uncommon to find someone working in a typical cubicle having significant responsibilities and being paid accordingly. That being said, however, you should consider some office geography factors:

- Those who have moved up and are still in cubicles are often in closer proximity to their boss.

- When your boss is on one floor and you are asked to move to another floor, there may be some negative significance to the move.

Right Move _____

Before you place any really serious weight on being moved either closer to or farther from your boss, consider all the placement elements of the office. A client of mine once reported that she had been moved a good distance away from her boss. This made her quite anxious until she learned that she was in line for a promotion that would put her under the jurisdiction of someone else, and the move was preparatory to the promotion.

What is often more significant than office size and location is the proximity of the office to services currently needed and that might be needed in the future. An accountant asked to work in an office in the marketing department should see this as a troublesome sign. A client of mine, a sales manager, was once moved to the floor that housed much of the legal staff. He saw this as a bad sign until he saw the office. It was a corner office, about twice the size of the office he had left. Consider all the variables, and don't jump to conclusions.

The Hidden Signs in Training and Transfer

When a company offers training or transfers to distant branches, it is usually sending the message that it is willing to spend money on you. Training costs money and so do transfers. If offered either, consider them as good signs. Unless, of course, the transfer is to Siberia. Even then, though, such a transfer might be a good sign. Siberia might need someone with your skills and the company feels that you are the one to turn Siberia into something a lot warmer and more productive.

More often than not, transfers are signs that you are moving up. I have yet to see a company transfer an productive employee to a less desirable location. You should look closely, however, at transfers from one department to another at the same location. Keep in mind that such transfers might be made because you are seen as productive, or possibly seen as not fulfilling the promise seen in you earlier. Reading these tea leaves is difficult unless, of course, you are told point-blank the reasons for the transfer.

> **Right Move**
>
> Check to see if the training being offered is such that it increases your value to the company, or is designed to correct a perceived flaw. Either way, the company sees value in you and is willing to spend money on your training.

◆ Check to see if the place to which you are being transferred has greater potential for growth than your present location. Even a lateral move in terms of job status could turn out to be a better opportunity than the opportunity offered where you are now.

◆ If moving creates personal problems, be sure to explain this to your boss. Turning down a good transfer can slow your growth, but most employers understand. As long as you are aware of the consequences, it probably won't reflect badly on your record.

Letters, Memos, and E-Mail

Interoffice paper memos and e-mail routings are good signs to use when evaluating your status within the company. I don't mean that you should ever read correspondence sent and received by others without explicit permission. However, it's not all that difficult to see who is and who is not on the various routing lists. When you see yourself being added to a list that ordinarily goes to those above your rank in the company, it's safe to assume your status is secure. When you are removed, it's usually not a good sign.

However, don't jump to any immediate conclusions. Try to discover why you are no longer receiving the routing. More often than not, the problem is not with you, but with the routing system. Computer glitches happen all the time! On the other hand, if it's not a glitch, it's a sign to be taken seriously.

Right Move

Most interoffice e-mail includes the names of the people on the routing list. It's no act of espionage to look at the routing list on the e-mail you get and to catch a glimpse of the routing lists on others' e-mail. This is a fast way to see how your boss and others think of you in terms of group structures.

A client of mine once set up a routing e-mail list to several co-workers in his office. It was nothing sinister, just a sublist of people whom he felt should be included on some of the information he had and received regularly. Within days, he was asked by several people why they had not been included. They were not included simply because my client didn't feel they needed the information and didn't want to add to the tons of e-mail that everyone gets daily. Such is the power of a routing list. But, the message here is not that it is a perfect indicator, but that many people actually think it is. Use it accordingly.

The Least You Need to Know

- One of the best sources of information on your status within the company is your performance and salary review.

- What your boss says informally can often be just as revealing as what he or she says formally, or doesn't say at all.

- The only gossip you can usually count on is that which deals with major issues that will probably affect others as well as you. Don't sweat the small stuff.

- Keep detailed records of all the praise and kudos you receive.

Chapter 5

Take Your Current Employer's Temperature

In This Chapter

- Discover where your company stands in its field
- Spot the trends that bode well and not so well for your career
- Check your personal goals against the corporate goals

Businesses and individual people have a lot in common. Some are risk-takers and others are risk-averse. Some are tightly focused on meeting well-defined goals whereas others take a more free-swinging view. Some focus on innovative ways to adapt their strengths to changing conditions, while others quickly abandon such strategies in favor of looking for ways to capitalize on new trends for more immediate advantage.

There is no one way that works best for all companies or all people. What usually works best for both, though, is an approach that capitalizes on the strategies that created current successes, yet allows for change to accommodate to anticipated and unanticipated events. Some business gurus are currently thinking about this in terms of some sort of corporate DNA. In simple terms, think about it in terms of your company's vital signs.

Taking the temperature—and blood pressure—of your current employer should be viewed in terms of your own career temperature and blood pressure. Are you comfortable in a free-swinging corporate environment, or would you prefer working in a more stable and possibly more predictable environment? As with companies, no one approach is right for everyone. But you should have a real grasp on what you feel the future will be like for you in the company that presently employs you before you make any drastic changes.

Career News

Many major companies often appear to be the perfect model of an open and free-swinging employment situation. Microsoft, for example is widely known for its indulgent care and feeding of the employees who create its software products. It is, however, really very traditional in its approach to business. Microsoft's overarching strategy has been that of establishing and owning a product standard and marketing it very aggressively through traditional channels. For technical people, it's something close to heaven. For others, it can be business as usual. Be sure you know just how your current employer sees itself and exactly how you see yourself in terms of your own career goals.

Hot, Cold, or Just Warm

"Hot" and "cold" are relative terms, at least in view of your career-planning needs. A company that has been on the skids for a couple of years and is suddenly showing vigor in ways that matter to your career needs may just be running to catch up. A company that has been coasting and now finds itself losing market share may have been in the hands of inefficient management. In short, you have to know the history and you have to know how the owners and managers see the future. Let's look at the major vital signs you can use to judge the company that may now employ you.

"Hot" Is When ...

- ◆ Your company is paying vendors on time.
- ◆ Your company projects sales at rates that exceed industry standards.
- ◆ Your company's cash flow exceeds projections for at least the past nine months.

- The turnover rate in middle and top management is seen as very stable over at least the last four quarters.

- Employee absenteeism is almost nonexistent.

- Your company's revenue stream is spread over a large number of customers.

- Your company is earning more on new customers that it did on those it may have lost.

Not every company is going to come up aces on all these points, but with enough of them on the positive side, you can be relatively sure that your employer is in pretty good shape. The owners may be planning to sell it to someone else, but at least it's a good bet that the business is not on the block.

"Cold" Is When …

- Your company's accounts payable are being stretched well past 90 days.

- Your company's operating expenses have increased as a percentage of revenue significantly over the past year.

- Your company's net profits have been below budget for more than nine months.

- Top management seems to think that "more of the same" is always the answer to problems that they are at least willing to acknowledge.

"Warm" Is When …

- Management acknowledges that there are problems, but presents less than exciting plans for correcting them.

- Management is flexible enough to see that yesterday's solutions to problems may not work in the current business climate.

- Customer complaints are relatively stable over the past year.

- The comments heard at the water cooler are focused on solving problems rather than in complaining about them.

- Vendors aren't treating you as second-class customers.

Start Looking for Signs You Can Use

When the doctor takes your temperature and it's above or below 98.6°, he or she knows that you have a problem. When you know that there are problems with your present employer, it doesn't always mean that the best medicine is a move. Your employer's problems could be your opportunities. If you are in a position to contribute to the solution of the problems, you could be in the catbird seat when things are finally put right. But when problems seem out of control, it is usually time to start looking out for number one. Before you take this dramatic step, let's look at exactly what you can do to evaluate the hot, cold, or warm symptoms.

Career planning and management is an ongoing process; it's not something you do once and forget about it. You change, your company changes, the business climate changes—everything changes. If it were possible to do one career plan early on and stick with it life would be pretty easy—and terribly boring.

Your career is like the engine in your car. When it's running well, you take it for granted. When some of the warning lights begin to blink, you probably ignore them and just hope they will go off without your having to do anything. When the blinking stops—along with the engine—you slap your forehead and finally acknowledge that you goofed. Since few jobs come with signs as obvious as blinking lights, how do you decide what is critical and what is not?

How To Look for the Signs That Are Important

The signs that most people feel are important are those that are closest to them. It's like looking under a streetlight for the keys you dropped a block away in the dark. Here are some "do's" and "don'ts" to help you:

◆ *Don't* seek information from those who are not in a position to give you valid information. Every office is loaded with people who either claim to have inside information or are at least perceived to have access to it. Listen to everything, but evaluate what you hear very critically.

◆ *Do* qualify the people whose information you think might be reliable. Keep in mind that good information can come from anyone, regardless of their rank or status within the company. It's up to you to decide whether or not you can trust what they say.

◆ *Don't* assume that all the bad news is valid and the good news isn't. Bad news is energizing, it makes you want to spring into immediate action. On the other hand, good news is calming and it's tempting to back off when the news sounds good. I'll talk later on how you can take steps to validate what you hear.

◆ *Do* look everywhere. It's tempting to look only in places where you assume the news, good or bad, should be coming from. Your search should be comprehensive. And ask others where they think you should look. Especially in larger companies, news that can affect your career can come from any number of different places. Don't ignore any of them.

Look at Both the "Hard" and "Soft" Signs

"Hard" signs most often come in the form of official company memoranda. You may have to read between the lines to get at the facts, but some of the most useable information you can have will be there. More important than individual memos is the progressive sequence of memos that relate to specific issues. You can often spot trends by looking at the information in sequence. Save those memos!

"Soft" signs are the most unreliable, yet they often convey an emotional impact that far exceeds their true value. React to them with caution—but don't ignore them. The soft signs that are worth investigating usually include people who visit corporate offices frequently and are shown right in. The implication being that management prefers that others not talk with them. When the external accountants and auditors start appearing at times other than their regular schedule, things might be happening that affect your career. Reports in the trade and business press are worth following. But unless the articles include direct quotes from people who are in positions to make important comments, take most of it with a grain of salt. Slow news days often call for articles that can be more speculative than factual.

Do Your Due Diligence

"Due diligence" is a term used most frequently by lawyers, and its first use was the result of the U.S. Securities Act of 1933. The term quite simply means gathering all the information you possibly can to protect your behind. In this case, you want to know everything you can about your employer that may have an impact on you and your career. Unless you work for a publicly traded corporation that has to publish an annual report, you may have to do a lot of research and even some snooping. Remember, snooping in the files of your employer is not only unethical, it can result in an unexpected vacation for you at public expense.

That being said, however, the following information is often readily available, whether or not you work for a publicly traded corporation. It's the trends you are interested in more than anything else.

♦ Customer history. Is the company retaining its better customers? Is it replacing those it loses, and with better quality customers?

♦ Market share. How much of the total market does your company "own?" How long has the company maintained its position and is the company maintaining its market share relative to industry trends?

♦ New products and services. Is your company a leader, follower, or a laggard when it comes to innovation? Being either a leader or a follower is okay, but being a laggard is not an especially good sign.

♦ How stable is the workforce, especially at the level at which you work? High turnover is not a healthy sign. On the other hand, a stable workforce could indicate a certain lethargy. Be sure you know the reasons for both.

♦ Check with your employer's suppliers. Your main interest will be in the stability of the relationships and the payment history.

Right Move _____

Typically, people change jobs more frequently when they are younger and just starting their careers. A study done at Ohio State University showed that half of most new young employees will have quit their jobs within the first 18 months of employment. After that, the quit-rate drops dramatically. What you want to look at is the rate at which older and more experienced people quit jobs at your company. There may be industry-specific factors that contribute to this, but in general when older and more experienced workers leave with greater frequency, it's time to ask why.

Reading Between the Lines

Spin is everywhere. Politicians do it. Even your friends and neighbors do it. If you were to judge the company that employs you just by its annual report, it would be like reading with one eye closed. It's a wink-wink world, but armed with a few of the tools of classical rhetoric, you can slice through the baloney and see just where your company stands on the issues that are critical in your career decision making. Needless to say, the same understanding will help you evaluate a future employer, but for the moment, let's think in terms of the company that puts beans on your table right now. The following tips apply to what's spoken or written by top management in its attempts to paint the company in a brighter picture than really exists.

Watch for the repetition of key words. Speakers and writers who are trying to convince you of something will consciously and unconsciously repeat key words and phrases. It really doesn't take a finely tuned ear to pick up on this tactic, but when you see it or hear it, start asking questions. Go for reality, and don't let the glittering generalities cloud your vision.

Watch for inappropriate use of metaphors and symbolism. This is a technique used to put a warm spin on a cold thought. The personnel manager who regularly refers to employees as family may have the best of intentions, but his superiors may not.

Watch for the use of the editorial "we." The CEO who tells employees that he is instituting such-and-such a plan is making a public commitment. But when the same person says, "We are planning such-and-such an operation," he is using weasel words. He or she is off the first-person singular hook.

Watch for the double-bind approach. One of the most frequently used techniques is to offer someone a choice between two alternatives when a choice really isn't necessary. "Would you prefer that we take a major loss this year or go ahead with the layoffs?" One may have nothing to do with the other, but when presented this way, most people assume that they have to make a choice.

Right Move

It's not easy to get the kind of information you may need from others in your company. Good employees don't like to betray a trust, even an implied trust. However, former employees are usually willing to talk more freely. Remember, though, those who left the company at the request of management usually have an ax to grind. Evaluate what they tell you very carefully. Those who left voluntarily are usually more willing to talk honestly about their experiences as employees. As with any other requests for personal information, use discretion and never put someone on the spot by asking questions he or she would prefer not to answer.

Judging Your Company by What Others Say

A balance sheet and an annual report can tell you a lot about your company relative to your career plans. But the people around you can often tell you more. But judging your company by hearsay puts you on very shaky ground. The term, judgment, implies that you accept some things and reject others. This, of course, means that you have some personal set of rules for accepting and rejecting what people tell you. And you are judging what they say in terms of the way you see things. I've discussed this in detail in Chapter 3, but let's take a look at how you can decide how much faith to put in what others tell you about your company.

Character Counts

In general, most people evaluate another's character by the way that person responds to challenges. Someone who caves to a challenge from another and hangs you out to dry is not to be trusted. A person who gives up easily is also thought by most to lack character. Neither of these types is to be trusted. If they do seem to have valid information that will help you, verify everything they say—never take what they say at face value.

By-the-Book People Are Difficult to Evaluate

People who adhere rigidly to the rules often find themselves conflicted. Should your boss tell you that you are one of the people scheduled for an upcoming layoff, even though he has been pledged to secrecy? This is a tough spot for anyone to be in. Most people who have a measure of character will try to find a way to let you know, but in a way that doesn't violate the trust placed in them. It is weaseling, but in this case most people are willing to forgive their transgressions.

Be Wary of Information from People You Do Not Know

Relying on third-party information is probably the riskiest way to learn anything at all about your company. People who pass along information from others usually say something about the source's character first, but you can see where this is going. The best advice I can offer is to take any such information with more than a few grains of salt.

The Least You Need to Know

◆ As exciting as a move may seem, the opportunities offered by your present employer may be better in the long run. Don't act impulsively.

◆ You need to know where your current employer is headed and how you fit into the scheme of things

◆ You need as much about your present employer as you do an employer for whom you are considering working.

◆ Much of the information you get by informal sources about your present employer will either be out of date or tainted with the opinions of the person sharing it with you.

Part 2

Begin with Yourself

A realistic career plan begins with you, what you want to do, what you are capable of doing, and how current employment conditions affect all of this. Self-assessment is more than a collection of checklists. It's a composite picture of you, relative to the needs of the employers who most need your skills and abilities right now. Personal style, communication style, and leadership abilities are key elements for creating your personal brand. The chapters in this part take you step by step from self-understanding to self-mastery.

Included is a detailed guide to creating your personal career toolkit, to be used any time to fine-tune your creative, interpersonal, management, and problem-solving skills.

Chapter 6

Why Take Stock of Yourself?

In This Chapter

- ◆ Creating a clear picture of where you have been, where you are, and where you want to go

- ◆ Drawing on your feelings as well as the real world for critical self-knowledge

- ◆ Deciding what you want more of and what you want less of

- ◆ Knowing what to do when you spot a flying pig

Remember when you were a kid and you visited the local firehouse with your dad? It was an open house, all the equipment was out, and the firemen were dressed in their uniforms and in fire-fighting gear. When you got home and your mom asked you how you liked the visit, I'm willing to bet that most of you replied, with great enthusiasm, "I'm going to be a fireman when I grow up!" Well, you're an adult now and you may actually be a firefighter, but, chances are, between that visit to the firehouse and today, you changed your plans at least a dozen times.

What happened along the way to make you change your mind? In simplest terms, you were exposed to lots of other opportunities that, for one reason or another, reshaped your idea of yourself in terms of what you wanted to make your life's work. Your parents, your teachers, your friends, and those whose lives you idolized all had an impact on your life. So did reality. And, as you will see in this chapter and the next, a reality check doesn't start today; it starts back at the firehouse.

Self Knowledge Is a Positive Tool

Tools have to be sharpened and maintained in order to do their work. Self-knowledge is one of the most important tools you have at your disposal, but my guess is that a lot of what you think you know about yourself is outdated, no longer useful, and maybe even dangerous if you try to use it.

An awful lot of what we think of ourselves comes from people who are trying to make us feel good, trying to make us feel bad, or even from people we never really know but who, nevertheless, have an impact on our lives. I remember coaching a young woman who worked as an accountant. She told me that she hated her work. It wasn't the job or the company or the boss—it was accounting. I asked her how she had come this far on her career path carrying that kind of heavy baggage. It turned out that she interpreted a casual remark her mom had made to her in high school as a sign that she could make her mom happy if she became an accountant. She did, but she really hated the work. There is more to this story, but for our purposes now, I think you can see how career decisions are often made for all the wrong reasons.

There is one more good reason to take stock of yourself now and throughout your working career, and that is because you are being evaluated regularly, whether formally or informally. This isn't a Big Brother thing, so don't get worked up. Everyone constantly evaluates everyone else. The best way to confirm this is to think about the people you consider friends and those at the other end of the scale. Good friends are good friends because you have made certain judgments that grant them that status. The others earned their position by behavior that gave you negative vibes. Therefore, a little self-analysis at this point is just one more tool you can use as you make important career decisions.

Your reality check is easy, maybe even fun, but it's going to take some thinking. You don't have to check any boxes or even write an essay. Go over the list below, think about each of the items in terms of what has brought you where you are now, doing what you do. In Chapter 3, I talked about feelings. Now, it's

> **Case in Point**
>
> Pearl Bailey, the great blues singer, said, "You never find yourself until you face the truth." The truth for most of us isn't some dark secret; it's usually something simple and uncomplicated. However, once we make a commitment to a thought or an idea, the real problem is not letting it take over our lives forever.

time to use some of what you learned about feelings to get a picture of just where you are in terms of your career and what happened to shape your work life as it is now.

- Go back to the firehouse, or the job that you first thought about doing at whatever age.

- What about that job excited you?

- What was the next job that captured your fancy?

- What was it that so excited you that you were willing to shift your sights?

- Go through all the jobs you had and considered having until now and think about what was so important about them that you were willing to consider making changes. Consider the people who might have influenced you, your own interests, and any external circumstances that had an impact on your decisions.

- Think about your present job and try to imagine how your feelings and life experiences got you to where you are now.

It should be apparent that the object of this exercise is for you to get a sense of the feelings you had for different career choices. Are there any common elements that might have been pointing you towards or away from certain career choices?

The Inside-Out Approach Opens Your Mind

There are no right or wrong responses, and no 1–9 scales to help you with this. As I said in Chapter 3, feelings are all but impossible to measure. But this doesn't mean that they aren't real and that they can't help you as you plan and manage your career. If you want and need something more solid, I suggest that you considering taking one or a few of the better occupational skills inventories. Many universities and independent career counselors offer them. A few of the schools that are better known for their work in this field are listed in the appendix.

In later chapters we will get down to the nuts and bolts, but for the time being it's important that you get to know yourself as a feeling and emotional person. This is who you are. Your feelings and emotions cause you to react to the realities of the world outside your skin. What you learned about feelings in Chapter 3 will provide the tools you will use to get closer to the nuts and bolts of later chapters. For now, you need to explore two areas. Think about what you would like to have more of, and what you would like to have less of.

The Reality of "More"

One of the things I discovered early in my work as a career counselor is that when I ask people what they would like to have more of, few mention money first. Although the other factors often mentioned deal with quality of life issues, they all can be traced one way or another to money issues.

> **Case in Point**
>
> Albert Schweitzer said, "Success is not the key to happiness. Happiness is the key to success. If you love what you are doing, you will be successful." Dr. Schweitzer was also heard to say, "Happiness is nothing more than good health and a bad memory."

Most people want to improve their life and work situation, which means they want to have more control over whatever gives them peace and pleasure. They're not looking for miracles; they know that what they want will only come as a result of their own hard work.

If it helps, make a list of the things you would like to have more of. Don't limit the list to the things you can touch; include the soft stuff like time to be by yourself, and greater understanding of things that may not relate directly to your career. You'll know when they are important if you paid attention to the chapter on feelings. Hold on to this list and refer to it as you read the rest of this book.

The Reality of "Less"

Most people want less of the things that give them stress. Few are looking for less of life's real responsibilities; they seem to want less of the emotional baggage that comes with these responsibilities. One person I counseled a number of years ago said, "I like having responsibility in my personal and work life. What bothers me is the fallout from this responsibility. I guess what I'm saying is that I don't like to fail at things because that's when the heat comes on." I must report that this person never stepped away from any responsibility. It's when you avoid responsibility because you fear failing that you shut off the motor of life. I think that Aristotle said it better than anyone when he said, "Happiness belongs to the self-sufficient."

Give Yourself All the Options

Taking stock of yourself involves peeking through both ends of the telescope. That is, you want to see the big picture and you want to see the detail. For example, suppose the big picture shows that you jumped from a relatively small job with your employer to one with far greater responsibility. That in itself is a comforting picture. But were you promoted because you deserved it, or were you given the job because no one else wanted it? As I said, you must be honest with yourself. Looking at your work life without a filter gives you the information you need to make sound decisions now and in the future.

Answer These Questions Honestly

Again, there are no right or wrong answers. But how you answer the questions should raise more questions about how you see yourself and how you see yourself in relation to your job and your career.

When your boss is out of the office, do you take advantage of the situation, or do you go on with work as usual?

No one is going to find fault if you take small liberties, such as leaving a little early at the end of the day. But, if you see the boss's absence as a license to do whatever you want and very little of what you are supposed to do, you should think very carefully about why you behave this way. If it's business as usual, chances are you don't have any serious issues with your boss, or probably with the company that employs both of you.

Do you update your CV regularly?

Relax, doing this is a sign that you are realistic about work and that you believe that being prepared is an important career move. You may be very happy with your job. But when you get a call out of the blue about making a major career enhancing move and the caller needs a CV immediately, you're ready. Don't feel guilty about this: keep that CV updated!

Where do you think your greatest career possibilities are? Within the company that now employs you, or elsewhere?

Some jobs just don't lead to the president's office. However, depending on the company itself and its size, the opportunities for people with certain specialties might be elsewhere. For example, if you are the top media buyer in an advertising agency, your chances for career advancement lie more in moving on than with your present company. Of course, the top job at your present company may be just what you want, so do your best and enjoy it. Not everyone is comfortable moving from job to job.

Are your skills and abilities in sync with your present job?

It's not uncommon to discover that, although you are doing difficult work that requires considerable skill, the work has become repetitive. And as it becomes repetitive, you become easily bored and distracted. This happens to highly skilled surgeons as well as to people whose work requires far less training and skill. Regardless of what you do, your work can become boring. Just how much boredom you are willing to tolerate will determine how restless you become in your job. This condition, however, usually requires learning new skills rather than moving on to another company. I'll talk about this in more detail later on in the book.

How do you spend your Sunday afternoons?

If work intrudes on your thoughts when you should be enjoying yourself, it's a sign of some problems. Those problems may not necessarily mean that you are unhappy with your job. But if a bright, sunny Sunday afternoon turns cloudy and ominous for you regularly, chances are you're not all that pleased with your job.

Try to determine just what it is about the job that ruins your Sundays. Try to separate the real from the imagined. The real may include a genuinely tyrannical boss, or company culture that stifles your creativity. The imagined may include perceived slights by bosses and co-workers. I'm not big on making lots of lists, but here is one place you might consider making lists. Determine whether the unpleasant events are routinely part of your work day, or if they come and go. The stuff that bugs you daily needs immediate attention. See what is behind the feelings. Try to determine where you have control and where you don't. Then make real efforts to see what you can do to neutralize those factors over which you do have some control. The big stuff over which you have little or no control may just be the reasons why you should consider making a change.

What is the real reason you don't leave your present job?

Case in Point

Alan Greenspan said, "I have found no greater satisfaction than achieving success through honest dealing and strict adherence to the view that, for you to gain, those you deal with should gain as well."

Apart from conditions over which you have no control, what keeps you from making a move now? We are, after all, talking about career planning, and career growth today is almost synonymous with moving on to move up. You may answer that you like your boss, your co-workers, the work environment, and even the compensation package. What else could there be? For one thing, there may be no opportunity for you to stretch your wings, to use skills and knowledge you have that are not called for by your present job. For another, you may prefer security and safety to the risk of moving to another company. You are perfectly normal if these reasons are in your list. Not everyone sees himself or herself at the top of the corporate heap. But, if you have the itch and you work for a large conglomerate, there may be more than a few opportunities to move from one operating unit to another to improve yourself both economically and emotionally. Being underused when you have untapped talents can eat away at your self-esteem. I'll be touching on this issue more than a few times in the rest of the book.

What does a really bad day at the office do to you?

No one is immune to the emotions a bad day can conjure up. And it's almost impossible to turn off these emotions when you leave the office at the end of the day. But do you tote this baggage home with you and let it ruin the rest of your day? And do you ruin the days of others when you unload on them about your bad day?

There's enough material in the professional literature to turn this chapter into several books, but for our purpose of getting to know yourself, try to reconstruct your typical bad day. Relive one right now in all its excruciating detail. Then ask yourself, did what you did to yourself and others as a result make any difference in the conditions that caused it? My guess is that the answer is no.

Bad days are a fact of life. You have to learn to deal with them. Occasional bad days are never a good reason to quit. However, bad days every Monday through Friday are a sign that something is seriously wrong. Again, it's beyond the scope of this book to help you in this area, but it is within its scope to help you determine whether or not your work conditions are such that you should move on or simply adapt to them. Everything in life involves some sort of trade-off. Only you can decide whether it's a fair trade.

Watch Out for Flying Pigs

Any measures of self satisfaction have to be seen relative to something real. That something real is usually called corporate culture, and it includes the difference between what is said in the employee handbook and what actually exists in the office or on the shop floor. In short, we are dealing with the warm and fuzzy stuff against a background of reality. The warm and fuzzy stuff can be thought of as the apocryphal flying pig, meaning that something will never happen. It's a gentler way of saying, "That something will only happen when hell freezes over." Whichever you prefer, I'm sure you get my meaning. Here are some of my favorite Flying Pigs, as they relate to happiness on the job.

- Employer and employee loyalty is a myth in much of American business today. You do owe it to your employer to perform as best you can. But you owe it to yourself to see to your own career development.

- You are the only one who can decide what is satisfying and irritation on the job. And the employer can and often does change the rules without asking for your advice.

- What you want from your job and what your employer can and may be willing to offer is never set in stone. It changes for any number of reasons. However, today you are more likely to look elsewhere for satisfaction than by waiting for your employer do what you want him or her to do.

I am not being cynical, I am being realistic. And I am not knocking employers. Many of my major clients are employers who use my services to help their employees grow within the company. However, no book on the subject of career management would be worth reading if it didn't acknowledge this reality. When you keep in mind that the employer also has the right to be dissatisfied with you, you can see that this is really a transactional situation. So it's up to both of you to seek either an accommodation to perceived needs, or to part company.

The Least You Need to Know

- Taking stock of yourself and your career is not a one-time activity.

- You should pay as much attention to feelings as you do to real-world events. But confirm your feelings whenever you can.

- Be honest with yourself about both the positive and negative things in your life.

- Your quest usually stresses what you want more of from life. However, knowing what you want less of is equally important.

- Flying pigs exist, but only in the minds of those who are trying to convince you that up is down.

Chapter 7

Beginning Your Self-Assessment

In This Chapter

- ◆ Reviewing your defining moments
- ◆ Looking back to look ahead
- ◆ Performance reviews and resumés create a road map
- ◆ Your friends and colleagues can help
- ◆ Why you need an empty shoebox

Using an analogy is not the best way to make an important point, but Sir Isaac Newton and the rest of the world have a lot in common when it comes to getting things done. Sir Isaac said (and I'm paraphrasing for those who failed Physics 101), "Things already in motion tend to remain in motion, and things not in motion sit on a couch and think about what they should really be doing." If I may be granted a little more scientific license, let me add that velocity—the speed at which things can move—can be changed whenever necessary. And here we are at the nub of things. It's up to you to get things moving if they are not already moving, and if they are moving it's up to make them move faster.

Throughout this book, you will see a number of small self-tests designed to give you insights in your career planning and management. None of the tests will give you the answers to guarantee that you will find the best job in the world and be happy ever after. This is not to denigrate career type tests, but they are best used when they are complex in that they get at the smaller details of your life. And they are most helpful when, after having taken them, you review them with a professional. I do suggest that you investigate some of these tests and I have listed them in the appendix of this book.

You Can Do It Yourself

When you think about it, you're taking stock of yourself all the time. You meet someone for the first time and you might like to get know them better. If you're like the rest of us, you immediately review what you said and how it might influence a possible acquaintanceship. In other words, you are awarding yourself bravos and blunders and setting a strategy for the next time you meet. See? You're already familiar with the process. However, when it comes to your career, it should be more structured and you should have specific goals in mind. If you keep your long-term goals clearly in mind, chances are good you'll seldom be frustrated by the short-term setbacks you encounter along the way.

Keep in mind that your goal in this self-assessment is to get a firm handle on what you like and don't like, and what you want more of and less of in your career. Forget all the other stuff that plagues all of us most the time. Stick to the career focus.

Looking Back to Look Ahead

You're looking for specific career information, not the nice things your first grade teacher said about you. This is not as easy as it might seem. Start with the elements that define your life today and work back toward their origins. Look for defining moments, paths taken when there was more than one path to choose.

Start with today, because today is what you know best, and you will be building on a base that is firm and immediately familiar to you. Contrary to the old saying that hindsight is always 20/20, it's not. Hindsight is loaded with all the rationales you ever used to make history appear better than it really was. In other words, it's a cloudy, rear-view mirror. So, try to stick to the facts. For now, we want to find some constants in your life that will help you see why and how things that happened in the past have contributed to who and what you are today, and whether they will be helpful in the future.

Now for the kicker! Don't think of this as only a list of your good traits and wise choices, like a resumé to use to impress a prospective employer. The good stuff is important, but you must also include all your blunders, false starts, mistakes, and screw-ups. It is just as important to know what you did wrong, why you did it, and how you got back on track. You're not going to show this to anyone else, so go at it fearlessly.

Case in Point

Henry Ford said, "Even a mistake may turn out to be the one thing necessary to a worthwhile achievement." Remember, the biggest mistake you can make is to do nothing. You can quote me on that one.

Start with Your Present Job Description

Your job description, even if it's not the job you aimed for or thought you were getting, is the best place to start. Make a list of the requirements your employer set for the job and another list of the skills you brought to the table. Then, make a list of your shortcomings and how you may have overcome them. Follow that with a description of what you would consider an ideal job for a person with your qualifications.

Don't try to analyze anything, just gather the facts. This isn't psychoanalysis; it's retracing a map of your career so far. Try to note the reasons for your decisions or actions at critical points. For example, if you had a choice of two jobs, what was it about each that affected your choice? What did you reject and what did you like about both jobs? Don't write any long essays, just the facts.

Now, look over all the performance reviews that have led to your present position. What was praised about your work, and what needed improvement? Pay particular attention to deficiencies in your work performance. If you honestly believe the comments were warranted, think back over what you did to overcome the problems. Think about how you might behave differently if you faced the same situation now.

Case in Point

Ben Franklin said, "It's hard for an empty bag to stand upright." Gather everything you can that will help you see where you have been and how you got there.

Review your present job description and note the changes from descriptions of previous jobs. Pay particular attention to trends in both the kind of work you have been doing and the skills needed to move from job to job. Look at your job description from the perspective of where you have gotten since you entered the world of work and where you are now. Is your path a straight line, or were there any detours? Don't assume that a straight line is necessarily a good indicator. It may be; however, diversions are also a sign that you might have been flexible enough to make course corrections as your work circumstances changed along the way. Remember, you are looking at yourself as a functioning human being, not a ruler to measure the distances between career events in your life.

Look at Your Old Resumés

Now, dig out your current resumé and all the other resumés you may have made in the past. Here is where you will see some important information. You created your resumés to put you in the best possible light with a potential employer. As you move from job to job, the employment requirements change, and you change, too.

The clues in this exercise are usually not all that obvious, but you should be able to spot points at which you were stressing credentials that would move you closer to the kind of work that is most attractive to you. Early on, all of us take jobs of convenience that get us into the workforce and into the fields where we think we want to spend our careers. As we gain experience and knowledge about career possibilities, we sharpen our focus and start more of an upward climb within our chosen field. All this information will help you more clearly see your career and your potential.

What Are Your Greatest Accomplishments?

Now, assemble a list of the personal accomplishments that are important to you. List professional accomplishments as well as things that gave you pleasure outside of work. Most people discover as much about themselves off the job as on it.

It may help to assemble this material under the headings "Aptitudes" and "Attitudes." Aptitudes are the skills and knowledge you have acquired on the way to where you are now. Attitudes are your feelings about what you have done, your positive achievements as well as the points where hard turns were needed to get you back on the road. How you deal with trouble spots is often more often indicative of future success than how you bask in the glory of your successes.

Your reactions to the events of your work life may have required immediate responses, or they may have called for decisions that resulted in more long-term changes. A key element in career management is the ability to decide when immediate action is needed and when you should modulate your responses and plan for a long haul. You can turn a speed boat almost instantly, but you have to plan ahead to turn a huge supertanker. Career management requires that you know when to turn hard and when to make the long, slow turns. We will get into more of this later when we begin analyzing your skills, abilities, and interests.

What Others May Say Will Help, Too

Friends and colleagues can be a big help if they understand that you are looking for real help, not just moral support. We all have friends we can trust to be honest and some who are more interested in being nice. Turn to those who will be truthful. Your friends and colleagues can often see things that you can't see—or prefer not to.

I have worked with more than a few clients who tell me good things their friends tell them that just don't ring true to me in my coaching role. It's always difficult to point this out, because they trust their friends and I'm pretty much a stranger. Just remember that your friends usually have the best motives, but they often don't understand that you are looking for real insights into your life and problems. Most people will level with you when you press them.

We seldom show or tell friends and work colleagues the same things about ourselves. We have one version for friends and another version for colleagues. We seldom lie when we tell the same story differently to different people, but we describe things in ways we see them perceiving the issues. If you were denied a promotion, for example, you would probably tell a work colleague about it in terms of office situations that would be familiar to both of you. Describing the denial to a friend, you would probably eliminate most of the detail and focus on the emotional side of the issue. In both cases you would probably be truthful, but you would be shading the issues to suit the relationship you have with each individual.

So, when you ask them for their thoughts and advice, be aware that how they respond will be determined by what you have told them and how they see you. In either case, assure friends and colleagues that even if they have negative things to say, it will not harm the friendship. Again, you can make lists, fill a pad of Post-It notes, or if you are better organized than most, collect these comments on your computer.

Now, Get an Empty Shoebox

I've suggested a lot of get-this and get-that in this chapter. Note, however, that I have avoided suggesting that you make any attempt at organizing all of this information. None of it really lends itself to lists and listing. However, all of it is important and you will be dipping into it in the chapters to come. Don't be tempted to do the gathering later as you read the chapters. Having your shoebox full and at your side as you read will not only speed things up, it will ensure that you keep reading. After all, the subject is you, and what more fascinating subject could there be?

The Least You Need to Know

- Where you are is probably not exactly where you wanted to be.
- Where you wanted to be is still within your grasp.
- Your missteps are as important in your planning as your successes.
- Judge what friends tell you about yourself differently from the way you judge what work colleagues tell you.
- A shoebox may be your most important career-management tool.

Chapter 8

Brush Up Your Basic Skills

In This Chapter

◆ Science reveals why you are a math schlumpf

◆ Why you only think you hear well and understand everything you think you hear

◆ Why the last memo you wrote sent everyone into gales of laughter

◆ How to get everyone's attention, even though you have never spoken to more than three people at a time

I was shocked! My lunch companion, a high level sales executive with a major international corporation, watched while I calculated the tip and signed the credit card receipt. "Wow," he said, "you figured that tip quickly and you did it in your head. How did you do it?" This was back when the typical tip was 15 percent. I told him that I started with 10 percent, divided it in half, and added that to 10 percent. "You did all that in your head?" he asked, and not with mock awe. He was as genuinely impressed with my skills as I was depressed at seeing how high someone could rise in business with such limited math ability.

As it turned out, he always carried a calculator and knew enough of the basics to use it when the numbers were beyond him. But however important the mechanics of math are, math is more than crunching numbers.

Math is a descriptive language with its own rules and symbols. I wondered what went on in his head when his colleagues began talking about profit margins relative to the average cost per sale. It must have been a fog to him. It turned out that he was a top salesman in the company. But as I discovered later, he never made it to management ranks. My guess is that this was due at least in part to his inability to understand the logic that is mathematics.

What's the point? The point is that you can survive and probably do fairly well without understanding much math. But it's a rare math-averse person who makes it to the top. I don't tell this story to give you any excuses. I tell it because I hope that you are reading this book with the idea of going a lot further than your fifth-grade algebra teacher ever thought you'd go.

Your Basic Skills Toolkit

Most of the chapters that follow will address the elements that you probably wanted most to understand when you bought this book. But as someone who has spent most of his working life in the field of career development, I can assure that no matter how outstanding your management style, no matter your ability to form and lead a group, your chances of making it and all the way up the ladder are slim if you lack any of the underlying skills your competitors will have.

Case in Point

When the National Assessment of Adult Literacy was administered in 1992 it was discovered that only 40 percent of U.S. college graduates scored at the "proficient" level. This means that 60 percent could not read lengthy texts in English well enough to draw accurate inferences. Pretty bad, isn't it? But, it got worse. When the test was administered again in 2003, only 31 percent were proficient. This means that 69 percent were a risk to themselves and to the companies that paid their salaries.

It gets even scarier. Three percent of the college grads who took the test showed up as actually being "below basic." For this test, below basic meant that they could not even perform the simplest reading exercises, such as locating fairly obvious information in short prose paragraphs.

You may have been able to satisfy your college requirement for a degree by taking a baby science course, or one of the many rehashes of high school math that many colleges offer. And you might have bypassed freshman comp by taking a walk through something like Survey of Twentieth Century Comic Books.

Don't feel too pleased with yourself. You got a degree, but did you get an education? Practical courses, such as those offered on computers are important. But even more important are the courses that teach you how to think and solve problems inductively and deductively. This is especially helpful when the manual that came with your computer was translated by someone whose first language is only spoken by a few thousand people. And the courses offered under the broad heading of "communications" are seldom helpful when your boss tells you to rewrite your report using the second person active voice.

It's not too late to sharpen the skills you may have learned but lost somewhere along the way. And it's never too late to learn them fresh. However, you first have to discover what you don't know before you can put yourself in the know. Fortunately, it's not necessary for everyone to go back to school to get the help they need at the basic skills level. Let's look at language first.

> **Case in Point**
>
> Gina Kolata in *The New York Times:* "Beyond arithmetic and geometry, quantitative literacy also requires logic, data analysis, and probability. It enables individuals to analyze evidence, to read graphs, to understand logical arguments, to detect logical fallacies, to understand evidence, and to evaluate risks. Quantitative literacy means knowing how to reason and how to think."

Reading Skills

Reading, writing, speaking, and listening are critical skills for success at any career level. Since I have no idea where each reader of this book stands on these skills, I'm starting in the middle, where most people are when they begin to think seriously about how best to manage their careers. I have not included any tests for you to use. Good tests are far too complex for a short book such as this. And a proper evaluation of their results requires someone with accredited skills.

A good reader understands what he or she has read on both a literal and a critical level. Literal comprehension means that you are able to grasp the main idea the writer is presenting and understand the material the writer has presented to support the main idea. This, of course, means that your vocabulary must be sufficient for the task, and that you can understand how

> **Case in Point**
>
> Woody Allen said, "Ninety percent of success is just showing up." Then, there's Dorio's corollary: "You can make that 90 percent by showing up on time."

the words are used in the context of the writing. Most people have very few problems at this level. It's when they try to read critically that many people have difficulty.

Case in Point _____

Harry Truman said, "Not all readers are leaders, but all leaders are readers." I like this one, too, by Groucho Marx: "Outside of a dog, a book is man's best friend. Inside of a dog, it's too dark to read."

Critical, or inferential, thinking is what you do when you want or need more than just the facts. If something you just read presents an argument or seems ambiguous, you need to be able to evaluate the writer's words on the basis of how well he or she has presented the material. You must also be able to judge the relevance of the material to the writer's main point. There's a lot more, but it's beyond the scope of this book. Check out the sources listed in the appendix, which include books on the basics as well as some advanced stuff.

Writing Skills

Good writing comes from having a large vocabulary, an understanding of basic grammar, and the ability to organize your thoughts in a logical way. You don't have to know what a gerund is and does. You don't even have to know how to spell well anymore, thanks to the computer spell checker. But you do have to know what you want to say, and you have to be able to express yourself simply, clearly, and thoroughly.

There are hundreds of good books on all aspects of writing. Most will help you when you have specific questions, but the best way to get up to speed quickly is to *read good writing*. There probably are people in your company whose memos are clear and even pleasant to read. Whether or not you know the parts of speech and how they work together, you will know good writing when you see it. And, you'll know bad writing just as well. Bad writing is usually awkward, error-prone, and too long, and often contains overly formal words and phrases.

Don't be embarrassed to copy the style of a good writer. In fact, it's the fastest way to improve the skills you already have. There are a few books listed in the appendix that will help you at whatever level you need.

Speaking Clearly

"I'd rather have a root canal without anesthetic than give a speech." It's a cliché and I've heard the same line from more than a few people, so I guess there really is something to the fear of public speaking. There's nothing I can do for you in a few sentences, but I can pass along a few do's and a few don'ts that will make it a more pleasant and successful experience. But before I do, let me urge you to learn to do it and do it well. You will be miles ahead of the guy competing for the same job who won't take to the podium.

Every experienced speaker will tell you that you have to get your audience's attention right away or, no matter how good your speech, you're dead meat. So here are some tips I've picked from the pros over the years:

If you plan to open with a joke, make it a very short one that relates directly to your topic. If you have some really startling information to relate, get right to the point. A slow build-up is slow death. It can help if you have a short quotation by someone your audience would recognize, but make sure the quote fits the topic of the talk. Don't open with, "Hi there, my name is ...." Never open with a rhetorical question—in fact, try not to use them at any point in your speech. Don't try too hard to win the audience. They will be with you if you have something interesting to say and you use words and phrases they understand immediately.

That's it, except for your exit. Don't thank them for being a good audience. Get out of the spotlight quickly. And, if you have an appropriate line and the talk wasn't about anything deadly serious, leave them laughing with a good joke. Again, make it a short one.

There you have it—the top secrets of some of the world's great speakers. The rest is up to you. Being a good speaker, whether you're addressing a group or only one person can be a critical factor in anyone's ascent to higher office. Check the appendix; I've listed a few sources of good information on public speaking, too.

> **Career Alert**
>
> Great speeches have three things in common. I call them the Three B's: be brief, be bright, and be gone. If you want proof, count the number of words in the Gettysburg Address, and read any historian's account of the event.

Listening Isn't Easy

In many ways, listening and reading are very much alike. You have to be able to understand what the writer or the speaker is saying. And you have to be able to analyze the thoughts being presented and to judge the speaker's or writer's reasons for wanting your attention. However, it's easier to put a book down whenever you want, and it's not that easy to walk out on someone who is talking to or with you.

Right Move _____

If you have any reason to think you might have a hearing problem, get it checked out quickly. You may think you hear everything, but even with minor hearing problems, you will miss the shades of meaning in what others say. English is a highly inflected language and inflection often carries as much information as the words themselves.

The major difference between reading and listening is that you can take what you are reading with you and read it again. Try doing that with a speaker. And don't think you can get away with not paying attention by taking a voice recorder with you. Voice recorders won't give you the nuance you need to understand what has been said.

There are two basic reasons why you should be a really good listener. The first is, of course, obvious; if you don't listen carefully to what is said to you or in your presence, you'll never fully understand what is happening around you. The second is that people tend to think more of people who pay attention than those who don't. Call it flattery, if you will. But, who among us is above just a little flattery once in a while?

You probably think you are a good listener. You come away from a conversation remembering all the facts and statistics you heard. However, have you been able to draw any conclusions from what you heard? Have you made any judgments that may have been required of you as a listener? And have you been able to make connections between what you heard and your thoughts and opinions on the speaker's topic?

Listening is a transactional activity when you and someone else can talk and respond to each other in real time. And this kind of transaction involves a lot more than words. Body language sends signals, as do the inflections of your words. There's so much to know in this area that I urge you to read some of the material I have listed in the appendix. For now, remember that being attentive will not only help you understand what is being said, it will also send positive signals to the person with whom you are speaking. Again, check the appendix for sources you can use to improve your listening skills.

The Dreaded Subject—Math

Henry Ford wasn't talking about mathematics when he said this, but he could have been: "If you think you can do it, or think you can't do it, you are right." Most people start out life with a bunch of preconceptions that hobble them forever. You were a little kid listening to your older brother talk with his pals about the algebra course they were taking in school. You heard lines like, "I'll never understand that stuff." "I don't have a head for numbers." Then, you probably heard the same crowd talk about complicated baseball statistics, and possibly about the measurements involved in something they were building out in the garage. Did it ever strike you that something was missing between their protestations about algebra and their use of some fairly complex statistical manipulations? Probably not. You just joined the I-hate-math-club, and repeated Algebra 1 in your junior year. Right?

I'm not going to tell you that math is easy. It isn't. But most people make it much more of a problem than it has to be. There's a whole body of work in developmental psychology that deals with the scripts people write for themselves. Trust me, when you jump on the I-Hate-Math Express, you are telling yourself things that are just plain wrong. And when you duck the math courses by taking some cushy elective, you are setting yourself up for future trouble.

There are all sorts of shortcuts and tricks to learning math, but one tip may help change your mind about math and, I hope, make it easier for you learn a little more about the subject.

My guess is that the day you finished the last math course you ever took, you either returned the textbook or retired it to the dumpster. Get a copy of a current textbook

> **Case in Point**
>
> Albert Einstein said, "If A equals success, then the formula is A equals X plus Y plus Z. X is work. Y is play. And Z is keep your mouth shut." See how easy it is?

for the highest level of math you attained. Don't buy it, just borrow it from a library, and dip into here and there. Unless I'm mistaken, you will understand most of it and be able to pick up what you don't understand quickly. I'm not saying you should read the entire book. I just want you to see for yourself that you did learn something, you remembered it, and that it wasn't all that awful. This will go a long way toward ending the lie you have been telling yourself that you just don't get it.

The Least You Need to Know

- Speaking in public isn't easy, but it's a key requirement the higher you get.
- The easiest way to improve your writing is to read good writing.
- The books you should read are never available on tape—improve your reading skills.
- Math skills are important. But more important is the ability to use and manipulate symbols and ideas. You can learn to do this without ever using a number. Try reading a basic book on symbolic logic.

Chapter 9

Analyze Your Personal Style

In This Chapter

- ◆ People are not always what they seem to be, and neither are you

- ◆ A simple test you can use to uncover your true personal style

- ◆ Create a TV promo of yourself that will put your career on firm footing

- ◆ Help in seeing what others really see in you

Remember in freshman psych when the prof asked each member of the class to rate a guest speaker by filling out a multiple-choice form? The prof told you that it was part of a larger study he was doing. At the next session, he provided all the students with a report summary of the questionnaire and explained that it really wasn't part of a study, but it was the best way to introduce you to the subject of perception. Unless your class was very different than most, the evaluations were all over the lot. In fact, I'll bet that no two people gave identical evaluations. This simple demonstration proved the point that even when two people experience the same thing, each experiences it differently.

What you experience is changed by any previous experience you have that might relates to the subject. In fact, it's changed by so many things so quickly, that you might describe it as the brain multitasking with multiple inputs. Everything you sense—sounds, smells, sight, touches—is subject to your own perceptual spin. And each time you experience something, you are automatically tapping your mental hard drive for all the relevant memories that are stored there. Those events are called to active memory and the process of reviewing them in context of the current stimulus is done in the blink of an eye.

This process is not limited to your perception of the world around you. It's just as relevant to your view of yourself, and that's the nub of this chapter: how you see yourself, and how to see yourself as others see you. In short, it's time to get a handle on your personal style. What you learn can not only help you in your daily dealings with others, but it can help you put your best face forward when you interview for a new job, or discuss the future you hope to have with your present employer.

No Two People Are Alike—Thankfully!

In 1955, two psychologists, Joseph Luft and Harry Ingham, developed a system to help people understand their interpersonal relationships. Named for the authors, the Johari Window is used extensively with self-help groups and in business personnel evaluation settings. It's well beyond the scope of this chapter to take you through the complete test, but it will be very helpful for you to see the four ways you can define yourself as a result of taking the full test. See the listings in the appendix if you would like more information on the test.

Those who take the test are given a list of adjectives that describe a wide range of human behavior. It starts with "able," and ends with "witty." There are 55 adjectives in all, including words such as "modest," "self-assertive," and "responsive." At the completion of the test, you have a picture of yourself in terms of your Public Self, your Private Self, your Blind Self, and your Undiscovered Self.

◆ Your Public Self is the part of you that you're pleased with and willing to share with others.

◆ Your Private Self is the part you're totally unwilling to share with anyone. These elements usually include things in your life that cause you shame, embarrassment, and even fear. To expose them to others would give you a serious sense of vulnerability.

◆ Your Blind Self describes areas in which your perception of yourself is at odds with what others may feel about you. You may think of yourself as a great manager, but those you actually manage may see you very differently.

◆ Your Undiscovered Self is that area that both you and others may be totally unaware of. These elements may be both positive and negative.

As you can see, this approach opens some very interesting windows through which you can see yourself on a number of different dimensions. There are many ways to interpret the results, and some novel and very productive interpretative systems are available to professionals who use the program in professional counseling or coaching settings.

Right Move _____

The Johari Window is a relatively powerful device in the hands of a skilled professional. It is quickly and easily administered, and its validity and reliability over the years speaks to its effectiveness. Check with your coach or counselor to see if he or she feels that it would be a helpful test for you to take.

Discovering Your Style on Your Own

As much as I want to encourage you to take at least one of the many excellent tests that get at your personal style, I recognize that many readers will be in a hurry, and others may just not be able to afford the cost of professional testing.

What follows are a few questions that, if answered honestly and thoroughly, will give you some idea of what your personal style is like, and how you can use that knowledge to move your career along a little faster. The questions are based on the topics that most of the major personal style inventories that career coaches use cover in depth. Remember that you are going to evaluate yourself, and that's not an easy job.

How do you prefer to make decisions?

Do you prefer to make them alone, or do you prefer to wait and see what decisions others in the group make? Generally speaking, those who prefer to decide without waiting for a consensus are more sure of themselves. Those who prefer to wait until they see what their fellow workers say

Case in Point _____

Homer Simpson, "It takes two to lie. One to lie and one to listen." Homer is right, and what he says goes double if you're fibbing to yourself.

are usually seen more as team players, while those who go it alone are thought of as risk takers. If the person considering you for a job seems to be seeking a team player and this isn't your style, be aware that there will be some rough edges if you take the job. At this point, just note which way you prefer to act in general.

Do you prefer to establish tight schedules for projects, or would you rather fly by the seat of your pants?

Some projects are so complex that schedules are absolutely necessary. But, what about the more routine work? Are schedules and firm deadlines more helpful to you than just keeping the dates in your head and hoping you get them done on time? Some employers would see being highly organized as being a bit rigid and possibly slowing the work flow. Others, however, see this as critical. Know what you are most comfortable with. Don't try to snow an employer by pretending to be what you are not. It will show up all too quickly, and both of you will be unhappy.

Do you look forward to meeting new people, or do you prefer making a few friends and sticking with them?

The obvious situation here is sales work. If you prefer the company of a few good friends, you are probably much better suited to work that involves a small group of people who work closely together.

Do you prefer solving problems using tried and true methods, or do you like to look for new and innovative ways to do things?

Even accountants can be creative without doing things that might attract the interest of the sheriff. So try to think about this from the perspective what gives you pleasure, not necessarily what the culture of your field might represent.

Do you like to do things on the spur of the moment, or do you prefer to plan everything carefully?

Spontaneity is critical for some jobs. However, under most circumstances, would you prefer to have advance notice of something? Do you feel threatened by being asked to do something without advance notice, or can you rise to the occasion with minimum stress? Airline pilots have to make immediate decisions, but the typical business executive usually has enough time to carefully evaluate all the alternatives in most situations.

Sizing Up Your Style

Professionally developed tests help you understand your personal style by asking the same questions in many different ways. Their aim is to ensure validity—that the test is testing what it is supposed to—and reliability—that it provides consistent results. You don't have that luxury when you take on the chore yourself. However, if you are honest with yourself, you can come close to the mark. If you really want to be certain that the picture you get is really accurate, see someone about professional testing. Now, let's see what you can make of yourself from the answers you gave to the few questions above.

Are you happiest in small and more familiar situations?

Typically, people who prefer small, stable situations tend to value thoroughness and dependability. They are generally practical in their approach to problems and enjoy structuring their work in an orderly fashion. Harmonious relationships with others are usually important, as is loyalty. They usually dislike conflict and prefer not to force their opinions and values on others. They often look for meaning in ideas and relationships and often have very original minds. Adaptability and flexibility are terms often applied to those who might be thought of as introverts.

Are you happiest in less structured situations where you might have frequent contact with many different people?

Those who generally fall into this category tend to take a pragmatic approach to problem solving and are more focused on immediate results. They are comfortable in almost any social situation and take pleasure in life's material comforts. They are usually enthusiastic and often very imaginative. They can be outspoken at times, especially when faced with illogical situations. Routine usually bores them, though they often operate using clear and systematically defined standards. At the extreme they are often quite forceful when discussing ideas with which others disagree.

I realize that this doesn't give you much more to go on than a typical magazine personality test, but if you take the time to carefully think about yourself within the dimensions I have outlined, you will at least be more than half way to getting a handle on your personal style. And this is often where the "ah-ha!" factor makes it appearance. Not that you will have a cut-in-stone picture of your style, but you will at least be able to see the pieces of your personality fitting together. It's like pushing a huge rock. It takes a lot of effort to get the rock moving, but once the rock gets rolling, the rest is easy.

The Thirty Second U-Promo

When you're watching a TV show and a commercial breaks in at a critical moment, that 30 second promo can seem to last for hours. However, in those 30 seconds the advertiser has passed along more information than you might think. Now, I want you to think like a TV ad producer. Write a promo of yourself that can be delivered in 30 seconds that will tell the millions of strangers out there in TV land just who you are. Don't write a job pitch, write a pitch that simply puts you in a clear light.

The promo should acknowledge your weaknesses as well as present your strengths. It should not be apologetic and it should not be a screaming banner for you. It should pitch you as you are right now. You can choose whatever you want to emphasize, what to include and what not to include, but whatever you include must be truly and honestly you.

You are doing this as a TV promo rather than as a simple essay because I want you to speak the words out loud to yourself as you write them. I want you to start a dialog with yourself. You are free to edit yourself at any time, and you can take as long as you like to write your promo.

When you write anything, whether it's a TV promo or a magazine article, you have to constantly think in terms of the person who will hear you or read your words. That person will judge you as believable or unbelievable, honest or dishonest, confident or lacking confidence, and sincere or insincere. Keep these factors in mind, but do not use any of the actual words I've just used to describe yourself. Use your own words and write to convince yourself that you are who you are.

Now comes the tricky part. Once you have a first draft, try to memorize it so you can deliver it in front of a mirror and watch yourself in the process. This may seem corny, but unless you can look yourself in the eye as you pitch yourself, you may be fudging something. Body language tells a lot about a person, and you can even tell a lot about yourself as you come face to face with you as you pitch you.

> **Case in Point**
>
> Dr. Joyce Brothers, "A strong, positive self-image is the best possible preparation for success."

Good poker players and successful sales people are expert in reading body language. They may come to this from experience, or they may have learned it from someone else. Either way, they all look for a "tell" in others, whether they are making a pitch or raising the ante in a card game.

A "tell" is a tic, something that is easily noticeable and appears in everyone when they are under some stress. It could be a tug of the ear, or a blink of the eyes. You'll know it when you see it because you will do it yourself when you tell yourself something that makes you uncomfortable. The only problem is that no one can see themselves blink in a mirror. Try it.

When you spot your "tell" as you pitch yourself in the mirror, or just feel uncomfortable about what you have said, you will know that this is an area where you need work. You are probably getting close to something sensitive, and it will be something you have to deal with. Again, be honest with yourself. Try rewriting your promo. See if you your "tell" has disappeared when you do the mirror test again. This is a strong first step to self-knowledge.

 Case in Point

Albert Einstein, "I know quite certainly that I myself have no special talent; curiosity, obsession, and dogged endurance combined with self-criticism have brought me to my ideas."

Yes, Yes, That's Me!

You may spend many hours writing this promo of yourself, and it will probably not exceed 300 words if it's to fit the 30 second time slot. However, it will be as close to you as you can get—if you are really being honest about yourself. Here's a quick test you can use to confirm that you are on the right track.

1. You find that you neither approve nor disapprove of yourself. Your feeling is that it is you, warts and all. In other words, you have not been judgmental. You are not harshly criticizing yourself for the things you have done that you not pleased with. And, you are not an overblown pitchman for your achievements.

2. You can see the paths that have led to where you are now, and you have a sense of where changes along the way might have made things different for you— either positively or negatively.

3. You have a good sense of the direction your life is taking and you can see where some course corrections might take you in more desirable directions.

Take a break. Put it aside for a few days and do something totally unrelated to career management. Then go back and see if it strikes you the same way as when you finished it. If you see any major issues, now is the time to correct them. But if you see some picky stuff, forget about it. At this point you can write and rewrite endlessly and get nowhere. There comes a time when you have to get the boat in the water, even if it has a few small leaks. You can patch the holes as you sail on.

Take Your Show on the Road

You have just completed a highly subjective study of yourself, and at this point you might want to get some input from others. When I discussed perception earlier, I mentioned that people seldom see eye to eye on everything. The people you select to hear your promo should be those you trust to tell the truth as they see it. Explain what you're doing so that their comments are aimed at helping you understand yourself, rather than offering help in rewriting the script. You can get the best help by asking them general questions, rather than digging into specifics. You are dealing with your image of yourself now, not trying to create a historically accurate picture of yourself.

You're not a psychologist, so don't overanalyze what people say. Just look for comments that seem to show up more frequently than others. These can be cues that you can't see for yourself and that you might consider thinking about for the future.

Adding It All Up

You are the sum of all your experiences and how you responded to them. Navigating a career is a matter of shooting the sun often enough to know when you are on or off course, and knowing when a course change might be prudent.

Probably the biggest mistake many people make is assuming the course they set for themselves years ago is still a true course. Flexibility is as important as maintaining a focus on cherished goals. Sometimes you have to sail around obstacles. At other times you just have to trim sails and head into a storm. If you took the time to write your promo, you have taken a major step in career management. In the next few chapters we will be getting into the details. Stick with me.

The Least You Need to Know

- The way you see yourself may not be the same as others see you.

- You can get to know the "real" by yourself—and with a little help from your friends.

- You should have a clear self-image before you move on to the practical details of career management.

- Take yourself seriously, but don't obsess over trivial details.

Chapter 10

Chart Your Communication Style

In This Chapter

- You may be a better communicator than you think you are—or you may not be

- You hear with your ears, but you listen with your brain

- Smile when you say that …

- Good writing is clear thinking on paper

Sometimes you have to dig into the really esoteric stuff to make a point. Communicating about communicating calls for some fancy footwork, so I thought I'd turn to a source most of us have learned to respect and trust. Winnie the Pooh said, "Don't underestimate the value of doing nothing, of just going along, listening to all the things you can't hear, and not bothering." Pooh Bear could have been describing many people we all know. They can appear disinterested in what you are saying, but when you wrap it up, they ask some of the most searching questions. Then, of course, there will always be a few glassy-eyed folks who just might have wandered into the wrong room. However, the glassy-eyed and distracted people may also have been the victims of someone who feels that the mark of a good speaker is to tell everything in excruciating detail and to throw in a few inappropriate jokes to substitute for content and or skill.

My guess is that you have been on both sides of the podium a few times yourself. In short, communicating—like life itself—is a series of transactions. And if there is one area that can put the chocks under your career wheels faster than being a poor communicator and a poor listener, I haven't heard of it. So this chapter is dedicated to all those good speakers and listeners we know, and all the poor speakers and listeners we also know, who provide us with the horrible examples we use to write books like this. Cheers to both!

This Is Only a Test

This is one area where a simple test can give you immediate and valuable feedback. And I'd like you to have some idea of where you stand in terms of interpersonal communications before we dig into the specifics. So grab a pencil and a piece of paper and begin. This is an open-book test—you are the book!

How Well Do You Communicate?

Think about how you interact daily with others at work. Read each statement carefully and rate yourself from 1 (Never) to 5 (Always).

1. I give my full attention to others when they are speaking. ___

2. I ask questions to help get clarification. ___

3. I paraphrase what others say to get "shared understanding." ___

4. People understand my instructions or requests for information. ___

5. I maintain good eye contact when in a conversation. ___

6. People tell me I'm an effective speaker. ___

7. I show respect to others when they are speaking. ___

8. I notice and am sensitive to another's nonverbals. ___

9. I speak up at team meetings. ___

10. I try to empathize with other's point of view. ___

11. I adjust my communication style to the needs of the individual or group. ___

12. I freely express my feelings to others. ___

13. I encourage further contribution from others when in a discussion. ___

14. I am aware of my nonverbals and use them effectively. ___

15. I give instructions that are clear and specific. ___

16. I refrain from sarcasm when making a point. ___

17. I enjoy making presentations. ___

18. People compliment me on my verbal communications skills. ___

19. People ask my advice on how they could be a more effective communicator. ___

20. I consider carefully the best way to package my message. ___

Total score: ___

90–100: Congratulations! You are an excellent communicator. Keep on doing what you're doing.

80–89: Your communication skills are good but you may need to do more in certain areas. Review your answers and take special note of your 3 ratings.

79 or below: The bad news is that your communication skills are in need of repair. The good news is that you can do something about it if you want to!

How Well Do You Listen?

For each item, rate yourself on how frequently you practice a particular behavior. Circle the appropriate letter.

1. I listen to the other person's entire message before I respond.
   a. Most of the time
   b. Occasionally
   c. Almost never

2. I paraphrase what the other person is saying to ensure understanding.
   a. Most of the time
   b. Occasionally
   c. Almost never

3. I take notes to help me focus and remember.
   a. Most of the time
   b. Occasionally
   c. Almost never

4. I try to "tune out" distractions when listening to someone.
   a. Most of the time
   b. Occasionally
   c. Almost never

5. I do not interrupt the speaker.
   a. Most of the time
   b. Occasionally
   c. Almost never

6. I refrain from day dreaming while another is talking.
   a. Most of the time
   b. Occasionally
   c. Almost never

7. I use nonverbal clues (nodding, for example) to show that I'm listening.
   a. Most of the time
   b. Occasionally
   c. Almost never

8. I try to learn something from each conversation.
   a. Most of the time
   b. Occasionally
   c. Almost never

9. I'm told by others that I am a good listener.
   a. Most of the time
   b. Occasionally
   c. Almost never

10. I listen even if what is being said is not of interest to me.
    a. Most of the time
    b. Occasionally
    c. Almost never

11. I listen to opposing points of view with an open mind.
    a. Most of the time
    b. Occasionally
    c. Almost never

12. I listen respectfully to others.
    a. Most of the time
    b. Occasionally
    c. Almost never

13. I ask questions to clarify.
    a. Most of the time
    b. Occasionally
    c. Almost never

14. I listen for both content as well as tone to gain understanding.
    a. Most of the time
    b. Occasionally
    c. Almost never

15. I reflect the underlying feelings of the speaker.
    a. Most of the time
    b. Occasionally
    c. Almost never

16. I consciously practice good listening techniques.
    a. Most of the time
    b. Occasionally
    c. Almost never

17. I allow others to vent their feelings before responding.
    a. Most of the time
    b. Occasionally
    c. Almost never

18. I am sought out by others as a sounding board.
    a. Most of the time
    b. Occasionally
    c. Almost never

19. I restate other's instructions or messages to be sure that I understand.
    a. Most of the time
    b. Occasionally
    c. Almost never

20. I avoid doing other things (such as working on my computer) when someone is speaking to me.
    a. Most of the time
    b. Occasionally
    c. Almost never

There is no numerical scale to this test. However, it is easy to review your answers and get a visceral feel for where you stand as an effective listener. I'll talk about listening skills a bit later.

How Well Do You Write?

A self-test of your writing skills is way beyond the scope of this book. However, it's not all that difficult for you to get a feel for your writing abilities by reading some of the sources I have included in the appendix. And it's not all that difficult to make major improvements in your writing skills by reading only one short book, *The Elements of Style*, by William Strunk and E. B. White. This book is about 100 pages long, devoid of theory and long on the practical aspects of writing. And, if you are aware of the areas where some improvement would be helpful in your writing, a few short chapters should do the job. See the appendix for publisher info. A blurb on the back cover of a copy of the third edition of this wonderful book appeared in the *Boston Globe:* "No book in shorter space, with fewer words, will help any writer more than this persistent little volume." Get it; it's even fun to read.

> **Case in Point**
>
> Mark Twain said, "The difference between the right word and almost the right word is the difference between lightning and the lightning bug."

Communicating Effectively Is a Shared Understanding

As you go through the rest of this chapter, it will be helpful to refer back to the way you answered the two quizzes you just took. Put yourself center stage, be your own critic and be your own coach. It's not as difficult as you may think. You should have more than a few "ah-ha" moments when you will see where you stand out and where some improvement is needed.

The "ah-ha" moments are just the beginning. Now, you have to do something about the problem areas. Fortunately there is a very simple technique you can use to get up to speed. I call it the ROC technique—Receipt Of Communications, based on a notion called shared understanding that is used effectively in group learning situations. You can use the ROC technique in any interactive situation, an actual group or even when you are engaged in conversations with yourself.

In simplest terms, the ROC technique is for both parties to acknowledge that they understand what has passed between them. You may not agree, but you both know where you are coming from. This, of course, invites questions and answers and should lead to better clarification. One of the major benefits of this approach is that it turns passive listeners to active listeners. I'll be talking more about this later on.

Nonverbal Communications—the 90 Percent Factor

A lot of research has shown that good speakers are often judged poorly, not because of what they have said, but because of how they behaved while saying it. We have all experienced the annoying bore who pretends to listen, but whose gaze is focused else-where, or by the especially annoying table-tapper. But the guy who gives you his full attention and then asks absurd questions gets the prize.

You've met them all. And so have the people who make the hiring decisions. Great resumés and years of experience go unnoticed as the job gatekeeper notices that you seem to be a million miles away when he tells you about the wonderful benefits pack-age of the job you are seeking. Use this checklist to test your skills at sending good signals via body language:

♦ **Eye contact:** Steady eye contact not only gives the impression that you are interested in what someone is saying, it adds some peripheral notes to the inter-change. Research on the subject has shown that it greatly increases your credibil-ity with the person who is speaking.

♦ **Facial expressions:** People need feedback from those with whom they talk. Try talking to a stone and see how quickly you burn out. However, and this is impor-tant, make sure that you send the appropriate facial expressions. Inappropriate facial expressions are among the most obvious examples of inattention you can send. A steady, frozen smile just won't do the trick.

♦ **Gestures:** Gestures should be appropriate to what you are saying, or responding to. However, unless the situation calls for extensive movement, you should con-trol them. Overacting gets people thrown out of play auditions and it does a lot to sink your employer interview.

♦ **Body orientation:** Lean a little forward and you tell the person you are speaking with that you are accessible. Lean too far forward and you may seem intimidat-ing. Everyone responds to signals differently, so pay particular attention to the response you get. If you notice that the person with whom you are talking backs off slightly, do the same. Measure the right social space and maintain it and you will be sending the right signal.

Career Alert

Those who are trained to interview potential employees are often highly skilled observers of body language. If you haven't been trained in this skill, be careful not to overanalyze what you see, and don't change your stance dramatically. Body language is subtle; the arched eyebrow, the slight smile offered at something you said that made an impression—these are the clues to look for. And remember, the interviewer is looking for these slight clues from you, too. Don't try to mask your emotions, but try to keep them in control within the context of the interview.

Changing the Way You Communicate

Any lifestyle change is difficult, mainly because you've spent years developing your life's good and bad habits. Starting at the bottom of the ladder in whatever field you have chosen required certain ways of communicating with your peers and your boss. As you moved up, further changes were often necessary. You probably weren't away of the changes that were taking place, but you were becoming a different person.

If you can anticipate the changes you will need to make in positions you see in your future, you will be ahead of those who don't. And one of the best places to address early is that of your personal communications. For example, watch how people in the positions to which you aspire greet each other, and compare it with how you and your current co-workers greet each other. It may be, "Hey, Bob, what's new with you?" at your current job, but at another level it may be a more formal, "Hello, Bob."

Getting a leg up on one aspect of the behavior that is deemed appropriate for the job you want can make the transitions a lot easier. Be an astute watcher of those whose job you wish you had. This isn't easy, mainly because you may just be put down by your co-workers as not "being one of them." But, there's a price for everything, and behaving appropriately is seldom too high a price to pay.

> **Case in Point**
>
> A Chinese proverb says, "Man who waits for roast duck to fly into mouth must wait very, very long time." In other words, make things happen here, now.

Moving up, over, or out in your career may be out of your control, or you may be in the comfortable position of being able to carefully plan each step. Either way, any change requires adjustments in your lifestyle. Fortunately, this is one area where most people can see first hand what they have to do, and how to do it.

Make changes in your communicating style carefully, if you can. Using different and unfamiliar words and communicating styles in an abrupt switch from your present style will not only be obvious, it will send the wrong signals. Take your time, get used to the changes in small steps so that they become second nature, not something you use one day and accidentally slip back into another.

Communication Skills and Your Up, Over, or Out Decision

Communicating with others is a skill like pitching a baseball. There is always room for improvement. This doesn't mean just learning new words and the lingo of your field. It means learning to read, write, and speak at a level that will not only communicate your thoughts clearly, but that will send the message that you think and express your thoughts clearly and succinctly.

The language you use should be appropriate for your individual work environment. We all adapt to our surroundings by communicating in styles and at levels we feel are appropriate for positive results. Anyone looking to move up should be aware that, although you probably won't be actually tested, your use of language will be an important factor at decision time.

Case in Point

Several years ago I was asked to sit in on a meeting that had been called by a client company to review credentials of several candidates for an important job in the marketing department. There were three candidates, two already employed by the company and one who had been proposed by an executive search firm. We had all been given copies of the candidates' resume[as]s and had been asked to interview each of them at the meeting. All three were perfectly well qualified and, judging by their resumés, you could have just flipped a coin to decide. However, because the job was in marketing and the person hired would have to deal directly with the company's customers, I and two people from the HR department were asked to help make the decision.

We agreed that the best way to get a feel for the candidate's communicating skills would be to apply an identical yardstick that involved communications. We gave each of them a copy of a typical marketing problem and asked them how they would solve it. I should point out that each performed solo, not in front of their competitors.

Of the three who looked like perfect candidates on paper, only one stood out in person. His solution to the problem was no better than those presented by the others, but his presentation was captivating. The others gave what one of the panel later called a lecture. The captivator got the job.

Two bulbs have to light up with any interviewer. One bulb signals intelligence, work history, and all the other factors. The other bulb illuminates the person who is going to make the best use of all those credentials. If you have any doubts at all about the level of your communicating skills, think seriously about getting professional help. One good source could be joining Toastmasters, an organization dedicated to helping people make better personal presentations. See the appendix for information on locating their nearest local chapter.

The Least You Need to Know

◆ You may be the best qualified candidate, but if you can't communicate that to the people who might hire you, you won't get the job.

◆ Without a shared understanding, even the best speaker or writer will not make his or her points.

◆ Poor nonverbal communication can sink a perfect speech.

◆ Your hearing may be perfect, but your "listening" may be out to lunch.

◆ Sadly, some terrible speakers insist on doing it and usually do themselves more harm than good.

Identify Your Leadership Style(s)

In This Chapter

- ◆ Learn to lead, regardless of where you are in the chain of command
- ◆ Know and understand the four styles of leadership, and learn to be flexible in their use
- ◆ Test your leadership skills now
- ◆ Identify the leadership styles of potential employers

There are leaders and there are managers. Both are needed in the world of work, but the difference between a leader and a manager lies mostly in the leader's willingness to do things against the so-called best advice of others. Not all managers share that quality. I'm not implying that the best course is always the one opposed by others, but when it is, the difference between a leader and a manager becomes obvious. When the chips are down, a leader does not choose to please everyone, but chooses to do what he or she sees as the best way to get a job done.

Leaders at any level have vision and are not afraid to act on it. A leader may occupy the last chair on the table of organization, and may not even be what his or her company calls a manager. But the leader I'm describing rises to occasions when more than managing skills is required, occasions that can make the difference between corporate success and failure, or between losing or retaining one small customer. In other words, leadership is a human characteristic that operates at all levels of business. Those who use it—and don't abuse it—usually fulfill whatever they choose as their definition of success.

Style Matters

Sadly, corporate praise and recognition is all too often given only to those who have made major contributions to corporate growth. This is unfortunate, because much of what we see today as corporate failure could probably have been prevented if leaders at all levels were recognized and encouraged. However, this works in your favor, because an act of leadership is usually more obvious to those who have a say in the trajectory of people's careers than just meeting corporate goals.

Case in Point

Jesse Jackson said, "Time is neutral and does not change things. With courage and initiative, leaders change things."

The major research has winnowed leadership down to four basic styles. Unfortunately, too many people see these styles as finite, and define themselves as one or the other type of leader. This may be effective in some situations, but one style does not fit all. The most successful people I've met in my years in this field are those who understand these styles clearly and adopt them easily as they are needed.

The Four Basic Styles of Leadership

Senator Everett Dirksen, a flamboyant and effective leader, was fond of saying, "I am a man of fixed and unbending principles, the first of which is to be flexible at all times." If you remember the late lawmaker, he was not a flip-flopper, and he approached every situation with the style its management demanded. The styles below are described as ways to address the variety of leadership situations most people will face in business. You may consider yourself stronger in one category than another, but to be a really successful leader, you must be able to lead effectively in a variety of different situations by using the appropriate style.

Right Move _____

No single leadership style works every time in all situations. The best leaders are able to size up problems clearly, take stock of the people involved, and choose a leadership style that will give the best results with the least disruption of the people involved. Regardless of the style chosen, a shared vision of the problem seems to be the major common element for a successful outcome.

The Task-Oriented Leader

This style of leadership usually calls for people to question their own leaders' tradition and the status quo. This can be difficult, especially when the entrenched leaders have been successful in the past. The typical task-oriented leader sets the bar higher than others might, but many will tell you that by setting the bar higher, they achieve what they really want to do. They are often seen as "slave drivers," an image some are comfortable with, but that others don't exactly cherish. In other words, tough decisions can make a leader quite uncomfortable and often quite unpopular.

The Motivating Leader

Motivating leaders are people-oriented. In most cases, they are willing to take on just about any task, whether it's within their specialty or not. They work by seeking out the people who have the skills needed and assembling effective teams. Unlike the other types of leaders, they are often considered to be "natural born leaders," and some may be, but this is a skill that can also be acquired, most often by working closely with someone who excels at this type of leadership.

Typical motivating leaders can be, in the extreme, obnoxious people. And they usually have a lot of difficulty doing the routine administrative work that goes with their projects. All too often, motivating leaders try to please too many people and end up pleasing no one.

Good motivating leaders succeed by convincing team members to share in the effort. Regardless of the level of their influence, most people will go to any length to support a project when they have been included on the team.

The Tactical Leader

Tactical leaders have a lot in common with motivating type leaders. Both are essentially people oriented, but they differ in the way they relate to people. The tactical leader is more political, and is often seen as more friendly and supportive than motivating leaders. They are generally quite concerned about the people they work with and the effects of their ideas. Tactical leaders are usually better team players, and they frequently gain the praise of other leaders within the organization.

In the extreme, however, tactical leaders can be so political that they often alienate those who hold opposing views.

The Analytical Leader

Some might consider this to be a subset of tactical leadership. I see it on its own mainly because many tactical leaders depend heavily on the analytical skills of the people they bring to the task. From my work with both large and small organizations, I see the analytical leader as one who seeks considerable input before making a move. Most analytical leaders are very self-disciplined, conscientious, and somewhat more cautious than others. This may be because they are seldom as interested in building support teams. They take on more of the responsibility for getting the job done themselves, so they want more facts on which to base their decisions.

Some might think of them as stodgy, more interested in fixing what's broken rather than in trying new ways to solve problems. In the light of the mantra that change is good for everything, they are often maligned unfairly. Change just isn't needed in all situations, and might even be harmful for the organization. Good analytical leaders can see this and often have problems with those for whom change is always the only answer.

Case in Point

A client I worked with recently had a good reputation as a leader in her firm. She was fair with everyone and most people respected her. She was a task-oriented leader. When there was a job to be done, she would see that it was done.

She had risen steadily in the company, but had been plateaued recently and was seeking coaching that would help her continue her career growth. After a few sessions, it was easy to see why she was one of the most effective executives in the company. However, she admitted that she struggled with the relational side of the job.

I pointed out that the simple act of consulting more actively with the people affected by her decisions would greatly diminish her image of being unreachable. She tried it and at our next session reported that the ice was melting. Further, she came to the next step on her own. She told me, "Marc, more than just talking to them, I give them some role in putting the plan in action once the decisions are made. It's amazing how things have changed." If there is one "magic" secret of successful task oriented leaders this is it.

Test Time!

Don't think in terms of fixed boundaries when it comes to defining your leadership skills. You may see yourself as being stronger as a tactical manager, but not every situation calls for those specific skills, and forcing the problem to conform to your style is a mistake. Adapt your style to the problem and you will gain more than you lose. Think of yourself as a leader—period!

The simple test that follows is designed to help you see where you might need some work on your leadership skills. There's no time limit—in fact, I suggest that you take a lot of time to answer all the questions. You will be searching through an open book— yourself—for honest and truthful answers.

Chart and Validate Your Leadership Style

Examine your leadership ability by answering the following questions with a Yes or No:

1. Do you set clear and specific goals for your associates? ___

2. Do you find ways to empower your associates? ___

3. Do you solicit ideas from your associates? ___

4. Do you delegate tasks that will develop your associates? ___

5. Do you take time to coach your associates? ___

6. Do you give timely and accurate feedback to your associates? ___

7. Do you solicit feedback from your associates about your leadership performance? ___

8. Do you recognize and reward good performance? ___

9. Do you address performance gaps in a timely manner? ___

10. Do you adjust your leadership style based on the needs of the individual and group? ___

11. Do you continually seek ways to improve as a leader? ___

12. Do you communicate effectively in both your verbal and written communication? ___

13. Do you actively listen to and show genuine interest in your associates? ___

14.   Do you involve your associates in decisions that will affect them? ___

15.   Do you maintain a calm, steady demeanor, even in stressful situations? ___

This simple test will give you an overall idea of where your leadership ability stands now. Since we are looking for areas for improvement, let's look at the down side. How many "No" answers did you provide? If you have more than four, you should seriously consider taking steps to improve in those areas.

You can't improve your leadership skills overnight. However, you can get a handle on what is needed right now in your specific work situation. I am frequently called upon to help managers in need of immediate help and I use what I call my 360 Degree Plan. This quick turn-around technique will set you on the right path, regardless of which management style you feel you are best at. It will help you immediately deal with leadership situations you may be facing, and help you see where you can polish the rough edges of your style in a more leisurely pace.

Do Your Own 360-Degree Leadership Assessment

The approach here is to seek input from five to seven people you work with regularly: your boss, peers, associates, even customers or clients. You will be surprised at how willing most people are to help you when you ask them. People are seldom willing to make unsolicited comments, but when asked they are often relieved to be able to share their thoughts, positive as well as negative. Be sure to tell them that what they tell you will be confidential and that you have asked them for their help because you feel that they would be comfortable helping. These are the questions:

◆ What do I do now that you feel I should continue to do as a leader?

◆ What do I do now that I should do more often?

◆ What do I do now that I should do less of or even stop doing?

◆ Is there anything I'm not doing that I should start doing now?

In my experience, you can get the best answers not by asking people to write their answers to these questions, but by asking them face to face. You might consider providing them the list of questions in advance so they give you more seriously considered answers rather than quick off-the-cuff responses.

If you are currently working with a coach, include him or her in the evaluation. It's
        the more the merrier, but getting too many people in the act can
        ings more complicated. Five to seven people has always seemed to me to
        umber.

As I said, the answers to these questions can help you make fast changes when they are needed. However, you can use the responses you get as a basis for your long term leadership development plans.

Now, I bet you wonder why I call this a 360-degree test. After all, that's a full turn and you end up going in the same direction. Well, the direction is not the issue, it's the exposure you get to fresh viewpoints you get as you make that full turn that does the trick.

> **Case in Point**
>
> Lao Tzu said, "The wicked leader is one who the people despise. The good leader is the one people revere. The great leader is one who people say, 'We did it ourselves.'"

Moving Up, Over, or Out

A major goal of this book is to help you decide whether it is best to move up within your company, over in your company, possibly to a subsidiary or another division with greater growth potential, or to move out to a different organization altogether. Leadership qualities may not be a big issue and the skills and experience required may be minimal, but leadership is a quality that gets more and more important as you rise to greater responsibility in any work situation.

Organizations, like individual people, have distinctive styles. Each organization has a set of unspoken rules that define how people work together. One organization may be seen as democratic with a decided flair for collaborative management. Another might be more authoritarian, with a very sharply defined, top-down management style. Another may appear to be leaderless, but underneath it succeeds by tapping the skills of several individuals to provide a sort of collective leadership. It is often critical to know right from the start what leadership qualities will work best for you. The bull-in-the-china-shop style of testing the waters is definitely not the way to go.

Getting a fix on the kind of leadership that flies well in any company isn't easy. However, one of the best ways to do this is to read the chairman's letter in the company's annual report. You won't get the whole picture, but in many cases you will be able spot broad elements of leadership style. Read what has been written about the company in the business press. Talk with colleagues who might have worked for the company at one time. And ask your headhunter. Talk to suppliers. In short, try to get as many views as you can. A composite picture can be very helpful. The opinion of a single unhappy person can poison the well.

Career Alert

If you have a pretty clear image of the dominant leadership style of a potential employer, and it seems as though you might be uncomfortable with it, don't take the job feeling that you can win them over to your way of thinking. You won't. If there is enough of a chasm, look elsewhere. Don't fall for the "challenge" notion.

Corporate culture changes over time. Organizations run by highly autocratic leaders can morph to the other end of the spectrum, often in a relatively short period of time. This shift often reflects a quite flexible outlook on the part of the leaders. This kind of flexibility is usually seen as a good sign. Management does what has to be done when conditions change. If you see yourself as a flexible person, don't be put off by companies that have undergone major shifts in corporate culture. On the other hand, look out for the companies that are so wedded to leadership styles that worked 20 years ago that they change nothing or those that have changed radically more than a few times.

The Least You Need to Know

◆ The major difference between a manager and a leader is that leaders are usually far more willing to take chances than managers.

◆ As important as risk taking may be, it is not always the prudent way to go.

◆ Leadership style matters, but so does flexibility.

◆ Leadership techniques can be learned, but experience is often the best teacher.

12

Assessing Your Accomplishments

In This Chapter

◆ See yourself as others want to see you

◆ Don't take your accomplishments for granted

◆ The one word you should use as little as possible

◆ Chart your accomplishments as a career reality check

By now, you probably have a pretty good picture of yourself as a person and how you relate to others. You've peeled the onion, so to speak. Now, we're going to look at the real-world things you have done, what they can mean to your career, and how you can use them to best advantage. Just as important, you're going to see that there are times when the things you might be proudest of might be better kept under wraps.

The typical resumé is mostly a narrative of what you have done, where you have worked and studied, and what other people might have been willing to say on your behalf. All this is, of course, important to any prospective employer, but so is the picture of *trajectory* your resumé projects. Have you been moving sideways, or can you show a history of growth and increasing responsibility?

Whether you are writing a resumé, or doing a face-to-face pitch to a prospective employer, you might want to think of Ravel's famous composition, *Bolero*. The music itself is simple, but the conductor's job is to slowly and imperceptibly raise the level of the sound from a barely audible pianissimo to a crashing forte. You are the conductor of your career. And you do it with the instruments best suited for the job—yourself and your accomplishments. Go ahead, get rave notices for your performance!

Don't Take Yourself for Granted

Despite the windbags we all encounter from time to time, most people are pretty modest. They tend to think that what they did or are doing is simply what their job calls for, so we don't get all excited about it. The truth is that we all tend see ourselves in a self-defined context. For example, when you brought in that big order for your company, you simply saw it as doing what you are paid to do. But if you had done the same thing at another company, you might have been raised to hero status. The problem you face is to know when horn-blowing sounds like bragging and when it sounds like you are doing really great things.

Probably the simplest test you can apply is that of judging the overall effect your work has had. Doubling sales for a company whose annual sales are five million dollars can be seen as something just short of miraculous. But bringing in a five million dollar order to a company whose annual sales are in the billions is another story. It's perspective that counts here.

Assess Your Accomplishments

Let's begin with a short quiz. Again, it's open book. And, again, don't rush. I suggest that you record and store your answers in that shoebox I suggested earlier. When the need for a resumé arises, you will have good information right at your fingertips.

How many of your accomplishments ...

❑ Affected some bottom-line indices, such as sales, profitability, quality, customer service, and so on?

❑ Were done without the help of others?

❑ Were done as a member of a team?

❑ Were recognized by customers or your company management?

❑ Led to an improvement or change in the way your organization or department did its work?

❑ Solved a critical problem?

❑ Positively affected morale, turnover, or other human resource business indicators?

Are there any outstanding events? Do your accomplishments show a clear pattern? Do they showcase any special skills or training you may have? Do they present a picture of yourself as you saw yourself before you started this test?

Look for achievements that were over and above what you were expected to do. Also look for achievements you initiated yourself that were not required by your job description. As I said earlier, managers meet and often exceed the goals set by their employers. Leaders, on the other hand, look for better ways to get a job done and are willing to take chances.

Impress Your Present Employer

If you are thinking of moving up or over in your current organization, the accomplishments you add to your shoebox should be closely related to the work you were expected to accomplish and the work that you did over and above what was expected of you. In short, you want to show your employers that their investment in you has paid off.

Case in Point

One of my clients kept meticulous records of the profits her division made above budget that were the result of her special efforts. As she explained it, "I could tell them that I worked most nights until at least seven, came up with the system that led to lower operating costs, and even designed the packaging. I would have gotten lots praise. But, rather than pitch the self-sacrifice thing, I gave them balance sheets that showed them directly what my effort had produced. They said that I should head up the new division, and that's just what I wanted." She rightly reasoned that profits spoke louder that anything with her top management.

Don't assume that your current employer is aware of the things you've accomplished in the line of duty. They may be, but an occasional reminder doesn't hurt—as long as you are not obvious about it. I have found that the best ways to remind employers of accomplishments without sounding like a braggart is to embed subtle messages from time to time in routine messages. Messages tucked away in written communication have the benefit of being filed while spoken messages don't. And, since most people are required from time to time to provide others with reports, the path is already there.

It isn't easy to describe subtle writing that would be appropriate for everyone. However, one rule seems to apply to all: don't use the personal pronoun, I, too often. For example, here is the kind of writing to avoid:

> "While I was in charge of the Domino Project, I was able to increase product output by 39 percent. I did this by using different suppliers."

Contrast that obvious puff writing with this writing:

> "The output of Domino Project now runs 39 percent above what it produced last year. This translates to nearly 40,000 more units shipped this year compared with last year when I first took over the project. Vendor costs are greatly reduced, too, as a result of the plans now in place."

The second paragraph has more specific information and only one personal mention. Even with fewer personal references, the personal impact is greater. It's the kind of writing that gets the attention of the people in your company who can make things happen for you.

Right Move _____

Get others to sing your praises. One of the best ways to do this is to speak well of them first. If, for example, you were part of a team that accomplished something important, send a quick e-mail to all your team mates acknowledging their contributions. I guarantee that by return e-mail you will have as many complimentary comments that you can add to your shoebox collection.

Don't spend too much time pitching the accomplishments your employer ordinarily expects from you. Rather, stress the things you have done above and beyond that which is expected. Stress the things that have added to your employer's bottom line, and throw in an occasional activity that rounds out the picture without being related to major corporate goals. Volunteering for charitable events that are corporate sponsored may earn points, but not big ones. Mentoring new employees is quite a bit farther up the scale.

Impress a Potential New Employer

You're going to have to work a little harder here simply because a potential employer probably has no record at all of what you have done and are doing for your present employer. You have to tread lightly when trying to impress a potential employer with your accomplishments to avoid giving away sensitive company information. While some potential employers would love to have access to information about your present employer, they seldom think highly of a snitch.

Most potential employers usually ask why you want to leave your present employer. Describe what you have done above and beyond what was required and explain that you are looking for a company that rewards initiative.

Humility Has Its Limitations

It's often said that if you don't blow your own horn, nobody will do it for you. There's a lot of truth to this. But there's also a lot of truth to the notion that people tune out a windbag very quickly. Where's the happy medium?

Sticking with the facts is a start. Cite your accomplishments in context of the situation and try not to seem smug. It's the golfer who hits the green with his first drive and makes it seem like it was nothing who is admired. The one who has to tell how he figured the wind speed, the lay of the land, and the torsion on the club shaft on the down swing is usually considered the buffoon. A little self-satisfaction is always allowed, but seldom tolerated when it goes on forever.

Do They Relate to Your Career Plans?

Reviewing your accomplishments gives you an excellent perspective from which to see how closely you are following a practical career path. Random events as well as carefully planned moves play roles in your career, and one way to get a handle on where you are heading is to take a careful look at your accomplishments.

Most people I know are working at things they never imagined in school. One man I know has degrees in experimental psychology, but today is a very successful ghostwriter. Several physicians I have counseled were English majors. When I ask them what happened, most of them say that early accomplishments had a significant impact on the path that led them to where they are now. The ghostwriter, for example, said that although he had serious interest in learning theory, he discovered that his professors praised him more for his writing style than for his work in psychology. As he put it, "It wasn't that I didn't realize that I enjoyed writing, I just never thought of it as a career. The writing accomplishments piled up, so I just went with the flow."

On the other hand, many I've met professionally have been rigidly following paths that led them to some level of success, but also led them to a point where their work is much less than satisfying. It's seldom too late to make career changes if you are willing to put in the effort and take some chances. And one way to get a handle on just what might be best for you is to look back at what you have accomplished so far.

What accomplishments have given you pleasure so far in your work and your life? Forget the usual stuff like the promotions and the attaboys you occasionally get from your boss. To answer this question, it's time to dig into your mental pleasure centers. Everything is fair game—hobbies, sports, family, whatever. Look for clues that kind of hang together to give you some general direction. This exercise won't give you nail-down answers, but you will come up with a list of accomplishments that made you personally happy. Remember, you're looking for real-world stuff, like the time you got first prize in a local amateur photography contest.

Again, make a list, collect little slips of paper, whatever, and add this information to your shoebox. But don't just put the stuff away and forget about. Think about how these accomplishments might be able to help you see whether you might want to change careers or refocus the one you already have. Is the shoebox getting full? I hope so. You're going to put it to good use later.

The Least You Need to Know

♦ Your accomplishments don't necessarily speak for themselves; sometimes you have to explain.

♦ Taking your accomplishments for granted is a mistake; tell all, but don't brag.

♦ Some things are better left unsaid, even though they may be very helpful to you.

♦ Your accomplishments may be a critical indicator of where your career should be headed.

Chapter 13

It's Not Just the Money

In This Chapter

♦ Discover what a satisfying job really is

♦ See why people who are generally satisfied by their life are often most satisfied with their work

♦ Learn what job satisfiers are most important for you

♦ Chart your overall job satisfaction score

♦ Discover which approach might be best for you—move up, over, or out

If you want to see how quickly attitudes toward work can change, read what people said about their work just a few years ago. You'll see that 20 years or so ago, people used words like challenge, achievement, self-satisfaction, and personal accomplishment a lot to describe what they looked for in work. Today, people seldom talk in these terms. The language they use these days is laced with acquisitive words, things they want to have. This can range from real stuff like a big car to a job title like vice president. Way back in the Depression era of the 1930s, job satisfaction was defined as work that would last more than a few weeks.

The point is this: job satisfaction is directly correlated with the economic conditions of the time. In fact, today some people would probably snicker if you spoke in terms of being happy in your work. Let me say right now that whatever the current vogue, unless you find some personal satisfaction other than financial reward in your work, life just won't be as pleasant as it could be. If job satisfaction is not a factor in your career plan, it should be.

What Makes for a Satisfying Job?

Frederick Herzberg's pioneering work 50 years ago in work satisfaction is still considered the turning point in understanding what makes people happy or unhappy at work. He simply asked a large sample of people two questions:

1. Think of a time when you felt especially good about your job. Why did you feel that way?

2. Think of a time when you felt especially bad about your job. Why did you feel that way?

From the thousands of responses he got, he concluded that job satisfaction depended on two key factors. He said that certain factors—he called them the *hygiene factors* —don't motivate people, but serve to minimize job dissatisfaction. The factors he included were company policies, supervision issues, working conditions, and salary.

The *motivation factors* included what we might call the "human factors" today: recognition, achievement, responsibility, advancement, and the nature of the work itself. His work stands the test of time.

I have included three simple quizzes later in this chapter to help you develop your job satisfaction profile. But first read through the following job satisfaction elements. No need to write answers or make notes. Just get a feel for the factors that are important and that you can use in creating your own profile later on.

- ◆ **Administrative policies:** Are the policies fair, consistently applied, and easy to understand?

- ◆ **Compensation:** Are salaries fair relative to those paid by competitors, and is the benefit package equitable?

- ◆ **Supervision:** Are you treated fairly, can you trust your supervisor, and do you get feedback on personal issues?

◆ **Working conditions:** Is your work space adequate for the work you perform, and is the equipment you use safe and up-to-date?

◆ **Interpersonal relationships:** Are you considered part of the team and is there an opportunity for you to socialize with co-workers during the day?

◆ **Advancement:** Has your employer defined a career path for you, and is promotion based on specific accomplishments. Is there any opportunity for continuing education?

◆ **Personal recognition:** Does your employer recognize you for both small and major accomplishments? Are bonuses paid for work above and beyond that which is routinely expected of you?

◆ **The work itself:** Do you get a sense of accomplishment from the work itself? Does your employer look for ways to improve working conditions?

Right Move _____

A lot of research has pointed to a positive correlation of job satisfaction with life satisfaction. In general, people who are reasonably satisfied with their life are satisfied with their work. The opposite is not always true. Think about how this finding might impact on you.

Again, these are the elements you will use to draw a picture of your personal job satisfaction. Keep them in mind.

What Do You Need for Job Satisfaction?

Okay, it's test time again. Rank the following 10 job satisfaction characteristics from 1 (what you need the most) to 10 (what you need the least).

___ Task variety

___ Authority to make decisions

___ Challenge

___ Recognition

___ Position

___ Personal growth

___ Achievement

___ Work environment

___ Money and rewards

___ Great boss

Any surprises? If so, what surprised you? Most people who do this exercise discover that there are no major surprises, but some discover that the order is different than they expected, or that it has changed somewhat from the last time they did the ranking. The lesson is that job satisfaction is not a very stable condition. That's why I encourage you to think of career planning as a lifetime project, not something you do once and then forget about it.

The changes you may have noticed could relate to something that is happening in your work life right now that didn't exist before. Or it could signal that your overall view of job satisfaction may be undergoing a longer term shift.

Now, do the test over, but this time pretend you are taking it while employed in your last job.

Then, do it just once more, but this time speculate wildly. Pretend that you have found the ultimate job.

You now have a sample of the past, the present, and what you would like the future to look like. Comparing the three sets of results, you now have a general index of the elements that are important to you in terms of the real world. Are you making progress toward your ideal situation? Have you sacrificed anything to gain something that is more important to you? Was the sacrifice worth it? And, do you think that you still might be able to improve your employment situation by moving to another company, by moving up with your present employer, or by looking for a lateral move within your present company that might bring you closer to a perfect picture of job satisfaction?

Career Alert

As important as money is, personal satisfaction is just as important. Research has shown that people who are personally happy with their work are less concerned about making more and more money. However, and this is a point to remember, most people in this category tend to make as much and often more than those who see money as a key element in defining their self-worth. So happiness does count!

Your Personal Job Satisfaction Scale

Now, we're getting down to the specifics. The questions you just answered give you a general view of what is and isn't important to you in terms of your career. The following inventory deals specifically with the job you currently have. Take your time. Think carefully about your answers. There's no rush.

Rate your level of satisfaction for each item below using the following scale:

5 = Very satisfied
4 = Somewhat satisfied
3 = Satisfied
2 = A little dissatisfied
1 = Very dissatisfied

____ My job duties and assignments

____ My rewards and recognitions

____ Opportunities for personal and professional growth

____ The importance of my work

____ The power I have to make decisions

____ The respect and fair treatment of my manager

____ My pay and benefits

____ The overall quality of my work life

____ = Total

30–40: Your job satisfaction exceeds the national average. Good for you!

20–29: You have some job satisfaction gaps but overall you are okay.

19 or below: You deserve better!

What Do You Need?

Now it's time to look at the general feelings the first test showed, and the number the second inventory showed. By the way, get out that shoebox again. You're going to add to it shortly.

Challenge

There are two elements to consider here, the kind of challenge, and the level. In general, the kind of challenge relates to skill and informational levels. At the skill level, everyone from a neurosurgeon to mechanic can and should strive to learn more and to do better and better work. Not only is it important from the purely practical point of view of what your employer might expect, it is important from the perspective of your own sense of self worth. Knowing more and doing your job better and better are very important components of your self-image.

Sharpening your skills and learning more are better done in small, steady steps. Small but regular doses of positive feedback make for more efficient learning than learning in big gulps. It has to do with incremental reinforcement, but this is an issue for Psych 101. Take my word for it—don't try to learn algebra in one sitting!

Position

You should always think of your professional aspirations in terms of what the job entails, not what you are called. I know people who are not vice presidents, but who make more money than many vice presidents. One client who is head of corporate communications of a medium-size company is not a VP, but she is paid more than some of those who carry the title of vice president. It may impress your golf buddies that you are a VP, but don't be upset when you learn that the duffer with the battered bag of clubs makes more money than you and he is not a VP.

Variety

Some people seem most happy when there is little variety in their lives. However, when you look closely at what they do, there is often considerable variety, it just exists on a less visible level. Others aren't happy unless variety is wide and often. Variety, then, is a necessary component of most people's lives. How much and how wide ranging is the key issue.

Some work provides an endless opportunity for variety and some work has no variety at all. Listen to yourself to determine how much variety makes you happy and how much has the opposite effect. Most people do have the capacity to seek and be happier with more or less variety in their work lives. But to intentionally move in giant steps either way can often be very counterproductive.

Authority

Unless you are the owner and president of the company, you will be subject to someone's authority. Even then, you will be subject to the authority of people outside the organization. In short, everyone reports to someone. In fact, if there is one problem I see most in my coaching sessions, it's some form of objectionable authority.

It's just not possible for so many bosses to be so awful, so there must be another answer—and there is. Most people perceive those who have some influence over them at work as either blocks to greater responsibility, or as people who are singling them out for torment. In the extreme, the term *paranoia* is often used. The truth is, however, that I've never encountered a situation where that clinical term could be honestly used.

So get used to it. People will bug you. There are people who can make your work life miserable. But the chances of you being the victim of some seriously deranged authority figures are extremely small.

The best way to deal with these people is the end-run approach. Don't take them head-on, get around them and do what has to be done. If your end runs are intentionally blocked, take up the issue with those who are in a position to objectively evaluate the situation. In other words, don't get into a fight.

Before I leave this topic, let me encourage you to think about your own style, relative to your career plans. How much frustration are you willing to bear to grow in your present job? Don't make rash moves. Make sure, first, that there is no way around the offending person before you start looking elsewhere. You may discover that others feel the same way about the offending individual and that he or she has already come to the attention of the people who have control in these matters.

Personal Growth

Forget the job for a moment. What gives you pleasure off the job? Your job and your growth within your chosen field are important, but just as important is your growth as a person. Sadly, far too many people leave school thinking they've learned everything they will ever need to know. They read *Beowulf*. They mastered differential equations. They may have even mastered the complexities of flying a jumbo jet or repairing an automobile engine. Whatever you have learned and mastered should make you curious about learning more, whether it relates to your work or your personal interests.

An executive I coached a few years ago had built a reputation in his profession and had mastered the art of jewelry making as hobby. Not only was he a capable artisan, he also knew the history of the kind of jewelry he made very well. I once asked him if this was an escape from the demands of his executive position and he told me that no escapes were necessary. "What I need is variety and different challenges," he said.

People are multidimensional. Some have many dimensions in their life with a great range of variety. Others have few. However, we all need to grow within the activities we have chosen. So, if tying flies and fishing is your thing, be the best at it that you can be. You'll be a lot happier for it.

Are You Motivated to Make a Major Career Change?

Life is more than work. It's more than hobbies and other personal interests. And if I were to try to give you the meaning of life, I'd be making it up. However, we're not operating at that lofty level, we're talking about you and your career. We're talking about the three ways to think about your career—should you move up in the company that employs you, should you look for a lateral move in that company, or is it time to pull up stakes and head elsewhere?

So back to reality, and here is the last quiz of this chapter. Get out the shoebox because I want you to store the answers you give to this little quiz. Rank the following 10 job satisfaction characteristics from 1 (What you need the most) to 10 (What you need the least).

___ Task variety

___ Authority to make decisions

___ Challenge

___ Recognition

___ Position

___ Personal growth

___ Achievement

___ Work environment

___ Money and rewards

___ Great boss

What did your ranking tell you about your job satisfaction needs? What surprised you? Are you beginning to see any patterns emerging when thinking about the other quizzes you have already taken?

What should be emerging is a pattern of yourself at a point in your career where you feel some changes might be needed. Looking at top two or three choices in the above quiz, ask yourself…

♦ Is there a place for me to achieve these choices within the structure of my present employment and job description? Is there an opportunity to move up?

♦ Is there an opportunity within my present company, but in a different department, division, or subsidiary company where I might move to put myself on track?

♦ Should I consider leaving my present job and looking for a place with a totally different company where I can fulfill the needs I have identified?

You may think that I am splitting hairs when I discuss moving over as a separate item. Given the way many conglomerates are structured, I think this differentiation represents opportunities many people are either unaware of or are skittish about approaching.

Most conglomerates are highly interactive. One of the areas in which this is often obvious is in human resources. While most frown on pirating personnel from each other, many are willing to help each other if it looks like a valued employee might be looking to leave. This is seldom done out of the goodness of their corporate hearts, but as an economic imperative. The cost of recruiting and training good people is high. If one company in a conglomerate has a need for someone who might be unhappy elsewhere within the family, recruiting costs disappear. And, depending on the level of the person being sought, those costs can be very high. So there you have it! It works for you and it works for the corporations.

Are You Motivated by the Right Reasons?

One of the more interesting things to come out of recent psychological research is the fact that bad things don't really affect us as deeply as we expect them to. In fact, the same is true of the good things as well. In other words, we tend to dramatize considerably when faced with problems as well as happiness.

The boss avoids your gaze. Terror strikes your heart. Time to call your headhunter, right? Wrong. The boss was distracted and didn't even know you were in the room. Then, you get a pat on the back from the CEO, whom you have only met once and he says, "Nice work, you really did a great job on the Zippo account." Bingo, you've made the A-list at corporate! Then he introduces you to the executive VP by saying, "You should really get to know Steve." Your name is Tom. Anyway, you get the picture.

Unless it has been forced on you, you should carefully plan any career move—but not so carefully that you plan and plan and plan, and never do anything about it. A key issue in all this discovery and planning you have been reading about in the earlier pages relates to control, the control you have over your career and the control others may have over you. Unless you are in a very unusual situation, you can seldom do much about the control that others may have over you. However, with a little planning and some concentrated effort, you can do a lot to maintain control over what you do—both actively and proactively.

Remember, it wasn't raining when Noah started building the ark.

Case in Point

One of my colleagues had a coaching client who was, as he put it, an obsessive "plan-aheader." He claimed that this man had actually made decision-tree charts of his career plans. Each step led to alternatives that led to more alternatives, on and on. As you might imagine, it's impossible to anticipate every possibility in any situation that involves the unknown future. So his decision tree always took him from one dead end to another. Then my colleague realized that this man really didn't want to move, he just enjoyed fantasizing about it and planning it in ways that always took him to blind alleys.

Don't let this happen to you. Plan ahead and have some fall-back positions, but always be prepared to make decisions based on what you have at hand. No amount of planning will give you the perfect answer. It will, however, give you the material you need to maintain some personal control. Then you must make the decisions yourself.

The goals you set should be realistic and yet they should give you enough wiggle room to assure that you keep moving. You may have more than a few of "the-lesser-of-two-evils" decisions in your plan, but at least the decisions made for this option will keep you moving in the right general direction.

The Least You Need to Know

◆ Nobody is ever fully satisfied with their job—but you can get close.

◆ Job satisfaction is mainly a question of what it is that decreases your satisfaction and what increases that satisfaction. It's the old saw—accentuate the positive and eliminate the negative.

◆ Knowing your frustration tolerance well is a key factor in career planning.

◆ Even when you reach the top, you will still find other mountains to climb.

Part 3

Putting Assessment Information to Work

Knowledge is power—but only when you put it to use! Armed with the information you have gathered in the previous two parts, you are now ready to begin the real work of creating your own personal brand. It's no secret that the first few minutes of a conversation with a stranger will be key to the impression that stranger will have of you. What few people realize is that whether it's a face-to-face encounter, a telephone conversation, or even a simple e-mail message, people form images quickly that may be accurate or downright harmful. The tips and techniques in the chapters that follow ensure that you will get noticed and make a favorable impression.

A career path is not a road map; it's a prescription for action and reaction. Your working life is made up of successes and blunders. Sometimes you'll succeed without trying, and sometimes you'll blunder no matter how hard you try to avoid it. Knowing what you can control and what you can't is the key issue of this part. It's different for everyone, but it's easy to learn where the roadblocks might be and where the buttons that trigger success are. Keep reading!

Chapter 14

Developing Your Personal Profile

In This Chapter

◆ Learn what puts a smile on your face and what makes you want to wring the boss's neck

◆ Your friends know more about you than you think

◆ Your personal profile is for your eyes only

◆ Do a personal mission statement to uncover your core values

◆ See yourself as a human being, not a cog in anyone's machine

Your personal profile is going to be a working tool, not something you will show to others, so let yourself go. You may find that rooting through your shoebox will help you remember things and point you in directions that can be helpful. In fact, think of this as a big grab bag all about you, your needs, your interests, and your skills. Think about your values and your relationships with other people. What gets your attention and what doesn't? And pay attention to the dark side as well. What bugs you? Who bugs you?

Why Do It?

Unless you've been extremely lucky, you're going to have to work for a good part of your life. So why not work at something you like? Or if you're pushed to the wall, at least try to work at something that gives you some pleasure. What gives you pleasure? Yeah, I know all about the house on the beach, the boat, and all that. Get real. What really gives you pleasure?

Case in Point

Thomas Jefferson: "I'm a great believer in luck and I have found that the harder I work, the more I have of it."

We all have needs. We need food and shelter as well as a sense of well being. As I mentioned earlier, meeting most needs helps prevent dissatisfaction with a job. Meeting other needs can provide you with the thing called job satisfaction. The personal profile you are about to create is all about the latter—what sends you home at the end of the day with a smile on your face. And what makes you happy when you are not working?

What Do You Value?

This may seem a little convoluted, but stick with me. I'm defining values here as the goals you set in order to satisfy a particular need. Some of your values will never change, but others may change frequently. For example, suppose your daughter comes home from school with the good news that she's been accepted by Harvard. Until that moment, you may not have valued job security very highly. But when you know what it's going to cost you, your value structure now spots job security as number one—at least for the next four years.

Your interests, on the other hand, show a preference for one activity over another. It's important to note that your interests are what led you to choose one type of career over another. Good math scores put your classmates on the technology track. A way with words put others on the road to journalism and publishing. You may share the same interests with your co-workers, but your values may be worlds apart. Get the picture?

Your close friends may be very helpful in assembling your personal values inventory. You may not realize it, but your friends and colleagues usually remember the stands you take on value issues. You surely know where you stand on specific issues, but your friends are in the best position to tell you how strongly you defend these values. They will remember more clearly than you the issues that made you angry or happy. People constantly look to others for clues on how to respond to them. They put these clues in their memory bank for future use. Tap those memories!

Putting Together the Profile

You are about halfway through this book and you have had something of a free ride so far. All I've asked is for answers to a few short quizzes and for you to start filling a shoebox with material that will help you plan and manage your career. Now, it's time to get a little neater.

Whether you do it with a pencil or a computer, start now to assemble your formal personal profile. No single format is better than another, so the organization is up to you. It's what you put in it that counts. But do organize it so that it is useful for you. Neatness counts—but only to the extent that it makes the job of using your profile as easy and as productive as possible.

Your Public Information

Your public information is what you are willing to share with anyone. This doesn't mean that it shouldn't include your dreams and fantasies. Why not say that you've always wanted to be a quarterback for the Giants? Remember, I'm not talking about the kind of information that is usually seen on a resumé. However, if you have any employment related accomplishments that have personal significance for you, they belong in your profile.

Case in Point _____

A mid-level manager I was coaching a few years ago included in his personal profile that he had always dreamed of having something to do with the art world. He had no art talent, but he just wanted to be part of that world. After several sessions, it emerged that he had a lot to offer artists from a business perspective. To make a long story short, he took a step down to work with an art gallery where he not only learned the business, but was able to buy the retiring owner out after a few years. So whether you tell someone else or not, put it on paper—now!

Here's a quick way to get at what can be on your public personal profile. What else would you like to tell a prospective employer in your formal resumé? You've probably done a good job of collecting all the basic information a prospective employer wants to see, but if you're like most other people, there are other things you would like to say about yourself. Most people tell me that they would list a lot of personal achievements. Many of these achievements don't speak to specific job requirements, but most of them say something about the applicant as a human being. Coaching a kids' ball club speaks to the subject of leadership as well as interest in others. What would you like to say about yourself?

For Your Eyes Only

Some of the most interesting reading is on the obituary pages of the world's major newspapers. Not to be morbid about it, but those who contribute to these obits are usually close friends who want to portray their departed friends in terms other than what the world has already seen. Most telling are those that recall the early life of the deceased. "Although he had risen to the top of his profession as a microbiologist," one I saw recently said, "he had always wanted to be a musician." You can only wonder if the subject of the obit had followed his dreams would he have been as successful as his obit seems to imply. What you never see in these pieces are the comments often heard about the deceased: that no matter how successful they had been, they really hated their work.

On that flatted note, let's get back to some major chords. If you weren't doing what you are now doing, what would make you really happy? Be realistic, but don't hesitate to record everything. Just so we are both playing on the same green, I'll tell you what I'd like to do—but you must have guessed: I'd like to be a pro golfer. There! Now, get at it, start the list!

Write Your Mission Statement

Most mission statements have been written for and about corporations. For example, the company that created the software that runs the computer I'm using, Microsoft, says this about itself, "To enable people and businesses throughout the world to realize their full potential." Lofty and a bit pretentious, but I think you get the point. A corporate mission statement is supposed to say something about purpose, goals, and values of the company. Your personal mission statement should do the same.

An author I know told me that that he thought writing a one-sentence mission statement about himself was more difficult than writing an entire book. He said, "Everything I'd write I'd revise. And I'd revise the revisions until I had probably written enough to write another whole book." He didn't mean that he had all that much to say about himself but, rather, that getting a handle on himself in 10 or 20 words is almost impossible. Even if you don't end up with a statement you like, the exercise will help you see more of what is in your head than hours and hours of counseling sessions might ever do.

Who Are You, Really?

This could be an interesting existential exercise, but let's steer clear of those marshes. Jonathan Swift could have set the tone for this section when he said, "Although men are accused of not knowing their own weaknesses, yet perhaps few know their own strengths."

When asked who they are, most people reply with labels. "I'm an accountant," for example. Press a little harder and many will peel away a few of the labels, but they still define themselves in a functional sense. They will tell you what they do. Few will tell you something like, "I'm a pretty happy guy."

So the next step is for you to write a few paragraphs about yourself, but without mentioning anything that might be on your resumé. Pretend you are interviewing yourself. Be tough. Nobody is going to see this but you. Ask yourself the kind of questions you would object to being asked in public.

 Case in Point

Eddie Murphy: "All men are sculptors, chipping away the unwanted parts of their lives, trying to create their version of a masterpiece."

What Is Your Purpose in Life?

You can define your purpose in life any way you want. Your religion may supply the clues. Your experience will provide other clues. Your dreams will provide others. It's easy to get corny here and come up with something that you might hear at a Miss America pageant, but that will be fine, too. The important thing is that you see yourself as you want to be in the world about you. A purpose in life can be seen as an organizing structure around which to organize your life. As Mother Theresa put it so clearly and succinctly, "Life is a promise. Fulfill it."

Your Goals in Life

Goals get us back to solid Earth. Goals should be achievable. They should, however, make you stretch. Achieving something you know you can do, does nothing for your self-esteem and it does little to move you along your career path.

Over the years I have noticed that people who have not set goals for themselves become devoted to trivia and minutia that gets them nowhere. Think about yourself from this perspective. Do you have a brass ring you are reaching for, or are you perpetually responding to the same old stuff?

Think of goals in terms of some meaning for your life. You may see yourself as striving for a certain skill or job level, but also think of the reasons for this. Think of goals in terms of your personal responsibilities, your family and friends, and even society in general. I don't want to get maudlin on this subject, but I do want you to have goals that have meaning and that will take more than a little effort to achieve.

> **Right Move** _____
>
> The unfamiliar is frightening. As much as we know that risks must be taken, we also see that failure hurts. However, small failures are easily forgotten and shouldn't keep you from trying again. If you really are risk-averse, plan your trips into the scary parts of life in small steps. Set your goals in smaller steps and be prepared for both failures and successes. And be prepared to learn from your failures and to reset your goals accordingly.

Okay, I've given you a lot to chew on. Let me summarize. All this has one goal, to help you create a picture of yourself as a person. Not to put too a fine point on it, too many people seldom look this closely at themselves, at least when they are doing any career planning. I just don't see how it's possible to take yourself as a person out of the equation. Maybe I'm old fashioned, but the dreams we have for ourselves should include a lot more than position and possessions. Give this some thought. In fact, I hope that you give it a lot of thought. But now back to the job at hand.

The Strength-and-Weakness Paradox

The brilliant management guru Peter Drucker has written widely on a theory that states a person's strengths can become his or her weaknesses. An example he uses often shows that the strength of self-confidence can easily tip over to become an issue of arrogance. He is also careful to explain that it is important to realize and accept that no matter how visible and important strengths may be, the weaknesses are still there and must be acknowledged and addressed.

We often see examples of this factor in leaders who arise in crises to become heroes of mythical proportions. However, when the danger passes, we see them much differently. Some of the most notable examples of this in historic memory are those military greats who were later rewarded with positions that they were totally unsuited for. Names aren't important, but think of the post-war failures of generals from every war we have ever fought.

The strength/weakness paradox operates at all levels of personal and career life. Now, as you continue to create your personal profile, I urge you to get real. Again, what you are doing is not for public view, it's for you and you alone.

List Your Personal Strengths and Weaknesses

You could take dozens of excellent tests, but most require a professional to analyze the answers for you. If you have the opportunity to take any of these tests, do so. However, I can give you enough help right here to at least get you thinking in a productive way about how to discover and analyze your personal strengths.

The paragraphs that follow describe a few personality types in very broad strokes. You will probably see bits and pieces of yourself in all of them. However, the job you have now is to see which of them describes you better than all the others. Throw away your preconceptions about yourself—not an easy thing to do, but give it a try. I have resisted giving each of these types a cute name mainly because the tests that do this send the message that you are either one or the other and you are not. Let the analysis begin!

- ◆ You think of yourself as dependable and loyal to the company that employs you. You work well and cooperate well with others. You try to avoid any confrontation, but are not afraid of it if it is absolutely necessary. You listen to others with care and often act as a calming force when others disagree vehemently. However, you are sometimes thought of as being indecisive and too slow to make decisions.

- ◆ You are a high achiever. Risk, even big risk, seldom stands in the way of your getting things done. You think of yourself as practical and might have been known to call others "dreamers" when you disagree with their solutions to problems. The problem at hand is usually more important to you than maintaining stable relationships with your co-workers. However, when you lose, you often feel that others might have ganged up on you intentionally. You are not overly concerned about being liked, but you are very sensitive about being respected.

- ◆ You speak well, write well, and find that your co-workers treat you with respect, even when they disagree with you. You can work well alone, but you prefer a team-centered type of activity. You have been known to inspire others, and people sometimes comment positively about your diplomatic skills. On the other hand, you can be impatient, especially with people who do not grasp your ideas quickly enough. You often prefer generalizations to specifics in discussions. However, some might think of you as being egotistical and sometimes more than a little abrasive. You appreciate praise, but seldom let harsh comments get you down.

◆ Perfection and precision are words you might use to describe forces that drive you. You are systematic and cautious, yet persistent when you are sure you are right and others might be wrong. More outgoing people might have branded you boring, but you can wear that badge with comfort. When accused of being indecisive, you can quickly point out that you are simply gathering enough information to make the best possible decision. What often bothers you most is being wrong and then being publicly criticized for it.

Do you see yourself in any of these profiles? Did any one profile seem to describe you better than others? Remember, the idea here is not to typecast yourself. The job is to envision yourself as a person, not as a job candidate.

It's Time to Write Your Profile

Here are the specs:

◆ No more than 600 words, no fewer than 300.

◆ Be specific, don't generalize.

◆ Use first person, active voice.

◆ Use as few adjectives and adverbs as possible.

◆ Present a broad picture of yourself; don't focus on any specific event.

◆ Don't obsess over style. You're not writing a novel. If you find writing in narrative style is difficult, do it as an outline.

◆ Don't be preachy.

◆ Include your goofs along with your positive accomplishments.

Let me warn you that this isn't easy. First, introspection itself is difficult enough. Second, unless you are a professional writer, putting words on paper isn't easy, and it's especially difficult when the subject is you. I would seriously suggest that you take at least a week to do it. Don't be afraid to revise again and again. Every time you revise, you are getting closer to your core. Anyone who writes a profile in one draft and thinks he or she has captured an accurate personal picture is deluded.

The Least You Need to Know

♦ Your personal profile will help you see yourself as you probably never have before—if you take your time and do a thorough job of it.

♦ You are probably somewhat surprised by what you discovered about what makes you happy and what is objectionable. You are probably more surprised at how well you dealt with some of life's problems.

♦ Your strengths can become your weaknesses if you are not careful.

♦ Perfection is not worth the effort, but getting close definitely worth it.

♦ There is no perfect person for every job. The best you can do is come close and then work hard to close the gap.

Chapter 15

Discovering Your "Helps" and "Hinders"

In This Chapter

- Discover the hidden "hinders" that can derail any career planning
- Learn how to turn "hinders" to "helps"
- Beware of the helps-to-hinders transformation
- Discover which "hinders" may be uncontrollable
- Are you ready to move from "you" to "them"?

By now, you should have a much clearer picture of yourself than you did when you first opened this book. Your shoebox should be full of career ideas and data about yourself. In the coming chapters, we will be getting down to brass tacks, but before we do, it's time to pull out the shoebox and start assembling yourself—on paper that is.

Until now, I have intentionally avoided suggesting that you organize anything you put in the box. Organizing as you go can force you into a mold too early on. Only when you have everything you need does it make sense to start assembling the picture. And now it's time!

Make Neat Piles

The way you choose to organize the information you collected is entirely up to you. One of the faults I've seen in most career management programs is that they try to fit people into rigid categories that define the system, rather than the person. These systems can be helpful, but most don't give you any real control over the emerging picture of yourself.

That said, I would like to suggest that you *loosely* organize your notes and ideas this way:

◆ **What you have done so far.** This section might include your education and training, as well as notes on the jobs you have held and might currently hold.

◆ **What you feel you are qualified to do now.** Remember, I asked you to go wild here. Be imaginative!

◆ **What you feel qualified to do in other fields.** Add to this pile whatever thoughts you have about the transferability of your present skills and qualifications.

◆ **Your career satisfactions so far.** This should include hard data, such as performance reports as well as your own feelings about your career.

◆ **Where you want to go.** In this section, add your thoughts about staying with your present company, moving up in that company or one of its subsidiaries, or making a clean break and moving to a totally different employer.

See Anything Emerging?

If you're like most people, you probably noticed that some items shifted from pile to pile. They just didn't seem to belong—that is, until another item was added that seemed to crystallize the "theme" of the pile. And when that happened, you had ah-ha moment. Something became clearer. Pieces were beginning to fall into place.

Now, look at each pile, item by item, slowly and carefully. Can some piles be combined? Maybe you need another pile? Don't hesitate to move and shift. You are creating a picture of yourself that could never be created with a more formal system.

Do you see any patterns emerging? Unless I miss my guess, you have some very different perceptions of yourself now than you did when you first started reading this book. A sense of general unrest about your job has probably emerged as a complex picture that gives you some focus. You may have even discovered that you are better off than you thought you were. Best of all, I'll bet you are more comfortable with yourself, whatever the results.

Making Your Personal "Helps" and "Hinders" List

Don't get too comfortable yet, there's more work to do. In each pile you create, you will discover areas where a little help is needed and where some things that are blocking your growth need to be removed. There probably aren't many of either, but they all need to be addressed.

Here are a couple of examples of what I'm talking about.

♦ From the notes in one of your piles you get a sense that you have everything you need to move up to greater responsibility in your career. However, you feel pigeonholed and find it difficult to convince people that you can and should be thought of in broader terms. Add this to your "hinders" list.

♦ Another note shows that you have people in your corner at the company, one of whom might be the one to approach about the "hinder" described above. Add this to your "help" list.

I could go on, but I'm sure you get the point. The lists I want you to create are basically the sum and substance of all the work you have been asked to do in the previous chapters. They will tell you in some detail, what you need to do to overcome the obstacles in your path. They will provide you with a list of the people you can turn to and the things you can use to help further your career. And, you've painted the picture yourself. It is you, not the result of some test that tried to fit you into one of ten categories, none of which remotely resemble how you see yourself.

How To Use Your Helps and Hinders

Prioritize the elements that can help you, especially those that are interdependent. Then, of course, think in terms of timing and how much effort each one will require. Don't fall into the trap of addressing the easy items first. Address the helps and hinders as they relate to your immediate and long-term goals. In short, set goals you can achieve, and organize your helps and hinders in progressions that will help you reach these goals.

You may find it helpful to ask some trusted co-workers or friends for help. Remember, your perspective is subjective. Others who are closely involved with you personally and at work may see things differently. And don't ask friends for instant answers. Ask them to think about a specific help or hinder and get back to you; you'll probably be able to put more stock in their responses.

Basically, what you want to do is bulk up the helps, see them in a clear perspective, and prioritize them in ways that will give you incremental improvement. Don't try to take on too much at one time. Career planning and management should be done so that it provides answers to the questions you have today, and guidelines for your future development. Nobody really knows what the future holds. Guidelines provide flexibility. Rigid goals for long-term growth seldom work out as planned. Think of life as a poker game played one hand at a time and you'll see what I mean. You know you want to leave the table as a winner, but the only way to do it is hand-by-hand.

Some Hinders May Seem Uncontrollable

It would be a just world if we had control over everything that crosses our paths, but we don't. However, most people tend to think of these roadblocks as either impossible to remove, or not worth the effort to try. It's isn't always necessary to smash through or ignore a hindering element. It's often possible to isolate the element so that it no longer is a problem, or to simply make an end run around it.

Case in Point

A client I coached a few years ago saw that her path was blocked by a limited education. Although her job specs didn't state it directly, she saw that everyone who was promoted had master's degrees. She had only a BA. When she realized this was holding her back, she signed up for an online Master's program from a major university and reported this to her employer. Not only did the employer offer to pick up part of the cost of the course, but they gave her a minor promotion and implied that good grades would be further rewarded. They were, and she is now on a fast track, even though she still has about 20 credits to complete for the degree.

Working Some Magic with Your "Hinders"

Let's say that one of the people you asked to help you create your personal profile told you that you seemed to put off making decisions. This person saw this as something that might hinder you and so might others. However, you may not have to change your habits at all if you simply say that while you may appear to be slower than others in making decisions, you probably give each problem far more careful consideration than those who make snap decisions. If possible, be able to point out where someone's snap decision caused more problems than it solved.

> ## Case in Point
>
> Recently one of my coaching clients found himself being criticized during a meeting for what the critic called "a squishy attitude" when the person thought he should be more hard-nosed. My client replied, "You may think of that as squishy, but I think of it in long terms. Long term, my approach builds team players. Your short-term approach may solve problems quickly, but you have to face them again and again. My way takes longer at first, but they never occur again. Call it squishy if you want, but I call it proactive problem solving." Needless to say, I was quite proud of him.

One of the characteristics of most successful people is that they know their strengths and weaknesses. They neither brag about their strengths, nor do they deny any weaknesses. However, those who make it to where they want to go are able to either resolve weaknesses by direct action, or they are able to turn them to strengths, as I've just shown.

Remain Flexible

Just because you may be that rare person who is able to wipe out all your hindering factors, don't think that others won't arise to plague you. You can take a breather, but don't let your guard down.

> ## Case in Point
>
> Tom Robbins, "Stay committed to your decisions, but remain flexible in your approach."

And Now for Something a Little Different ...

With apologies (and thanks) to John Cleese and the Monty Python regulars, we move from you—sorry about that—to Part 4 of the book where we focus on the real world. Here you will meet the dragons that stand in your way, and the good knights who are more than willing to help you out. We're going to delve into the sources of information that few have access to, and we are going to tell you where to get the information that your present employer doesn't want you to have.

Before we bid fond adieu to the person you now know as you, let's take one final look at what you should know.

◆ You should have some firm ideas about whether it's best for you to stay where you are, look for a transfer within your company, or start looking for opportunities outside your current company.

- You should have a pretty good idea of where you stand in the hierarchy of your present company, and where you stand with people doing similar work with other companies.

- You should have a clear picture of the path within your company that leads to where you want to be, and what "helps" and "hinders" you will encounter. In the chapters that follow, we will show you how to scope out the opportunities outside your present company.

- You should know whether the itch you want to scratch is real, or just something that will pass.

- You should know everything there is to know about your present employer, at least as it relates to you and your future.

- You should have a realistic picture of yourself in terms of skills, accomplishments, and abilities.

- You should know which of your skills and abilities are needed in the open marketplace, and which of your skills are transferable.

- You should have assembled your skills tool kit and you should be able to demonstrate that you can swing a hammer and hit a nail on the head, literally or figuratively.

- You should know your style. If you don't remember what I mean by this, go back to Chapter 9 before you go any farther.

- You should have a very clear idea of your communicative abilities.

- You should know where you stand in terms of leadership qualifications. Not all jobs demand dynamic leaders, but some of the most successful leaders never thought of themselves as leaders until they had to lead.

- You should have a solid picture of your accomplishments that are important in any move up, over, or out program.

- You should know what gives you job satisfaction and what turns you off. You should know just how much satisfaction you are willing to sacrifice for growth.

The Least You Need to Know

I've just told you!

Part 4

Finding the Information You Need

The Navy has ships called minesweepers, small ships that sail into waters strewn with explosive mines to find and destroy them so that the larger ships can make safe passage. As you can imagine, this is dangerous work. Think of your search for career information in terms of being a mine-sweeper. The explosives you must avoid are the sources that aren't helpful, or are just plain dangerous. A lot of what is on the Internet is helpful, but just as much of it isn't, and it's even possibly dangerous.

In the chapters that follow, I show you how to avoid the mines, how to clear the passage and even how to avoid having to abandon ship should you accidentally hit a mine. Keep in mind that the Internet is only one source of career information. The sources I discuss take you beyond this source into the real-time sources that few people even know exist. I hate to use the word *secret* but in many ways these sources are secret—not because anyone intended them to be but because they take a little work to dig up. But when the average person watches TV for nearly 40 hours a week, a couple of hours digging where I tell you to will be a small price to pay. Besides, you can record the shows you miss and play them later.

Chapter 16

Develop Your Job Search Information Checklist

In This Chapter

◆ Ben Franklin made it easy for you to evaluate career search information

◆ The critical path method can cut your time in half and save you a lot of work

◆ Your nine-point job information checklist is in this chapter

◆ Seven ways to avoid making bad decisions

The six chapters that follow this one are all about how to gather job-specific information. Unless you plan carefully right at the start, you will probably find yourself with much, much more than you need—which will be a problem if you're not careful. So before we get into the search, it might be a good idea to look at how to decide what to include and what to chuck. In other words, let's set up your personal decision rules. If you're in a hurry, skip to the end of the chapter for "The Least You Need to Know." But I warn you, you do so at your peril. So hang in, this is a short chapter.

Staying Focused

You can always flip a coin. The decisions I'm talking about involve simply whether to use or not use certain information in your career planning. As any statistician will tell you, if you have enough choices, flipping a coin may be as good as any other complex decision-making process. However, I don't think that most people who are making career decisions would take me very seriously if I suggested you flip coins, so let's look at a better way.

Although he didn't invent it, Ben Franklin is credited for popularizing a system based on listing the positive and negative attributes of decisions. Systematically eliminating the weaker attributes should leave you with a good decision. If it was good enough for Ben, it's good enough for you and me.

You will be deciding whether to include or not include the sources you will discover in the chapters to follow, and later you will use the same system to decide whether to use the information you get from these sources. This may seem like a huge undertaking, but it really isn't. You should be able to make most of the decisions quickly.

Here are the elements that you must address:

- **The let's-get-on-with-it factor:** When we are pressed for time, most of us make snap decisions. Do this too often and you will lose good information. The best advice I can give is that everything is important until you prove that it isn't. Take your time.

- **The if-it-was-good-enough-then factor:** The information you are considering using may have been excellent in the past, but times change. Always look at the data in light of what is relevant now.

- **The I-know-better factor:** Called selective perception by psychologists, those who fall victim to it tend to rule out material prematurely because it fails to support closely held ideas.

- **The source-credibility factor:** Of all the issues you will face when making career decisions today, this may be the one that is easiest to fall victim to. You'll find a lot of material to make your career decisions on the Internet. And a lot of it will appeal to you by virtue of the credentials of the person who puts it on the net. I'm not saying everybody lies, but more than a few individuals truly believe in what they say, but are close to clueless. My advice is to check out any individual whose data you plan to use very carefully.

◆ **The I-keep-seeing-it factor:** Much of what is seen on the Internet is unverified. Written for a blog by one person and picked up by others, it quickly assumes unjustified validity. If you have any doubt at all, check it out.

◆ **The group-think factor:** When you belong to any formal or informal group, you tend to think that its collective thinking is valid. It may be, and it may not be. Don't let yourself be pressured into accepting something uncritically.

Constructing Your List

First of all, avoid taking the easy way out by using any of the many canned checklists available from any number of sources, including the Internet. Many can be used as general guidelines, but to be most effective your checklist has to be about you and you alone. Think of it like buying an off-the-rack suit, and having one tailor-made just for you. The off-the-rack suit may look okay, but the tailor-made suit fits you perfectly.

Your personal job search information checklist will help you to ...

◆ Decide whether you should consider moving up in your present job, moving to other opportunities within your company, or start looking elsewhere.

◆ Evaluate whether your chosen career is the place to be, or whether you should think about making a change in the focus of your career.

◆ Evaluate your personal abilities and accomplishments in terms of the requirements of your chosen field, or other fields that seem more attractive.

◆ Evaluate the short- and long-term potential for growth of the fields in which you work or would like to work.

> **Right Move**
>
> At this point, focus on gathering information to meet your short term goals. Your short-term goals should be tightly focused, and your long-term goals should be more generalized. As you grow in your career, you will see opportunities you may not even be aware of today. Plan ahead but stay flexible!

Any good career counselor would address these areas in personal sessions. These sessions do have the benefit of a live professional to guide you, and there's probably no substitute for first-class professional career coaching, but if you take it seriously and stick to the plan I am outlining, you should do very well by yourself. The key is really persistence. Don't make career planning something you do when you have nothing else to do. The major advantage of using the CPM approach is that you must set dates by which to accomplish the various tasks you set for yourself.

Your Career Information Guidelines

The critical path method is far more sophisticated than it appears here. It was originally developed to organize a large number of complex tasks to ensure on-time and effective completion of a project. If you have the time, you might want to read further on it. For now, however, we are just using the main ideas to get you from where you are now to where you would like to be. Many of the critical path plans I have seen included graphic representations of the work to be accomplished. I'm going to skip that. It just adds work that really isn't needed. Here's what you should be investigating:

- ◆ Economic and competitive conditions of my current field of work.

- ◆ Economic and competitive conditions of my current employer.

- ◆ Projected economic status of my current field of work.

- ◆ Projected economic status of my current employer.

- ◆ A picture of my personal work status and history.

- ◆ A picture of my potential with my present company in my current job.

- ◆ A picture of employment potential with my current employer by changing careers or moving to other divisions or subsidiaries.

- ◆ A picture of the potential that exists for employment with other organizations.

- ◆ A picture of the personal elements I will encounter in making major employment changes.

Note that I am anchoring these points in economic and competitive issues. You may find great pleasure in your present field, but if that field is in decline, you may simply find yourself moving from one declining company to another. Biting the bullet isn't easy, but there are times when you have to do it. Think of the industries and specialized fields that employed thousands just a few years ago that have simply disappeared. Remember when day-trading was the wave of the future? As I write this, there are more than a few people who had made excellent livings in real estate who are not working. Anything else you can think of?

> **Case in Point**
>
> A number of years ago I met a man who was the sales manager of a small but leading electronics company. He was not a client, but in getting to know him I discovered that he had moved here from France where he had a small chain of jewelry stores. Before living in France, he lived in Israel, where he obtained advanced degrees in solid state physics and had been head of technology for a major player in the field. This was a man with an unusual career history, to say the least. His philosophy was simply to determine which fields were strong and growing and to move into them. He explained the jewelry stores by saying, "There was no need for physicists in France at the time, but the jewelry market was strong and easy to learn about." This man's approach is exactly what I am talking about here. Planning and flexibility!

I hope you're seeing a pattern emerging at this point. We started right from Chapter 1 with a rather broad focus. Chapter by chapter, I've been narrowing this focus and I have tried to do this for you with as little effort on your part as possible. All of the information you have put in your career shoebox should provide you with what you need on the personal side.

Now we are moving into the real world of jobs. The critical path checklist you are creating will not only help you find the work you want, but it should help you find work that is meaningful and personally rewarding.

The next step is to establish a sequence for your information search. You have to establish your own checklist here; only you know what is important and less important, and only you can set up a meaningful and workable timetables. If you're currently working in engineering and doing a master's in marketing on a part-time basis, only you can determine the right time sequence to follow up on your career change plans.

Once you know what you need to look for and the sequence in which the information will help you, you need to set dates to have the material in hand. Be reasonable; don't set dates you know will be very difficult to meet. And of course, don't set dates so far in advance that the information you finally gather will be useless.

Your Final Critical Path Date

If you're unfamiliar with the critical path system, you have probably been wondering why such a simple procedure as I have been describing has such a fancy name. The answer is that the actual critical path is longest time path in your system. It's the search path that you feel will take the most time and the most effort. As such, you simply cannot delay any elements in this path without endangering the entire project. You may be able to let deadlines slip on some of the projects not in the critical path without endangering the completion date, but you cannot monkey with any of the projects on your critical path. Get the picture?

> ### Career News
>
> Most successful people never dreamed of being where they are today. Although most planned individual steps carefully, few ever ended up doing what they aspired to early on. Don't believe me? Frank Stanton, former president of CBS, started as a psychologist. See what I mean?

Managing Your Critical Path Information Search

Most critical path plans seem to add more work than is really needed. And, I'm sure that you might have that feeling about what I am proposing. But let me assure you that the few hours you spend up front will save you much more time on the back end, and your work will be far less frustrating as you do it. I can truthfully say that most people who give up on career planning partway through do so because they were doing it willy-nilly. I gave you a lot of latitude in the earlier chapters by suggesting the shoebox system of career planning management. Now that you have a lot of the heavy lifting behind you, it's time to get organized.

Getting Started

The simplest way to get started and to keep your search going is to get nine file folders or large manila envelopes and label each with the titles I have listed. Keep them together and in a safe place. That's all there is to it. For the next six chapters you will simply be collecting and filing information. When you complete Chapter 30, you will have everything you need to create and activate your career plan.

Just to summarize, your career planning program should now include the following:

- ◆ All the personal information you have been putting in the shoebox
- ◆ File #1—Economic and competitive data on your current field of work
- ◆ File #2—Economic and competitive data on your current employer
- ◆ File #3—Economic data on your current field of work

- File #4—Projected economic data on your current employer

- File #5—Data on your current employment status and history

- File #6—Data on where you stand with your present employer

- File #7—Data on possible moves within the organization that presently employs you

- File #8—Data on employment potential with other organizations

- File #9—Data on all the personal elements that can impact any decision you might make regarding employment

The equation that is developing is this:

pf + rwf = scp

Where:

pf = personal factors

rwf = real world factors

scp = successful career plan

Are all the bits and pieces starting to make sense? I hope so. You could do your career planning without taking any of the steps I am suggesting, and you could be very successful at it. That success would depend on two factors. The first is an incredible ability to collect and organize data in your head. The second is just plain luck that what you want from life will come to you without even trying. Trust me, the second is a one-in-a-million shot. The first probably includes one half of one percent of the people seeking to improve their careers. For the rest of us, it's work. But it's work worth doing.

The Least You Need to Know

- Most of the real-world information you need to manage your career is economic.

- Using the nine-point checklist will help you gather information quickly.

- You are halfway there. Congratulations!

Chapter 17

Find the Information That Will Help

In This Chapter

- ◆ The Internet isn't all it's cracked up to be

- ◆ Four questions to ask about every piece of information you will use to make career decisions

- ◆ How to validate career information

- ◆ How to use out-of-date information to start your search

- ◆ The who-says? test that clears up much doubt about career-related information

The Internet is a blessing as well as a curse. Because of it, more information is now available to help you plan and manage your career than ever before. However, not all of this information is trustworthy. I'm not condemning the Internet at all; I'm simply warning you to be as careful using it as you are of using any other source. We tend to think of something new and high tech as perhaps better and more reliable than other sources. Well, it is and it isn't.

Don't rush through this chapter. You won't find much actual career management help in it, but you should end up with a focus that will help you spot the good stuff and chuck the useless stuff quickly. You will put these skills to good use as you complete your reading of this book.

You should ask four questions about the data you will use to manage your career-development program:

♦ Is the information readily accessible?

♦ How current is the information?

♦ Is the information practical and relevant to your needs?

♦ Is the information factual and reliable?

Let's look as each at each of these in some detail.

Is the Information Accessible?

You may think that random walks down the information superhighway might ultimately lead you to the mother lode. You should live so long! You've got to have a map and you have to start from point A.

Point A isn't just a metaphor; it has to be based on the information you have in hand and the information you think you need. This means you should first determine whether your existing information is relevant to your present goals and whether it's timely.

So it's time to sort, save, and chuck. Keep the stuff you know is valid and helpful and throw out the rest. Start stuffing the folders or envelops you created as you read Chapter 16. Yes, I know, one more thing to do. But in case you haven't noticed, all the checklists and chores I've given you so far are focused on the nine-point checklist and the folders you created in the last chapter. You're in the homestretch.

Case in Point _____

One of my coaching clients once asked me, "Can I do the research in my pajamas?" He was half-kidding and half-serious. It turned out that he was a morning person and knew that his Internet connection was a lot faster at 4 in the morning than it was in the afternoon when the kids landed on the net. So he really did a lot of his research in his pajamas. However, I did warn him that the Internet was by no means the only source he should use, no matter how easy it is to use.

You will discover that a lot of information you need is proprietary—owned by some-one. This includes such data as salaries, conditions of employment, and actual figures on benefits. It is usually useable only under certain circumstances. Those conditions often include membership in the organization that produced it, or the payment of cer-tain user fees. Here is where you have to be careful when using the Internet. Much of the free information is helpful, but the really valuable information usually comes at a price. You need to determine whether the information you need is important enough to pay for it and whether the price asked is fair. I wish I could give you a checklist to help you make these decisions, but every situation is different so you are on your own here.

Career Alert

Be careful about asking friends who belong to organizations that have information you want. Most organizations pledge paying members to make use of it only for themselves. Don't put a friendship in jeopardy by asking. However, many organizations have different levels of membership. Check out what is available to you at different levels. The company you work for might even have a corporate membership that allows you to access information. Check your college alumni membership to see if it grants you access to the library.

Depending on where you are in your career planning cycle, you may need information quickly. When this happens, most people tend to overlook the validity and reliability of the information they discover and use. You may be pressured for decisions, so you often take data at face value. This is especially true of salary information and employ-ment statistical data. If you find yourself in this pickle, decide which information is really time sensitive and focus on it. Know where you can afford to base decisions on less reliable information. But have the facts you need for critical choices.

Is the Information Current?

One of the major advantages of the Internet as a source of career information is that it's usually up to date. This is a major source of problems for traditional book publish-ers. Their reference books are out of date the day they are published. And as time goes on, more and more of the information they contain goes stale.

Bound-book sources, however, are probably the best place to start your search. Either you or the library has paid the price of entry—the book has been bought and paid for. What you can get from these books is ideas and directions to go for more current information, often available on the internet free or for less money than you might have to pay to buy the original print source. All the research done by the authors is right there, ink on paper. You will probably see many paths to venture down that you had not considered before. The data may be out of date, but now you know what is available and you can seek ways to get information that is more current than that in the book.

Right Move

Many libraries chuck outdated reference books as they acquire new and updated editions. Ask your librarian to save those that will be of use to you, rather than to throw them out. The information may be outdated, but you will still find information, ideas, and data sources that had never occurred to you. Look to other sources for updates—free if possible, or for less than you might have to pay for the current edition of the published book.

Most major newspapers are excellent sources of statistical information, such as overall economic trends. Articles on career development researched by staff reporters usually include current statistical data. Depending on the newspaper, you can probably do a keyword search on their online database and pull up articles with current data relevant to your career plans.

Trade and professional magazines are excellent sources, too, but their focus will be much narrower than that of general-interest newspapers. Whatever your field or profession, there is probably at least one magazine covering it, and most of these magazines have a Web presence, too. Some sites grant immediate access to previously published articles, others list titles and synopses. Some require you to register with them and others insist on paid subscriptions. Looking in a magazine aimed at sales professionals, for example, my guess is that you would find more than enough articles published in the last few months to give you just about everything you needed to know to judge employment potential in the field. You might even get a pretty good idea of the salaries and benefits being offered.

Again, the key is finding *timely* material. Later I will talk more about these search areas, but for now, just remember that information must be current to be really helpful.

What's Relevant and What Isn't?

Who would think that information on the availability of silicon would be important to an accountant's career management? It might be important for engineers and scientists, but an accountant? Well, if you worked for a computer chip maker and the price of raw silicon suddenly doubled, it would be safe to assume that your employer might look to outsource some operations to a country where silicon was available at better prices. That move would affect everyone who worked for the company, including accountants. I'll talk in more detail later on this topic, but for now, you should remember that your career management program could be affected by events as remote as this.

The cliché, "Think outside the box", has real meaning when it comes to deciding what information will have an effect on your career. On the other hand, it's important not to obsess over minutia.

Right Move

Computer search engines work by linking words to words. Many of these links can be laughable, but most will take you in very productive directions. For example, following links from the word "chemist" a few moments ago landed me on a site with current national salary data. A few links further put me on a site that adults usually block their kids from seeing. Learn not only how to use these searches, but how to judge their quality and reliability.

To paraphrase an old saying, "Relevancy is in the eye of the beholder." In simple terms, what your friends tell you may be relevant to them but may be useless to you in terms of your career needs. When people offer help, they usually feel compelled to defend their input. My solution to this potentially friend-losing situation is just to offer thanks and avoid any further discussion.

What's Reliable and What Isn't?

You usually discover that information you have chosen to use is either reliable or unreliable only after the fact. So pessimists are usually more helpful than optimists because of their perpetual lament, "Don't count on that!" However, you can bump up the odds of the information you gather being reliable considerably by using these simple tricks:

- ◆ The who-says? test. When your neighbor, an accountant, tries to tell you that the sky is falling in the microbiology field, take the advice with a grain of salt. However, if a dozen accountants tell you the same story, pay attention; they may be on to something. Check your sources carefully.

♦ The consistency test. The banner headline in the journal that covers your field screams gloom and doom. Are they right or wrong? If they have successfully predicted gloom-and-doom before, you should pay attention. The more often they have been right, the better the chances they are now.

There are other ways to put a sharper edge on the reliability of career information you may want to use, but if you stick with the two I have just given you, you will be ahead of the game—and ahead of others who might compete with you for the prize job.

Career Alert _____

Emerson said, "A foolish consistency is the hobgoblin of little minds." You will see a lot of stuff on the Internet that appears to make the same statement. Just keep in mind that errors are just as easily propagated as reliable facts. Emerson's use of the word *foolish* is the key here. Keep an open mind and check out any information, no matter how often you see it repeated, that just doesn't seem right to you.

The Price of Raw Lumber in Norway

A friend with a wry sense of humor once showed me two elaborately plotted graphs. One charted the price of raw lumber in Norway for the past 20 years. The other charted the average compensation rates of senior vice presidents of major U.S. banks over the same period. If you placed one curve over the other, they were almost identical. Ergo, following the price of lumber in Norway was all you needed to do to predict salary trends of senior bank vice presidents in the United States. Don't laugh! Many people buy stocks and bonds based on even sillier research. And I'm sure as many people make career decisions after carefully evaluating everything—but without verifying the facts they use.

Let me tell you what can happen to facts on their way to your ear. Those teaching social psychology like to introduce the course to their new students with this simple experiment. They whisper a simple statement with two or three points to the student sitting at the head of the first column of students. That person is then told to whisper the information to the person behind him or her. The process continues until the whispered information reaches the last person in the class. That person is then asked to repeat the story. In most cases, the facts are completely distorted, the point of view is changed, and little remains of the story whispered to the first person.

The point? When there is even a whiff of doubt, go to the source.

I told you this would be a short chapter. But, it's a very important one. You are going to be making very important career decisions based on information you get from friends, co-workers, and plenty of other sources. Check it out carefully. A little mistake now could turn into a big problem later on.

The Least You Need to Know

- The Internet is a great source of career information, but some say half of it is inaccurate. Your job is to determine which half you can use.

- To be useful, career information must be current, valid, reliable, and directly related to your needs.

- Career information facts can become fiction overnight. Check, recheck, and check again on every fact that you plan to rely on.

Chapter 18

Looking Close to Home

In This Chapter

- ◆ Rating the best employer for you
- ◆ Insider's guide to your employer's financial health
- ◆ Your employer doesn't have to be number one in its field to be the best place for you to work
- ◆ Your immediate supervisor may not have the authority you think
- ◆ Avoid management fads at all costs

It's easy to lament the "good old days," when many people spent their whole career with one employer. Whether those days really were that good is open to serious debate, but what has replaced them certainly offers much more opportunity for personal and economic growth. Much of that opportunity actually exists because of what so many condemn—merged, acquired, and segmented companies.

Stymied for growth in your present position? Maybe there's a faster track in another division, a subsidiary, or a company in which your employer has a major interest. Most of the conglomerates I know and consult with are very open to interdepartmental and even intercompany transfers for bright and ambitious people. If you can't move up where you are, many organizations give you the option of moving to other holdings with better opportunities. Remember, the central idea of your planning is based on the notion of moving up, over, or out.

This chapter focuses on how your present employer might help you make appropriate up, over, or out move decisions. You may think you know everything you need to know about your employer, but I'll bet I'll have a few surprises for you in the pages that follow. You may want to quickly read Chapter 5 again, in which I discussed the personal side of your current employer.

What Do You Know About Your Employer?

Unless your employer is the local candy store, you may actually know very little about your employer. Your business card may say that you are the sales manager of Ultimate Dynamic Corporation, but the payer on your paycheck may read something entirely different. And you may even get interoffice memos with yet another heading. Some of these entities may be divisions of the company named on your card, some may be subsidiaries, and others may just be loosely affiliated organizations. It can get complex, but you need to get as clear a picture of the entire corporate structure as possible.

Although I am focusing on your present employer, you will need to know as much about any other organization you might consider working for. However, this book is not about job hunting. That's a totally different subject and there are plenty of very good books in print to help you. Check the appendix for some that I feel are especially helpful.

Does the Perfect Employer Really Exist?

I don't think there is such a thing as a perfect employer. However, I do think that many companies, large and small, come close. Let's look broadly at the characteristics that I think put some companies on the four-star list.

- **Stability:** Stable companies give employees a chance to grow and prosper and pay attention to time-tested core concepts without jumping in and out of the hot field *du jour*. However, they are also often known for being very innovative. If they are publicly traded corporations, financial analysts don't hesitate to add them to clients' portfolios at any level. They can be big and complex, or they can be small and simple. Stability comes in all sizes.

- **Management:** Those who run the company are respected for their special abilities as well as for their understanding and dealings with employees as groups as well as individuals. The two words that come to mind immediately are "fair" and "intelligent."

♦ **Industry position:** The field or fields of the company are growing and expanding. If any of their operations include areas that might peak and decline quickly, their portfolio includes enough operations in other fields to counterbalance possible losses.

♦ **Personal growth:** There are opportunities for personal and financial growth. Especially important, the company provides opportunities to learn more and to polish existing skills. The company values people as key assets.

♦ **Fair compensation:** Compensation for work at your level is at least at the national average for your field. Beware of companies paying outrageous salaries. They may be staffing up for a short-term push that might not include a need for your services once they reach their goal.

♦ **Reputation:** If it's a publicly traded company, its public history is clean and impressive. If it's a privately held company, it won't be easy to get an acceptable comfort factor, but it can be done.

It isn't easy to be objective about the company that presently employs you. You already have many opinions firmly in place. But you might want to try this: pretend you are applying for your present job with your present employer and are just now thinking about the points I have just discussed. How does your employer shape up? Unless you are terribly dissatisfied with your job, I'll wager that you may be happier about some factors and a bit more dissatisfied with some others. Whatever your answer, remember it and remember your reasons for answering the way you did. It will be a baseline for some important decisions.

Who Do You Really Work For?

I'm not talking about your immediate boss. If you work for a corporation, it may be owned by a company that is owned by yet another company. It's important to have a clear picture of the entire corporate structure. One failing subsidiary could sink the whole kettle of fish. Or one extremely profitable operation could carry the losers until they get their act together.

The overall picture is important, but it's even more important to know the status of your company within any larger corporate structure. You could be working for a division or subsidiary that is on the block because it failed to meet its corporate goals, or it could be sold because there are investors willing to pay outrageous prices for organizations that they lack in their own corporate structure.

> **Right Move**
>
> A lot of what you need to know is available in public records, especially if you work for a publicly traded company. If you don't already own any stock in the company that employs you, you should buy at least one share. That will entitle you to all the publicly distributed information on the company's financial health.

This may sound like a bit of gloom and doom, but if you are planning to work for a long time with your present employer, you will see and possibly fall victim to changes over which you have no control. If your division is fantastically successful, someone may try to buy it. If your division loses enough money or business in any particular quarter, the directors may put your division on the block. There's no way to predict how either possibility might affect you, so just be prepared.

If the company you work for is part of a widely diversified organization, your chances of long-term employment are not that good, unless your organization is key to the success of enough of the other holdings. Poor performance of the operation is not a good sign. Other companies might be interested in an underperforming operation if it's at a fire-sale price. And when that happens, more than a few careers will probably be disrupted.

If you work for a closely held private corporation whose owners and managers are a tad long in the tooth, you may find yourself working for someone else one day. About the best way to protect yourself if you want to be with the company regardless of who owns or manages it is to make yourself indispensable. This is not easy to do, but even if your best efforts are of no avail, the reputation you establish will go a long way to helping you find new employment.

Your Employer's Financial Status

You don't have to be an accountant to know something about the financial health of your employer. In fact, you can gather a lot of what you need to know without ever seeing a balance sheet or a financial statement. If your company hires and fires large numbers of people as the company's fortunes rise and fall, you should view it with more than a little financial skepticism. Those that hire for specific and well-defined growth plans and tend to retain employees during downturns are usually seen as being in good financial hands. Regular layoffs when the company fails to meet some quarterly goals should be a warning to you. Also when the only answer management has to the profit demands of investors is cost cutting, you might want to keep your resumé up-to-date.

It's important to know whether your company has easy access to capital, whether it's for planned growth or to weather one of the downturns that seem to be coming with more and more regularity these days.

The higher your level of responsibility, the greater will be your need for accurate financial information. Unless you know all the budgeting details, you may not know that your longevity is predicated on goals that are impossible to reach. This is seldom a problem in publicly held corporations, but it can be a problem with privately held companies where the owners are loath to share financial information with anyone.

Career Alert

There are very profitable companies that treat employees badly, and poorly managed companies that treat their employees very well. Avoid both if you can!

It's usually a lot easier to get financial information on the company that already employs you than it is from one you are thinking of working for. You probably already know some people in the financial department. It wouldn't be discrete to ask anyone for information they are pledged to keep secret, but you can nibble around the edges by asking questions that they can usually answer. For example, corporate profits can usually be easily estimated by asking where the company stands relative to some of its major competitors. If the competitors are publicly traded, get the information from their quarterly and annual reports, and then position your company relative to the numbers. You won't have dollars-and-cents information, but you will know whether to be thinking "out" rather than "over" or "up."

Most major corporations publish elaborate annual reports that include a lot of impressive pictures and graphics. It's easy to be wowed by the statements made and elaborate illustrations, but you should keep in mind that the numbers in them record the company's financial status as of the day their fiscal year ends. By the time these reports are written and printed, a few months can go by, and the financial picture can change dramatically. You can get more accurate figures by getting your hands on the quarterly reports, which are usually available on the Internet.

Federal law states that every corporation must submit its financial report to an independent auditor, whose statement has to be included within the pages of its annual report. It's very important to read their statement. Much of what you read will sound like boilerplate, but look out for any terms other than "clean opinion." When the auditor spots problems that are at the whim of some future events, they will issue a "subject to" statement. This isn't a good sign, but the really bad sign is a report that states that auditors have a "going concern" for the financial health of the company. If you're already working for a company whose annual report is of concern to its auditor, get your resumé up-to-date and start looking.

A profit-and-loss statement is a marvel of misdirection. Whatever it's called in the report, you need to discover how much money the company took in for·the period and how much money the company made as profit or how much it lost. In simplest terms, income less expenses equals either a profit or a loss. Look for the line labeled Net Income or Loss.

If only it were as simple as a profit or a loss, career decisions would be easy to make, but life isn't quite that accommodating. If you find that your company is reporting a profit, you need to get answers to these questions:

◆ How was the profit calculated and what were the sources of the income? Profit calculation for a company on an accrual accounting basis might mean something entirely different from the same number based on the use of cash basis accounting. It's far too complicated to explain at this point, but if you see problems in other areas, get a crash course in balance sheet analysis and make appropriate use of the information you learn.

◆ Is the profit reasonable? You need information on industry standards and the numbers turned by your employer's competitors to see this number in its proper light. Don't be impressed by millions unless you know that your competitors are not reporting profits in the billions.

◆ How does the profit compare with previous reports? Here you will need historical data to get a clear picture of the health of your employer. Look for steady growth. If your company shows a net loss, find out why. Maybe they invested heavily in machinery that was needed to handle recently acquired business that will turn a bigger profit to be reported next time.

◆ Are the profits pretty much the same year after year? This could mean a lot of things, but one sinister thing to consider is accounting magic. The books may not be cooked and what the company is doing may be perfectly legal, but few companies show the same figures regularly year after year. Check the CEO's compensation and see if it, too, is stable. Obvious upward variations should send you deeper into your company's financial records.

◆ How was the profit made? A sudden jump in profits may imply that the company is on a major roll, or it could be a nonrecurring event. Glowing statements in the president's message often try to portray a random event as a sign of more great things to come. Could be! But check it out.

If your company is reporting losses, a sudden slip to the negative side could be signaling some restructuring losses. If your employer announces a new strategic plan at the same time it reports a significant loss, you should dig into the reasons. They could be legitimate, or they could be the result of management mistakes or just plain mismanagement.

A profit of a million dollars may seem like a lot to you, but it could be chump change for your employer. Examine your employer's profits relative to profits made by other companies in your field, preferably those that compete directly. The number that will help you most is not the actual value of the profit, but the return on investment (ROI). This figure more or less lets you put your company on a reasonable basis for relative comparisons. It is way beyond the scope of this book to explain this figure, how to get it, and how to use it. However, your banker or investment counselor can probably get

Career Alert _____

Don't think of profit or loss on the balance sheet as a go/no-go kind of decision. There can be good reasons for both in healthy corporations. Get the entire picture before you make any major decisions.

Career Alert _____

Watch for an announcement that your company is restating its previous year's earnings downward, that key executives might be leaving "to spend more time with their families," or, worse, that the SEC is poking around the books. Any of these events is a good sign of long-term problems, not just a temporary glitch.

you all the information you need. Just remember that the figure you get on your employer should exceed the percentage of return on 30-year government bonds (the accepted standard), or there may be problems.

As important as profit is, it pales when compared with the information you can gather when you review your company's cash-flow records. This information is known by various names, but most often it will be seen as "The Utilization of Funds," or "Statement of Cash Flow." This reports to shareholders the sources of the company's income and the places where the company has spent its money. It can be complicated even for an accountant, but the final number is always clearly reported at the end of the report as whether the company ended up its reporting period with more or less cash that it had at the beginning of the period. Just keep in mind that a negative cash flow is not necessarily a danger signal. It can be if the company reports negative figures for too many periods, or for other reasons that are too complex to explain here. A line-by-line reading of this report can tell you a lot about how and where the company makes and spends its money.

Keep in mind that most employers are usually quite willing to give employees the financial information I have just described. If there is anything to be hidden, it's probably so well hidden that even the auditors or the IRS might miss it. So while it's important to know where your employer stands financially, obsessing over minutia that you are unlikely to uncover could be a waste to time. That said, the more footnotes your employer's financial has and the more complex they are, the greater the likelihood that something is in the wind. Read them carefully and if you are really concerned, talk with your banker or your financial counselor.

How Healthy Is Your Field?

The field in which you work can be as important to your career as the company for which you work. You could be working for a highly respected company in a shrinking industry. Unless the industry is shrinking slowly enough, you could be in a precarious position. It's unfortunate, but people are often typecast by industry. Even though their skills and abilities are easily transferable to other industries, they often have a difficult time convincing potential employers. The longer you spend in a shrinking field, the more difficult it will be for you to convince a potential employer that your skills and abilities are transferable. Most of your business contacts will be within your specific field, so if your field is shrinking, they may not be of much help.

> **Right Move**
>
> Whether you are just starting out or have considerable work experience, pay as much attention to the field in which you work as to your employer's position in it. Your goal should be to find an employer with a good reputation in a field that is expanding. Don't stay too long in a field that has peaked, even if you really like the field.

On the other hand, working in an expanding field provides opportunities for less experienced people to grow, and even greater opportunities for those with recognized talents. Since most people realize that they will have more than one job during their working lifetime, it does seem to make sense to seek work in an expanding industry, even though the field you may prefer has a stronger personal interest to you.

Your Field and Its Image

It isn't easy to clearly define a field of business any more. For example, any career counselor will tell you that healthcare is growing and will continue to grow. Depending on who writes the definition of the field, it could include hospital maintenance workers as well as neurosurgeons.

Define your industry as only those people or other companies that directly compete with you or with your current employer. In healthcare, for example, the demand for hospital administrators might be growing while the need for nurses might be going soft. They are both healthcare jobs and both subject to the same overall market fluctuations, but within each specialty demand can vary considerably.

Most fields of employment have at least one trade or professional association or magazine. These magazines and associations are often the best source of current employment information. However, keep in mind that both magazines and associations can be mere cheerleaders for their fields. Look carefully at the numbers they make available, and read their editorials with an eye to the reason for the existence of the magazine or association.

Career Alert

If you have ruled out an up or over move within your own company and are looking for another employer, beware of this. There are companies and even employment counselors who will eagerly grant you interview mainly for inside information they think you may be willing to provide on your present employer. Don't fall for this ploy! Always be seen as someone with integrity!

The image of any industry and the companies that are part of it may live on long after the real bloom has faded. This is partly because there are people and other industries that have a real stake in the field's survival. For example, it isn't easy to get a clear picture of a company in a shrinking field from a stockbroker who may have a lot of paper he or she wants to move. I'm not talking about out and out fraud, just the notion of wishful thinking and the drive for financial success. Some might call it greed that drives this factor and it may be in some cases. However, it's not that easy to tell greed from honest optimism in many cases. My advice? Check anything and everything that nudges your sense of credibility even a little.

Playing on a Shifting Field

I've already stated that consolidations in general provide more career benefits than those that existed when people spent lifetimes with one company. There is, however, a downside and this is a good point to complete the picture. Good people lose good jobs when an acquired company has to be blended with other holdings and "redundancies" (jobs) must be "eliminated" (cut). There's no way to prevent these dislocations, but there are ways to prepare from them and to even benefit from them.

Mergers and acquisitions take place for a number of reasons. If your current employer has a history of acquiring and merging, you should be prepared to move on at some point in your career. You may be able to move to another division or subsidiary of your current employer, or you may not have that opportunity. Whatever the case, being prepared is important.

If your current employer has a history that leads to job losses, you should really try to negotiate a generous severance package. This is usually done at the time you take your job with the company, but sometimes you can do this after the fact. Almost anything legal is negotiable, and if you don't have a severance package, or if the one you have isn't generous, consider asking for what you want in lieu of an offered raise. Just remember that, by seeking this package, you are sending a message to your employer that you don't see your employment as being all that long term. However, your employer by its obvious business practices probably isn't giving you a warm and fuzzy feeling, either.

The People You Work For and With

The people you work for and with will probably run the gamut, from kind, intelligent, and understanding to mean, duplicitous, and humorless. They, like you, will have their quirks and idiosyncrasies. Just keep in mind that they have to put up with you, too—unless, of course, you're perfect. And if you're perfect, you really don't need this book, so please pass it on to someone who does.

The head honcho could be called the CEO and he or she could be running everything, including divisions and subsidiaries. Or if you are working for a smaller company, that person may just be called the president. Whatever the title, and even if you never have any direct contact with the top dog, his or her style and approach will have some effect on you. Just keep in mind that the people between you and number one are there to carry out his or her plans and ideas. Most corporate leaders welcome ideas and suggestions from the ranks, even if they may be at odds with current policy. However, most don't take kindly to criticism that doesn't include positive suggestions.

If you are working for a company headed by a CEO who has been on the job for a while, it's relatively easy to get a feel for his or her style. However, the real problem occurs when your company changes heads and the new guy is an unknown factor. It's common practice for people at this level to want to make an immediate impression on the company, its customers, and the investment community. Profits and the price of the company stock are the fastest way to get the attention of Wall Street, and sadly it doesn't take many layoffs to improve the company's bottom line.

A CEO's decisions can have a major effect on you, but the people you work for directly will be more involved in your future. Keep in mind that all executives operate within some proscribed framework. Your boss may have direct control over your day-to-day work, but may not have the authority to fire you or to promote you. You will probably have to work though your immediate boss to get what you want, so even though your boss may lack the authority, you ignore him or her at your peril.

Every company, large or small, is organized differently. Your company may have a formal organization chart that shows where and how you fit in, or it may be small and relatively unstructured. Whichever the case, it's important to fully understand how your company is organized. First, to determine who has authority over you in case of any disputes. But, more important, to see the career path that leads from your current position to higher levels of responsibility.

Career Alert

If the company you work for doesn't have a formal organization table, it may just be small enough or well enough organized to function without one. However, if it does have one and refuses to let you see it, this can be a cause for alarm. If other documents, such as the master plan, are kept hidden as well, it just might be time to think about moving out.

Here are some tips for evaluating your company's table of organization:

- **Reporting relationships:** If you report to more than one person, you're in a difficult spot. Even though some charts attempt to create levels of reporting by using solid lines for primary reporting and dotted lines for secondary, there will be conflicts that could spell trouble for you. Satisfy one person and slight the other, and even excellent performance zeros out. If you can, ask to report to only one person. Lines should be clear and direct. Any indirect reporting responsibility should be avoided.

- **Number of people reporting to your boss:** If you see that your boss has a lot of people reporting to him or her, be aware that you will have trouble getting attention when you need it.

- **Departmental commonality:** When the accounting department and the head of engineering report to the same executive, ask why. If it's temporary, it's probably okay, but if this is the way it is, your company is putting too much faith in one person and jeopardizing the work of the people who report to him or her.

Organizational Fads and Folderol

I'm long enough in the tooth to remember some of the major management fads that gripped American business. Created by well-respected consultants, all promised the moon. Some were actually quite good, but most failed miserably. There are a number of reasons for the failures, but what's important is that you don't allow yourself to get in a position where your career depends on the success of a system installed by an executive who wants to make a fast impression on his higher-ups. You may do a spectacular job, but the system may fail, and take you down with it.

The Least You Need to Know

- Mergers and acquisitions have provided more career benefits than you may think.

- The perfect employer doesn't exist, but many companies come close.

- It's not necessarily who you report to that is important, but how you get your message to the right people.

- Your employer's profit picture is important, but more important is the overall history of profits and losses.

- Your company doesn't have to be big and glitzy to be the best company for you to work for.

19

Sources Most People Overlook

In This Chapter

- Discover how your employer's staffing projections can help you see where your career might be headed
- Learn when to trust and not to trust the company rumor mill
- See why recruiters might be your best source of planning information
- Uncover information in virtual libraries you need to plan for both the short and long term
- See how your college or school can help, even if you graduated years ago

You could search the Amazon rain forest for the rest of your life and never find a moose. You could talk with every employment agency within 100 miles and never learn a thing that would help you. Knowing what you are looking for is the first step. Knowing where to look for the information completes the picture. And that's what this chapter is all about: where to look.

Many of the sources I discuss provide information without charge, but some charge. You can often get answers to your general questions without paying anyone, but you may end up paying for some of the more specific information. If you have a broad enough base of general information, the pay-for information you need may not end up being all that expensive. And of course, it's up to you to decide just how a fine a point you need on your information to make realistic decisions.

Many companies, organizations, and individuals are in the business of providing career information and services. Employment and career management information changes rapidly, almost from day to day in some fields. It costs money to gather, reduce, and analyze the information you may need. It's unreasonable to think that you should be given everything you need without charge. That said, your job is to make sure that you trust the source before you spend any money. In the meantime, make as much use as you can of the free information that many offer.

What Else Is Available from Your Employer?

In the last chapter, I went into detail about the obvious sources of career information you should be able to get from your employer. Now let's take a look at some of the stuff that's usually available, but not necessarily advertised. Annual reports are public information and I've already mentioned them several times. However, there are internal reports that are not necessarily hidden, but that are seldom made available to employees unless they are asked for. And even if you ask about some of this information, you may have some difficulty getting your hands on it.

Job Postings

Most companies ask their employees to suggest people they know for open positions. In smaller firms, this could be as simple as a notice on the company bulletin board or website, or even an employee newsletter. In larger companies this could be a major production that lists openings within the division of the firm you work for and within other divisions and subsidiaries.

Quite apart from the primary purpose, these postings can be a very interesting source of career information for you. Suppose you're a lab tech in a division of a large conglomerate. The job postings show that one of the other companies of the family is recruiting aggressively for lab techs. This should raise all sorts of questions. Was there a sudden departure of lab techs in that operation and why did they leave? Is the other operation scaling up for short-term or long-term projects?

If you're really anxious about leaving your current job but would like to stay in the corporate family, see if you can get the inside track on jobs before they are even posted. A contact in the department responsible for publishing the postings could put you at the head of the line. Don't compromise anyone, but a hint here and there is often all you need.

Career Alert

Asking for sensitive information directly could alert your employer that you are getting restless. If you know the people who have routine access to this information well enough, ask them to get it for you. Their motives won't be questioned—yours might.

Staffing Projections

Staffing projections usually precede major organizational changes by quite a bit of time. The numbers and job descriptions in these predictions are usually a key element in expansion or acquisition planning. If you're not in a hurry to make a move and want to stay within the corporate family, knowing the future staffing needs could be a great way to plan a move both up and over.

You might be blocked for promotion in your present job. A staffing projection for another operation in the corporate family could give you a lead on an automatic promotion as well as the possibility of a relatively clear path for even further growth.

Staffing projections for new or greatly expanded operations are usually closely guarded, so it may be difficult to learn what is happening. However, if you're in the habit of monitoring your employer's publicly offered information, you might be able to spot economic data that would indicate the kind of growth plans that precede any actual moves. Even if you are not, the office scuttlebutt is usually full of hints that can put you wise.

Right Move

Try to have at least one friend in the finance department and one in whichever department is charged with corporate planning. Never ask them to betray a trust, but from the general things each says you can often combine the information into a nugget that will put you well ahead of everyone else.

Headhunters and recruiters can be a good source of information, too. I'll discuss them later in this chapter, but, for now, keep in mind that while they often have accurate information that might help you, they won't divulge it. Discretion is a key factor in their success. They might be able to act on confidential information they have, but the better ones will keep confidences.

Who's Hot, Who's Not

Most companies have some form of company newsletter. It may be a blog, a single sheet included with your paycheck, or an elaborate company magazine. Whatever, it can be an excellent source of what's happening on your company.

You have to read these publications like a detective looking for clues. What actually appears won't always be of interest, but what the information implies may be important. Why was so-and-so moved to a key spot in another division? Why was a guy whose experience has been mainly in marketing been hired from the outside to head up the manufacturing operation? There are reasons for everything. Some of them might make you wonder whether you are really working for the right company and others will give you the clues you need to make your up, over, or out decision.

Be sure to see what is being said in the business press about your company. If your company is on the stock market, there should be quite a bit of information available that will be of career interest to you.

You may not read *The Wall Street Journal* regularly, and your company may never be mentioned in its pages, but it's probably covered by the business journals that cover your field. If the journals are not available to you, you can usually get much of the information they publish in the regular print edition on their website. Most magazines that post their material on the Internet just give the major stories in brief form and list titles or brief synopses of all the other articles. Bookmark all the sites on which your employer is seen and check these sources regularly. You might consider downloading and saving the information that is relevant to your specific needs. Paper printouts are a good idea, too. Paper can be easily carried on the train or bus to work if you prefer not to lug and use a laptop.

Employee Grapevines, Blogs, and Scuttlebutt

A scuttlebutt, at least in the Navy, is a drinking fountain. Naval officers learn early in their careers not to allow too many sailors to gather around one for too long. Managers used to have the same problem with the ubiquitous water coolers in offices. Now however, everybody carries their own bottle of designer water (there's a joke in that somewhere) and they congregate electronically. Scarcely a company today doesn't have an informal electronic watering hole, and it's a far better source of information than the water fountain.

What makes most of these sites most interesting is that the users are often anonymous, so they're free to say things that the company would not want said and protect themselves from retribution. This also means that a lot of what you see is probably far less trustworthy than the stuff passed personally at the water cooler. Anonymity also allows for cranks to pass intentional or accidental misinformation at will. In short, you have to take it all with a grain of salt. But I'd strongly suggest that you confirm information that is of direct interest to you. Even a crank can have something important to say.

The larger the organization you work for, the larger the number of informal networks. I was told of a network that really was a network of networks that existed at a major international corporation. The individual networks evolved based on job functions. Engineers talked with engineers, sales people talked to sales people. Then one day someone realized that each of these informal Internet networks could be connected to share with each other. I imagine it still exists and my guess is that it drives corporate management crazy.

Career Alert

Never put anything on the Internet that you don't want everyone to see. And, whether you want it seen by others or not, never use your own name.

Suppliers: A Mine of (Mis)Information

Most suppliers respect the need for keeping quiet when they have access to confidential information. There are however, always a few who are willing to pass on information that they shouldn't. I'd suggest that you listen to what they say, but discount most of it. It's sort of like the class snitch in grade school; everyone's usually happy when he or she fingers the class bully, but there are few personal points for doing so.

That said, the suppliers who work with your company are often an excellent source of information on what is happening at your employer's competitors. Most won't pass on really sensitive information, but news of hirings and firings, staffing up, and new products are the currency of existence for suppliers in most fields. If you are unhappy where you currently work and think you might be happier working for your employer's competitor, listen to the supplier grapevine. Keep in mind that if you do move to the competitor as a result of information from a supplier, keep the source of the contact to yourself. You won't be doing a favor for the supplier who did you the favor of sharing information. But then, you already knew that—didn't you?

Headhunters Are Not Cannibals

It's unfortunate that those who provide professional services to both employers and those seeking employment have ended up with the sobriquet *headhunter*. (It's also unfortunate that few people realize that the word *sobriquet* means a name given affectionately.) Whether you call them headhunters, recruiters, consultants, or staffing specialists, they represent a major source of help and information for both parties.

Like lawyers, most refuse to disclose confidential information, but most are judged not just by the success of their assignments, but by being major sources of information about their clients. In most cases the information you can gather from consultants is not confidential, but it's not exactly news that made the papers. Any good consultant will use whatever information he or she has about a company to help a client make a connection, but most stop short of telling you anything that could compromise his or her client, or their relationship. Everyone understands this. You may think of this as a wink-wink situation if you like; despite the occasional story of leaked confidential information, most employment consultants are honest and very respectable people. Don't make a fool of yourself by pressing one for confidential information. If you do, you will lose whatever reputation you have with the consultant and you may even be the subject of inter-consultant chit-chat. They do talk with each other, you know!

What are consultants willing to divulge about their corporate clients that may help you? The answer is simple. They will tell you whatever you need to know to have a favorable image of their corporate client. They will not divulge confidential information. And you may have to pry a bit for them to tell you anything negative about the corporate client they represent. This doesn't make them bad people. When was the last time you bought a painting from a reputable art dealer and paid a million more than you should have? Never? Okay, when was the last time you bought a car and paid for the undercoating—which is totally useless. Everyone is naïve when they are out of their own field, so don't feel that withholding some information is a major disgrace. It's really up to you to know what you need to know and to recognize when the information will be valuable and reliable and when it won't.

Recruiters tend to specialize in fields of work, geographic regions, and levels of employment. The information they have and might share with you is usually specific within these categories. However, some of the better firms have offices in different locations that probably specialize in the dominant fields in the areas they serve. A look at their ads on the Internet can give you a clue about their location, specialization, and levels of searches.

Keep in mind that most recruiters specialize, so they tend to gather an awful lot of information about the fields they cover. Some even provide databases of information they make available to clients. It's not uncommon for executives on the rise, as well as those near the top, to maintain a connection with a favored headhunter. They may not be actively looking for a job, but these executives realize that headhunters are often the only source used by some organizations for their staffing. This, of course, means that you will know a lot more about what's going on in your field than you would if you weren't on the headhunter's client list.

Headhunters will tell you that even though you are listed with them, you are never obligated to follow up on any of the leads they provide you. However, wouldn't you like to know what's going on, even if that knowledge only reinforces your resolve to stick with your current employer? You're safe in the hands of most headhunters. Any breach of trust is instant knowledge in your field and they might as well as close up shop.

Virtual Libraries and Online Directories

If you haven't been in the job market for a while, you may have wondered what has happened to all the classified ads in newspapers that used to bulk up a lot of local and national papers. Your first thought probably was that the employment picture is pretty bleak. Well, it isn't in most cases. It's just that the Internet has replaced print classified ads. Unless you are a total technophobe, you will see that this shift has been a fantastic thing for job seekers as well as for those planning or managing ongoing careers.

The current search engines, Google, Yahoo, and most of the others, can put you in touch with information that is precisely targeted to your needs and instantly use-able. If, for example, you live in New York and want to work in Seattle as an attorney, simply type this in your browser window: "Seattle, WA legal employment opportuni-ties." Literally hundreds of sources of information are right at your fingertips. This is as helpful for the career planning or managing reader as it is for the person who is actively looking for work. Both the commercial sources and the government informa-tion sources you will find provide all sorts of information from current employment trends and compensation to historical employment data that you can use for both short- and long-term career planning.

I'm not going to take you by the hand and show you how to use a computer search engine. I will, however, give you advice you must take to heart when you use the Internet to search for career related information. Search engines will put you in touch with the sources you will actually use, but you may be asked to provide information that might get back to your employer. There's a book-length explanation of how this might happen, so just trust me—play it safe.

Let's look first at the safest way you can use your search engine. Every search engine drops "cookies" into a file that are supposed to speed up further searches and to help you return quickly to previous sites you searched. There's no denying that this can be a very helpful service, but it also leaves a trail that anyone can follow on your computer. If for example, you type "executive search" in the browser of your computer at work, the trail has been laid out. Anyone who has access to your computer can simply begin to type the words and by the time they reach "execu …," the window opens and you have been exposed. So first and foremost, don't do risky searches on your office computer. It's better to be discovered peeking at X-rated pictures than visiting a recruiter's website on your office computer.

Career Alert

Most search engines will allow you to block the sites you visit from depositing cookies in your computer. However, that usually includes blocking the "good" and the "bad" cookies together. Check the online instructions that come with your search engine for details. I highly recommend Mozilla Firefox, because it is one of the simplest to set up when you want to block or clear cookies. Others may be as good or even better; I just haven't tried them all.

Don't provide any personal information to any of the sites you visit. You might consider setting up an entirely fictional personal name and address. Most search engines allow you to have several addresses, so this probably won't be a problem. Whatever name you use, however, many sites will ask for information that cannot be faked, like an address or telephone number. You will only know how far you can go with the deception by giving each site as little information as possible. It's usually the phone number where you can get hung up. But see what you can do.

You can do much more to protect your identity on the net, but unless you really have a twinge of paranoia, it's not worth the effort. I doubt that you will ever find a company that spends the time and the money to discover whether their employees are job-hunting. The fact usually turns up accidentally. You might have signed into a headhunter's site and provided all the information they requested. Some of that information could possibly find its way to an active site that might be shown to your employer who might be seeking to add to your department or, heaven forbid, to replace you. However, I could get rich betting that would never happen.

Blogs, Boards, and Career Centers

The next time you sit down at your computer, type this into the search window: "accountant employment blog." You will be rewarded with enough sites to keep you busy for an entire weekend. Substitute your field for the word "accountant", and see what you get. The narrower and more specialized your field, the fewer the sites you will find, but I'll bet almost no employment description doesn't have at least a couple of pages of sources willing and ready to do business with you that just might be able to provide you with some critical career information.

Just for the heck of it, I just logged into half a dozen sites at random in the "accountant" category and had immediate access to excellent information that related to compensation statistics, specialty trends, geographical distribution of workers in the field, and projected staffing needs for several very desirable places to work. All this sure beats the old classified ad pages, with their tiny type and no links to more information. Viva the electronic age!

College and Other School Career Centers

Most colleges and vocational schools have always provided a placement center. These have traditionally been of modest benefit to recent graduates looking for their first job. Lately however, you will see that many of these schools have expanded their services to include those well past graduation who are in an advanced career search and management mode. I've been told that some continue to provide this service to all graduates at any time without asking for compensation, but many others ask for a fee. This seems only fair; it's a lot of work helping people find jobs and manage careers.

One of the major benefits of these services is that they often have access to employment information that other sources do not have. Most colleges and universities have ongoing research programs that spin off data that can be invaluable for career management purposes, as well as providing direct career related services. And when they do actual placement work, a graduate of a prestigious school comes with the additional glow that goes with the school that provided the degree.

Quite apart from the placement services, many colleges and professional schools offer access to their current research to graduates who maintain their membership in the alumni association. This is not only an excellent source of helpful information; it's also a splendid source of social and professional networking. Don't overlook your old school as one of the best sources of career related information.

Right Move _____

Even if you didn't get your degree from a major school, many of the biggies offer continuing-education courses in many fields. A hidden benefit in this is that as a registered student, most schools will give you full access to their library and other information and data sources. For a modest fee, you will get an awful lot more that you paid for.

Many courses in continuing education are taught by adjunct faculty, people who work in their field, but teach one or two courses. If you ever wanted direct contact with professionals who are already successful in their—and your—field, this can be the place to get it.

Other Social and Business Networking

You have probably checked out and might even be listed in social networking sites like MySpace and Facebook. I suppose these can be helpful, but from a purely time-use perspective, I'd suggest that you narrow your search for information by doing as narrowly focused a search as possible. These sites are fun, but think about them after you do some serious, well-focused research on the sites that count.

The Least You Need to Know

- ◆ Your present employer's job postings and staffing projections can tell you a lot about the company's plans and how you should think about your future relationship.

- ◆ Listen carefully on the company grapevine, but never make decisions on what you hear with out solid confirmation.

- ◆ Outside employment services and consultants can supply you with good and timely information, but don't expect them to share confidential information.

- ◆ You can go back to school for help with your career planning.

20

What Your Employer Doesn't Want You to Know

In This Chapter

◆ See how your current employer stacks up with competitors

◆ The short and long-term picture for your field of work

◆ Discover what others in other jobs are being paid for doing the same work as you do

◆ Uncover your employer's plans for growth or downsizing, and learn how mergers and acquisitions can boost your career

◆ Why you should take what former employees tell you about your company with a grain of salt

Unless you work for a small company that shares business information freely with you, you probably know very little about your employer. Sure, you have all the stuff the human resources people gave you a few years ago when you took your present job. You read the annual and quarterly reports. And you get that warm and fuzzy feeling when you read your company's employee newsletter, especially the folksy message from the president. But what do you "really" know about your employer? You know the old saying, "It's what you don't know that can hurt you."

For example, do you know how your employer stacks up with its key competitors? Your company may show millions in profits, but what if your company's competitors show profits in billions? Actual numbers are important, but the numbers must be evaluated relative to companies that may be in a position to put your employer out of business.

Your employer may pay you more than you thought you'd ever earn, but what are the folks who are doing the same work as you being paid by your company's competitors?

Your company may have invented the product that started the revolution, but what does your competition have up its sleeve that will obsolete that product?

Who knows when owners and stockholders may decide that it's time to cash in their chips? Would you be comfortable if your small, happy firm were to be acquired by a big, faceless conglomerate?

Okay, have I scared you enough? I hope so, because these are the things that are more likely to affect your career than the things you pay too much attention to, like the snub you got from your usually friendly boss.

Interview for Your Present Job—Again!

One of the best ways to get your act together is to do a little play-acting. Put yourself in the role of someone who is applying for your job. What questions would you ask of your employer? What inside and outside information would you go after? What criteria would you use to determine the validity and reliability of the information you get?

You may be surprised at what you turn up. And you may be more surprised to realize how much you didn't know when you took the job. This isn't unusual. There's a lot of wishful thinking that goes into any employment change situation. You want that job, and most of us are willing to accept information uncritically when it confirms what we want to believe. However, you should see where the glitches are more clearly now that the pressure to be employed is off.

I don't suggest that you actually re-create your interview. Rather, I suggest that simply get yourself in the mind-set of an applicant for your job. If you have any business experience at all, you've probably been involved in some sort of role-play training situation.

How Does Your Employer Stack Up?

A typical competitive analysis is a detailed and lengthy report. If you can get your hands on research your employer has already done, you probably won't have to do this yourself, but you do want to be sure the information in the company files is up-to-date, especially if your field is in a state of rapid and regular change. If it's out of date, it can still be useful, mainly as a guide to just what to look for to bring it up-to-date.

Make a list of your present employer's competitors. Those that compete directly will be pretty obvious. Those that compete indirectly may not be all that obvious. And those companies that may be poised to become competitors of your employer are of key interest. My guess is that your employer's competitive file makes no mention of the companies that could eat their lunch in the near future.

Career Alert

The companies that could become competitive with your present employer should be of special interest. First, they could pose problems for your present job, and second, they just might be opportunities for someone with your experience. About the only way you can gather the information you need here is by following the trends reported in the business press, and with information passed along from your network of contacts.

The Competition's Products and Services

This information is usually pretty easy to get just by reviewing competitor's catalogs, literature, and service brochures. The tough part is getting a handle on how your competitors' customers and clients see the quality of those products and services. The best source is probably your employer's sales and marketing departments. If they are on the ball, they will not only have the facts, but they should be able to provide you with their speculation about competitive activity that might be valuable to you as you plan your career moves.

The best way to make use of this information is to do a product-by-product or service-by-service comparison of what your employer provides and what competitors offer. Your goal is to get a sense of whether your present employer is competitive enough for you to make long-term plans.

Right Move _____

The ad agency that handles your employer's account can often help you get competitor's information. Most agencies keep files of sales literature of products which compete with those made by their clients. If your firm is larger enough to make use of outside market research services, check with these suppliers, too. And, of course, many companies make their sales and promotional material available for immediate download on the Internet.

Next, identify your competition's strengths and weaknesses. The competitive factors of most interest will not necessarily be simple comparisons of your product's features with your competitors'. You really want to know how your competitors exploit what they have to put your employer's products at a disadvantage. For example, they may have an inferior product, but are able to market it better than your employer markets its superior products. From a career perspective, this can be a critical issue in your planning. You may prefer to work for a company that makes a better product, but the one that makes the most of what they have is going to be around a lot longer!

You also need to understand the outlook for the market in general. Knowing whether a market is expanding, contracting, or remaining flat is just a start. You need to plug in the competitive information you have and view the complex picture before you can make any good career decisions. Don't be scared off by a flat or a declining market. A declining market may be in a slow enough decline that it can be productive for many years to come, especially if your company's competitors are obviously abandoning it. A flat market, shared by companies that also recognize the situation, can work as long as no supplier decides that it wants to eat everyone else's lunch. The key factor for your career implications lie in viewing market outlook figures in terms of what a loss of market share would mean for your future.

Learn to follow other competitive strategies. I hate to keep repeating this, but by owning just one share of stock of each of your employer's competitors gives you excellent competitive information. Beyond that, however, keeping up with what is written in the business press will give you a good idea of how your employers' strategies are played out. When you see executives from competitive companies quoted frequently in the press, but your top guys prefer to remain in the shadows, you should try to find out why.

How Does the Competition Pay?

Actually, pay is only one factor to consider. Think in terms of total compensation when you want to see where your employer stands relative to competitors. Sure salary is important, but so are some of the benefits that are often offered. Bonuses and profit sharing plans, for example, can make a smaller salary loom quite large in terms of what actually accrues to an employee's bank account. Medical plans and other insurance plans can also make a big difference in what you currently receive and what others in other companies may be paid for doing similar work.

Case in Point

A coaching client of mine recently expressed serious concern when she discovered that someone doing work similar to hers in a competitive firm was being paid nearly 30 percent more than she was. I suggested that she check out the value of the benefits package she had and compare it with that of the person she felt was being grossly overpaid. It took some snooping on her part, but she did come up with what she needed and the net numbers actually put her ahead of the previously envied competitor by a little more than 12 percent per year. Her firm was far more generous with its benefits program than was the competitor. Check with your human resources department; many can give you the numbers you need to make reliable comparisons.

Every company has a different take on its compensation package. This, of course, means that the typical salary survey can be meaningless unless you know everything and its cash value before you make any comparisons.

But how can you get this information? Most of it will come from grapevine sources simply because every company prefers, with good reason, to keep its compensation information secret. Your present employer probably has much of this competitive information in its files already. It gathers this information in bits and pieces as it interviews job candidates who are or were employed by competitors. Most of the information is probably out of date, but at least it has comparative data to work with. I wouldn't suggest that you ask it to share this with you. Not a good career move! However, if you are in the process of a compensation review, you could ask what competitors pay. Your company may share the information and it may not. But it's worth asking.

Career Alert

Today, many people and the companies that employ them are adding an element to the compensation package that doesn't have an actually dollar value. More and more people are interested in employment factors that interface with their private lives. Time off for child birth, sabbaticals, even a day off on your birthday has become as much an element of the package as the money you take home. In fact, when money compensation is no longer a competitive issue, these human factors become very important. Don't fail to factor this into your plans. You could make a move for a higher salary, but find yourself working in a sweat shop.

If you are like most people, you only look at the highlights of the medical coverage your employer offers. You may not even know that the company has a stock option plan or that it offers low-cost loans for the college education of employees' family members. This may be a good time to dig out all that stuff you picked up on your first day. In fact, if you have been on the job for more than a year, it's a good idea to head over to human resources and ask for an update. It might make that "out" decision you were thinking about look a little less appealing. It could also be the kind of information your employer had hoped you wouldn't ask for.

Your Employer's Idea of the Future

Peter Drucker said, "The best way to predict the future is to create it." Wise, indeed. And to create your future you need to know what the owners of your company are planning to do. I doubt that they will tell you outright what their plans are. However, there is one good way to see just how actively and attentively they are planning ahead, and that is by analyzing their business forecasting. The larger the company, the more complex the forecasting should be. Don't pay an awful lot of attention to the president's messages that accompany the quarterly and annual reports. Do however, look at the numbers. If you are a stockholder, you are entitled to a lot of good information; as an employee of a small privately held company, you're on your own.

It's unlikely that you will be able to discover any information on a planned merger or acquisition unless you have access to someone on the inside. However, when you have access to reliable financial information, you can often see the blips that will tell you that the owners have more on their mind than the businesses that currently allow them to light their cigars with twenty dollar bills. Money piled up in a line-item account that doesn't seem to relate to any current activity should tell you that something is afoot.

Keep in mind that all financial projections are based on some notion of what will happen given a set of anticipated conditions. When you see an unusual amount of money being allocated to recruit nuclear physicists, you can be sure that the hamburger-franchising company you work for has more in mind than getting into the fried-chicken business.

Watch the working capital figures carefully. When you notice too little attention being paid to working capital requirements, you might want to see what other accounts might have been beefed up. Accounting can be creative, and that doesn't necessarily imply that the popular notion of the concept is in play. Budgeting is, in reality, a creative process. Those who write the budgets are guessing creatively what will happen if they allocate funds one way and not another. Your employer's view of the future can be seen in the numbers. The grapevine stories can often be confirmed or consigned to the rubbish pile simply by watching how the money is allocated and how it is ultimately spent.

Despite the value of good financial information as a clue to where your company stands and what it might be up to in the future, there is no substitute for good judgment in the executive suite. If you work for a company whose executives have been around long enough to have a track record, the only thing you need is your own good judgment to make career decisions. However, if your company is in the hands of new people, make sure you know everything you can about them. What did they do of note before joining your company? Why did they make the jump? What have they been saying publicly about their plans for the company, and what does the grapevine have to say. Remember what I have been saying about depending too heavily on the grapevine. Just verify whatever scuttlebutt you get by way of it, and you will be better off than you might be otherwise when it comes to making career decisions.

Things That Can End or Enhance a Career

If you think merger and acquisition madness hits hardest at your career level, check some of the websites devoted to physicians talking about careers. One writer, a psychiatrist with stellar credentials who practiced as an employee of managed care organizations, stated that he had changed jobs six times without ever being fired. Market forces over which he had no control made him redundant that often. As he stated, bluntly, "The current deal is to work as long as the company needs you and you need the company."

As the old story goes, there is no such thing as a depression until it's your job that is eliminated. And that applies to people with the skills and education of a physician as well as to anyone else, regardless of where they are on any economic scale. Yes, I know, up front I said that this sort of thing was actually beneficial, and I still say it is. However, it's not the system that's at fault, it's the misuse of the system by some people that often makes life miserable for so many people. I wish I knew how to deal with that, but I don't. So life must go on, and so will mergers and acquisitions.

Getting News You Can Use

In general, those who are in positions that directly affect revenue production are usually less likely to find themselves on the outside than those on the service side of the company. Cost centers such as finance, legal, public relations, and human resources are usually among the first targets for post-merger staffing reductions. And here is where you are most likely to find your employer playing its cards close to the vest.

Everyone is usually needed until the merger takes place, and then the thinning of the herd takes place. Mergers and acquisitions are seldom announced out of the blue. The news is around both publicly and privately for quite a while before the deed is done. The chances are that you will have plenty of time to get a sense of where you might fit in, if at all.

Headhunters are often the best source of guidance in this case. Few will share privileged information with you, but they will use it themselves to help clients. If you don't have a connection with a headhunter now, I'd suggest that you establish one now. Do this whether or not the specter of a merger or an acquisition is on the horizon. You will be ahead of the pack when and if it happens. Good headhunters will be in touch from time just to check in. They often use the ploy of calling you to see if you can recommend someone for a spot that they are recruiting for. They are usually hoping that person will be you, but this prevents them from being accused of piracy if you should take the job.

In addition to establishing a working contact with a reputable headhunter, think about establishing a contact with a senior colleague in your firm. Do not impose on this relationship by asking for privileged information. Rather look to this person as an informal mentor who can guide you through the changes that will take place. This connection may not be able to prevent an inevitable dislocation, or a less desirable repositioning within with new organization, but it can help you see the future more clearly than you might see it without this person's guidance.

Landing on Your Feet

If you are offered a spot on the merger transition team, jump at it. It may not ensure that you are one of the survivors, but it will definitely put you in a position to have information that can help you plan your career with more certainty than you might if you don't have the information.

The one thing you can be sure of, if your job is secure and you survive the merger you will have more work to do than you did before. In some cases, this might put you in a better position for growth than you might have had prior to the merger. It also gives you a better opportunity to see where you stand with the new management. Remember, information is probably more important to you at this point than whether or not you get to do the work of two people on your present salary.

> **Right Move** _____
>
> If the merger or acquisition is inevitable, consider presenting yourself as being for it. Staff reductions are based on all sorts of check lists, and many include an item that asks the rater whether the person being rated supports or opposes the merger. Okay, so you fib a little! It's safe to assume that you haven't been given all the facts, anyway. I'm not saying that you are being lied to—heaven forbid! Just suggesting that you may not have been told everything and you really don't know which questions to ask. So you didn't hear it from me. okay?

It's tempting to duck and cover during a merger. This is not a good move. Make yourself visible and make positive contributions to the process, even if you have to hold your nose while doing it. Unless of course, you know that your job loss is a foregone conclusion. Then, unless you have a great offer on the table from another employer, do whatever has to be done to negotiate the best possible severance package.

Downsizing, Outsourcing, and Other Nasty Corporate Behavior

Although job loss is always a possibility with a merger or an acquisition, there can often be significant career benefits for the individuals who are retained. This is rarely the case when a company decides to downsize. The last quarter of the twentieth century saw massive downsizing almost across the board in American business. This has been attributed variously to increased per-worker productivity, technological advances, and the availability of lower cost labor available outside of the United States. All are valid reasons. Downsizing is frequently a corporate desperation move, or a move that is motivated by pure greed. Whatever the case, downsizing is not a good sign, even for those who might retain their jobs and who might even win promotions in the process.

Unlike most mergers and acquisitions, which usually become public knowledge long before the deed is done, downsizing is most often planned in complete secrecy and sprung on employees with all the fury of a hurricane. The scenes on the nightly TV news of people being escorted from their employers' buildings by security guards holding paper bags containing only their personal belongings are just as chilling as the photos of the workers on breadlines during the Depression.

Informed Is Prepared

This is not the place to argue the rights, wrongs, and excesses of downsizing, so I will not hop on my soap box. My job—and your job—is to know as much about what your company is doing, why it is doing what it is doing, and what you can do to accommodate it in your career plans. As you might have guessed from what I have been saying, downsizing is a wild card. It's hard to predict, but it can and should be planned for.

One thing that is seldom mentioned is that all companies that have downsized have spent as much effort preserving their intellectual capital as they have in reducing other labor costs. Just knowing this should give you a clue as to whether your employer might or might not be thinking of downsizing you. The other clues, of course, are economic.

If you work for a publicly traded company, watching the financial reports, both public and private, can help you see what may be happening. Keep in mind that Wall Street has one goal in mind for all of its clients: profit. Their financial analysts are most anxious to present the issuers of the stocks they sell as profit centered. Any news of offshore shifts of labor will be eagerly reported. Their good news can be your bad news. Read the papers and understand what they are saying about your employer.

Let's be frank: downsizing is not what used to be called temporary layoffs, it's outright firings. Those escorted to the door aren't coming back. As you might imagine, the key players in this activity are the corporate lawyers. Their goal is to reduce the possibility of litigation and to handle that which does take place expeditiously. Therefore, the one source you can probably depend on to have the information is the legal department. However, you surely can't count on the company lawyers to spill the beans.

Short of any legally actionable espionage, just watch out for the sudden or regular appearance of people in dark suits carrying stuffed briefcases who might arrive by some less visible entrance than the front door. The office grapevine will work overtime at any signs of unusual activity. Listen, and check it out, but don't let yourself be panicked. This doesn't mean that a call to your headhunter should be put off. Now is probably the best time to switch from passive to active in your relationship with your recruiter.

Not as Bad as It Could Be

Not all downsizing is as dramatic and disastrous to people's careers as it might seem from what I have just said. Many companies, when faced with the need to downsize, do it with genuine care for their employees. Some do it without any firings by simply not replacing people who retire. Those companies that go this route are generally in better shape than those which pull the plug dramatically. They are usually able to manage whatever economic problems they may be having by slowly reducing overhead.

Early retirement programs are another approach taken by companies that are in less precarious positions. Doing this, they offer benefit packages to employees who voluntarily agree to leave. You can generally tell something about the company's health by how liberal or sparse the early retirement packages are. Companies that go this route have to do a lot of planning in advance of the downsizing announcement, so it's quite likely that a lot of information will be circulating via the grapevine.

Listen to Former Employees at Your Peril

Those who move on for reasons other than being fired might seem to be good sources of information to use in your career planning. This is seldom the case for several reasons. First, the information they're passing on may be out of date, even if they have left the company only recently. Second, people tend to be expansive in the service of their own needs and goals. Your friend Joe may have quit and moved on to a bigger and better job, or the bigger and better job may be a figment of Joe's imagination and he might have quit just a few days ahead of the ax. And your friend Sally, who was fired, has a personal need for you to see the right perspective (hers) on the situation.

It's not always easy to tell fiction from fact in the stories handed down anecdotally. However, when you hear a number of stories from former employees that seem to confirm each other, you might be on safe ground to add the information to your stockpile of company information.

When your best friend, who recently left the company, refuses to give you information you know he or she has, it's probably because of an employment contract. Don't sacrifice a good friendship by pushing your friend.

The Least You Need to Know

- Mergers and acquisitions can be benefit your career, but downsizing has few advantages.

- Others may be paid more for doing the same work as you, but you may be in a better career position than you think.

- Your employer may be competitively weak, but this could be a better place to work.

- If your present employer is going nowhere and has no real plans, it's time to move on.

- Downsizing may actually have some career benefits.

Chapter 21

How To See Yourself in the Big Picture

In This Chapter

- ◆ Where and how to find up-to-date data to plan and manage your career
- ◆ Why you should avoid some of the "popular" careers
- ◆ How to use free statistics that others never thought of to fine-tune your career
- ◆ How to use free insurance claim data to predict employment trends

There are two reasons you should plan your career carefully. The first is to set goals. The second is to anticipate problems you may encounter on the way to achieving your goals. Both require good information.

The federal government and many state and local government agencies spend vast amounts of money doing economic research. The Fed provides excellent overall economic data, and state and local governments provide the regionally specific data you need. And, of course, local governments are interested in attracting the best employees for the businesses and other organizations in their areas.

There are, however, two problems in this. First, there is so much information available that it's often difficult to decide what is really important and what isn't. Second, the information is mostly historical. It may only be a day or two old or it could be more than a few years old, depending on how regularly it gets updated. But this is far better than not having any information at all.

There are plenty of other private and commercial sources of employment information. However, no matter how objective the organization that prepares it is, you have to assume some bias. I don't mean to imply that you shouldn't trust commercially prepared research data, but you should understand that the free lunch you get may not be prime rib. Still, a hamburger is better than nothing.

Real Numbers and What They Mean

But before we get into the meat of this chapter, I want to urge you to verify the source of any data you use in your career planning. Most statistics you can use are easy to understand, and most organizations that publish the data are telling the truth. However, you will occasionally see information that makes a point but lacks the appropriate contextual background you need to see it clearly. I know, you're shocked, *shocked!* But trust me on this. They do mean well.

All of us use the word *average*. But it can be defined several ways. Depending on which definition you use, the same data can mean very different things. This is the only math you will encounter in the book, but please, please pay careful attention.

Add the following numbers:

9
9
15
17
<u>20</u>
70

If you divide the sum, 70, by the number of figures, 5, you will get the *mean average*, which is 14.

If you identify the middlemost number of the rank order you will find the *median average*, which is 15.

If you identify the number most often repeated you will have the *mode average*, which is 9.

In this example the mean and the median are close, but the mode is far less than both the mean and the median. In general, this is the way most normally distributed data looks.

The mean is the statistic most often used as the average in employment statistics. There are valid reasons for expressing averages in terms of the median and the mode. But when it's done, most people and organizations will tell you what they are doing and why they are doing it. But there are times when someone with a specific point of view finds that the median or the mode makes their point better. Make sure you understand what they are doing and why.

That's it! The math lesson is over. You've been warned. Now, on to what you really want to know.

> **Career News**
>
> Be sure to read *How to Lie With Statistics,* a short book written by Darrell Huff and published by W. W. Norton. No math skills required, only a sense of curiosity and a willingness to admit you might have made some pretty stupid decisions based on what you thought was truth. It's really a lot of fun.

Learn the Employment Trends

As I have said before, the key issues to lifetime career planning should be based on solid economic factors. Most skills and training are transferable, and personal flexibility is more important today than it ever has been. You can, for example, work as an accountant in almost any field. An artist can work in advertising, publishing, the movies, and many other rewarding fields. Both accountants and artists can also work for themselves. However, the narrower your field, the more difficult this becomes and the more the need for careful planning.

You will need to know what is happening in specific career fields, in the industries in which you can be employed, and in the general economy. The best source of occupational information is the *Occupational Outlook Handbook*, published by the U.S. Department of Labor. It's free and available online, and anyone can learn to use it—even those who have mastered nothing more than tic-tac-toe on their computer. Just type "Occupational Outlook Handbook" in your computer's search window and it will appear—if you're online, of course. Unlike the income tax form and other confusing government documents, this has been thought out and designed to be completely intuitive. It's hard to go wrong, but if you do find your way into a blind alley, just hit the Home button and you will be right back to square one. It's that easy.

The following categories in the handbook are those that will be of most interest to you.

The Fastest Growing Occupations

One report you will have at your fingertips when you open the Occupational Outlook Handbook is titled "Fastest Growing Occupations." The most recent data projects growth from 2006 to 2016. This data refers to the projected rate of change, and the listings are in rank order of the percentage of growth rate over the ten year period. Number one on the list, showing a projected growth of 53.4 percent is "Network systems and data communications analyst." It doesn't exactly come as a surprise, given the phenomenal use of computers in business and other organizations.

Take a wild guess what the Department of Labor is projecting as number two, the next fastest growing occupation in the United States. I'm willing to bet that unless you have been reading these reports already, you never would have guessed that it is "Personal and home care aids." The projection for this group is 50.6 percent over the same ten year period.

The reason for this surprise will become clearer as we look at some of the other statistics available in the DOL report. But before we move on to the next category, I should report that this section of the report also includes a section on the most significant post-secondary education or training for the rated categories. As you might expect, systems analysts should have a minimum of a Bachelor's degree. Those in the number two ranking, personal and home care aids, require only some short-term training and on-the-job experience.

But don't stop there. You now have two statistics to play with, one of which describes the growth rate of two widely divergent careers. What can you draw from this? Does the need for systems analysts relate at all to the projected demand for home health care workers?

Occupations with the Greatest Job Growth

This report projects occupations in terms of the number of people employed for the period of the report. The previous report projects rate of growth; this report projects the number of people who are projected to be employed over the same period. Note that these files report earnings using the "median" statistic. This is an appropriate use of this statistic and is more helpful than might be a mean or a modal average.

You will see that there are occupations listed in this report that are not listed in the report on rate of growth. Just keep in mind that the first table describes rate of growth. The second describes amounts. The numbers of people and the rates of growth do not necessarily go hand in hand.

Right Move

When you view these statistics, don't just check those you feel might move in the same direction as the field that interests you. Look at those that are moving in opposite directions. Gains and losses are not a zero-sum function here, but the activity they show can be help you make good choices, or at least help you to avoid making bad ones.

Some Fast Growing Fields Should Be Avoided

This entry in the Handbook puts you in the bigger picture, that which describes major industrial categories in which you might already be working or where you might be seeking employment. It's organized along broad categories, which helps you picture where you might and might not want to work. For example, the leading area of a growth field is "Management, scientific, and technical consulting services." The current report projects an annual growth of 5.9 percent for the next 10 years.

The category of "Cut and sew apparel manufacturing" leads the pack of the most rapidly declining fields with a decline of -8.9 percent each year over the next 10 years. This is a field that employs both highly skilled people as well as people with minimal skills.

Just because an industry may be in decline doesn't mean you should never think of working in the field. For example, in the current report, "Pulp, paper, and paperboard mills" are projected to decline by -3.6 percent annually over the next 20 years. Yet, just today (May 8, 2008), I read an article in *The New York Times* about a new paper mill just going on-line in upstate New York. The article painted quite an exciting picture of the venture and its chances of success. If you have always wanted to work in upstate New York—it really is beautiful country—and have the skills needed, go for it. When I get to the wind-up of this book, I'll talk about the quality-of-life trade-offs that we often make. Life isn't all that interesting without taking a few chances, as long as you are prepared for everything.

Industries with the Largest Wage and Salary Employment Growth and Decline

This report highlights the economic picture in terms of actual gains and losses. Compare this with the previous table, which reports on the same industries, but in terms of the growth rate. The report on my screen now shows that the food and beverage service categories are at the top, showing an increase of 1,023,000 jobs. The industry that showed the largest loss was crop production. I wonder how much this will change in the next few years because of the sudden demand for fermentable crops that can be converted to ethanol.

Clues Most People Overlook

Okay, economics probably isn't your strong suit. It isn't mine, either. However, hidden in this freely available data are clues that most people overlook completely, and you don't have to be an economist to see and make use of them. For example, the category of food service includes everything from burger flippers to senior-level executive management. If you are an accountant for a farm cooperative, which would have been in the largest losing field of crop production, it would certainly make sense to think about a shift to food service. You may not know a grain elevator from dumbwaiter, but the need for your services would probably overshadow the need for any highly specialized knowledge.

This is the kind of flexibility I have been talking about all along. Far too many people fail to take advantage of opportunities that are right in front of them. They define themselves so narrowly that it's almost impossible for them to either avoid losing out as their industry declines, or moving up in areas they would never consider.

The information I've discussed so far is but a very small part of the *Occupational Outlook Handbook*. Please, please, use it, whether you see it online, in a library, wherever. Knowledge really is power, and this is the basic knowledge you will need to plan carefully.

There are other sources of economic data you can use to put a sharper point on your career planning. This data is more general that the information in the *Occupational Outlook Handbook*. However, the more carefully you plan, the better your chances of working at what you like in a field that you enjoy. So check out the sources that follow.

> **Case in Point**
>
> A colleague of mine was coaching a biologist who had moved from the lab to administrative management in a large health-care firm. It was a good move at the time, but after a while he became redundant for reasons that had no relation to his ability. In short, another talented person fell victim to cost cutting because the stockholders wanted more. He spent the better part of a year looking for an administrative job with another company in the same field. Then, at the urging of my colleague, he looked elsewhere and ended up as the top administrator in a large physician's cooperative, a place he had never even thought of. He now makes more money, has less pressure, and does volunteer counseling of others who found themselves in the same pickle. The moral: opportunities exist everywhere. You have to think imaginatively of yourself in broad terms, and be willing to take some chances.

Other Economic Information Sources

It's possible to build a house with only a hammer and a saw. But if you had a power saw, a pneumatic hammer, and every other tool carpenters use today, you could do it a lot faster and maybe a lot better. I just gave you the power saw and the pneumatic hammer: it's called the *Occupational Outlook Handbook*. Now let's add the rest of the tools you need—but don't just jump in, read, and move on to the next chapter. The sources that follow are all available online and I strongly suggest that you check each out as you read. Take your time; get the feel of the report and the data being reported. You may pick up some information that will be of immediate help, but I'd be happy if you just got yourself comfortable with the tools so you can use them when you need them. To mix some metaphors, learn to ski before you try to ski jump.

The Employment Situation

The Employment Situation is published monthly by the Department of Labor's Bureau of Labor Statistics. *The Occupational Outlook Handbook* gives you the big picture projections; *The Employment Situation* gives you a comprehensive report of the contemporary employment scene.

If the country is in an economic decline, as it is as I write this, rising employment figures can signal that a recovery is under way. There is even a positive correlation with inflation under certain circumstances. Rising unemployment figures, conversely, usually signal a slowdown. Of particular interest to career planners are the figures describing the average workweek in manufacturing. Changes in workers' hours are considered reliable indictors of near-term hiring activity. The payroll diffusion figures can often foreshadow major shifts in overall employment, not just in manufacturing.

Just type "The Employment Situation" in an online search window and you will have it on your screen.

Unemployment Insurance Claims

This weekly report produced by the Department of Labor gives you access to the number of new filings for state unemployment benefits for the previous week as well as the total number of people who have received payments for the week before the current report figures.

This report tells you immediately whether employment is up or down. The number of new claims, when viewed historically, will give you the trend. The report doesn't report by industries, but it does give you the broad view of the country's current employment status, and tells you which states had increases or decreases of more than a thousand. Labor economists consider this report one of the key indicators of the health of the labor market.

Keep in mind that this report doesn't fully reflect the unemployment situation. It deals only with those filing and those currently receiving claims. It doesn't include those who have exhausted the allotted period during which they can collect benefits, but who still remain unemployed. Still, the information it gives you should be part of your planning, especially if you live in any of the states that are reported in the increase/decrease statistics.

Just type "Unemployment Insurance Claims" in your online search window and open the report.

Help-Wanted Advertising Index

This is published by The Conference Board, a large and respected economic research organization. It is not a government organization, but it does make available a lot of good information. Its *Help-Wanted Advertising Index* surveys the help-wanted advertising in 51 major newspapers across the country once a month.

It has been shown over the years that help-wanted advertising volume is significantly correlated with various labor market conditions. It's used by businesses to track changes in the regional and national supply of jobs. You can use it to put a sharper point on the data you get from the other sources I have already described.

In addition to the numbers, each issue of the report offers significant interpretations that can be very helpful in your career planning. For example, I have the May 29, 2008, report on my desk and Ken Goldstein, the labor economist at the Conference Board, provides a concise and insightful analysis of the current period of slow economic growth and labor market conditions. He concludes that the numbers reported are the reason why consumer confidence is at a 16-year low. This kind of information and insight should be extremely help for everyone's career planning activity, whether it focuses on executives or shop floor positions.

Just type "Help-Wanted Advertising Index" in your online search window and open the report.

Help-Wanted OnLine Data Series

This is also produced by The Conference Board and is available without charge online.

The *Help-Wanted OnLine Data Series* serves pretty much the same purpose of the Conference Board's Help Wanted Advertising Index I have just described, except that it surveys and reports online employment listing statistics. The report on my desk as I write this is dated June 2, 2008. It reports that there were 2,743,700 new online ads posted in May of the year. This report, too, includes analyses and comments by The Conference Board's economists. The economist writing in this issue states that, "This lackluster job outlook is clearly contributing factor in a shrinking consumer confidence." The Conference Board is well known and respected for the quality of its research and the insight it offers in its interpretation. I'd suggest that you bookmark its site in your computer and check it regularly.

Just type "Help-Wanted Online Data Series" in your online search window and open the report.

Personal Income

The Bureau of Economic Analysis at the U.S. Department of Commerce is the source of this monthly report.

Changes in real income are frequently seen as indicators of consumer spending patterns. When you consider that consumer spending has a direct effect on overall economic growth, it's a good idea to consider this information in your longer term career planning. When you consider that two thirds of the nation's gross domestic product is based on personal consumption, you can see that significant movement in either direction can be a strong factor to use in your career planning and management.

Just type "Personal Income and Outlays" in your online search window and open the report.

Making Economic Decisions

I hope you haven't come to the conclusion that with the right economic information you will automatically make the right decision. You won't. But armed with good data choices and a realistic plan for making decisions, you will be much better off than the coin-flippers. Good data is valid data, which means it measures what it's supposed to measure.

Good data must also be reliable data, which means it yields consistent results. In simple terms, if you were to measure the same thing several times, the results would be consistent. The notion of validity and reliability can get very complicated, but if you stick with these basic definitions you will have what you need to decide on which economic data to use when you make your career decisions.

There are many ways to make decisions, but I suggest that you use a simple four-step system. You probably use this system yourself intuitively even when you have to make simple decisions like whether to go to the movies or stay home and read a book.

1. Define the issues.

The first question you have to ask yourself is this, what is the most important outcome of the decision for your career planning purposes? If, for example, you are thinking about changing fields but want to continue doing the same kind of work, the outcome of your decision would be whether or not you made a wise move. There are other issues, of course. But keep the issues simple and clear at first.

2. Identify all the sources.

As I have pointed out and as you have probably discovered from digging in the few sources I have described, there is more than enough economic data on just about every subject. The best way to address this is to start with a wide view and work your way down. If you are looking for the rate of projected growth in a particular field of employment, start with the data available from the Bureau of Labor Statistics and narrow your focus until you get to the sources that seem to be most valuable. At this point you will probably have access to both government information and information provided by the various organizations that serve the field that interests you. Gather the reports and move on to the next step.

3. Evaluate the sources and the material they provide.

Here's where the process slows down a little and where you should be careful not to make quick judgments. Remember, I mentioned that a lot of data available for career management is collected and reported by individuals and organizations that have specific interests. I have yet to see any organization in any field publish outright lies, but they all present their data in the best possible light.

Remember what I said earlier about the three ways to present a number as an average? In the example I used, an organization that used the mean average would be presenting its data in a way that would be best for most users. An organization that presented its data as a modal average would probably have its own reasons for doing so, but it probably wouldn't be in the best interest of most people who might have need of the information.

In addition to the choice of statistical evaluation, look carefully at the size of the sample. In general, the larger the number of individuals sampled, the better the data will be. And, of course, be sure that the information is current. You can and should also check out the organization; most have names that imply trustworthiness, but this can be semantic wizardry. The best test is to check out each organization you have never heard of, even though it might sound familiar.

It's best to do this evaluation in steps. Say you've turned up 20 reports that purport to tell you what you want to know. Don't select the one that might look best right off the bat. Your first cut might eliminate half of the sources. Put the rejects aside; don't throw them away yet. Reduce the remaining 10 to 5, and then reduce the remaining 5 one at a time until you have the report in which you have the most faith. If you have any questions about the one you have chosen, go back to the ones you eliminated that might resolve your issue. You probably won't find one in which you have absolute faith, but by looking at all, you should be willing to move with what you have.

4. Make your decision.

The decision you made in the last step was to accept the information in one or several statistics. Now, with the accepted information, you are in a position to make whatever other decision you need to make. Say, for example, that decision led you to conclude that the field that interests you is growing, but that the number of people working in it is shrinking. There, as you might imagine, is a contradiction that needs further investigation, which might show that although the number of people working in the field is diminishing, the salaries of those who remain are growing.

Here is where you and the numbers part company. At this point you can make an informed decision, or you can continue to look for more data. There are no rules to help you with this decision—or help you decide when to decide. At some point you just have to do something, and it's better to do it with solid research than with a coin flip.

You and the Business Cycle

Business expands or it contracts; it rarely stays steady for any length of time. In simple terms, the state of business at any given time is reflected in the gross domestic product and other economic variables. Some economic trends move in sync with the overall cycle, others move in the opposite direction. Others have no relation to the cycle at all. If you have any interest in economics, you might want to learn more about the business cycle. But you should be in shape to make good decisions with the sources I have just given you.

The Least You Need to Know

- Federal, state, and local governments are the best sources of the statistical information you need to plan and manage your career.

- Commercial and nonprofit organizations are most useful for specific employment statistics and trend analyses.

- Always use more than one source of employment data before you make major decisions.

- Economic information about your field is and will always be the best information you can use. Keep checking your sources regularly, even if you are not thinking of making a move.

Chapter 22

Money and Other Things

In This Chapter

- ◆ The clues you need to negotiate the best compensation package
- ◆ What your employer, or prospective employer doesn't want you to know about compensation
- ◆ How to know when you have negotiation wiggle room
- ◆ Why salary may not be the best way to judge an employment offer
- ◆ Why companies you never heard of offer over-the-top salaries

Here's where you and realty come face to face. You probably have some idea of what you are worth to an employer, but if you're like most people, you're thinking mainly in terms of salary. You have a pretty good idea of what other employers are paying for the same work. In your employer's ledger, salaries are seen as a cost of doing business. That cost is more than just your salary. It includes a benefits package, the cost of training, even the purchase of equipment, a car, relocation, and any number of other things.

Whether you are interviewing with a prospective employer or negotiating for a raise, promotion, or transfer within your present company, you and your employer have a different picture of what you're worth. However, most negotiations center on salary, and this can be a major mistake on your part. Read on and you'll find out why.

Your First Clues

The salary figure first offered is usually one of the best clues you'll ever get as to how an employer thinks about compensation. A low offer might say that the company's entire salary structure is not competitive. It's usually a safe bet that any better numbers you are able to negotiate will not be reflected in future raises.

On the other hand, remember that salary is only one element of a compensation package. Some companies offer extraordinary benefits packages to compensate for a lower salary. Generally speaking, those companies that offer excellent benefits, including retirement plans, are more concerned about keeping and promoting people than those companies that offer the moon and the stars as salary.

You can get a feel for this issue by asking how long others in the department where you might work have stayed with the company. Ask about the promote-from-within statistics relative to hiring from the outside. Most people are willing to stay with companies when they know they have a future and will be paid more as their performance improves.

The Guessing Game

Employers large and small base their compensation strategy on history as well as what they know and think they know about how their competitors are compensating their employees. In short, it's something of a guessing game, but they're fairly educated guesses. They look at industry surveys and the salaries expected by people applying for their own job openings. And they factor in industry scuttlebutt, but only after verifying it.

They usually find the appropriate levels by averaging all this information and looking at their employee retention rates. When people leave and give insufficient salaries as a reason, and potential replacements are asking for more than the company now pays, the message becomes clear. Keep in mind that the improvements may be in terms of salary or benefits or both, but remember that no company lasts for any length of time by throwing money around without good reason, *or* by pitching its compensation too far below industry standards.

Getting inside information on compensation isn't easy. But it's become a lot easier now that fewer people plan their lifetime careers with one company. The freedom of movement has resulted in a much larger and more reliable grapevine than ever existed when companies had more paternalistic views. I'm sure you have checked into many of the thousands of Internet blogs started by both happy and unhappy employees. You can get a lot of good information on these blogs, but *do not* do anything drastic based on what you read until you verify everything.

Career Alert

When your employer or potential employer claims an inability to pay at least to industry standards, it may not necessarily signal overall financial problems. It might be that paying you more would cause unrest in the ranks. You might prefer a company with a lower salary scale but a sound financial base to one that offers dazzling compensation but may be gone tomorrow. Look at everything. Salary is important, but so are stability and other benefits.

The Way Some Employers Think

Some employers think that by offering higher compensation packages than their competitors they will attract better talent. This is usually done by smaller and more naïve employers anxious to attract top talent. They don't realize that a job opening is a job opening and those with or without the skills and credentials will apply. In addition to not having good compensation advice to draw on, they usually lack the skills needed to select the best qualified workers for the job and can end up with an expensive and inexperienced employee. This is a plan for disaster.

The companies that pitch their compensation program below industry standards may be able to hire good people, but the people they hire seldom stick with the company. So, as you might have guessed, the companies that hit the mid mark in terms of total compensation usually end up with the best people.

I have known companies with well-conceived compensation plans to bypass their guidelines in an effort to attract a particularly well-qualified candidate. When they do attract, hire, and overcompensate the desired employee, it's usually impossible to keep the numbers a secret. As you might imagine, this can and does often cause considerable unhappiness within the ranks.

Right Move

The higher we go up the ladder, the more likely a larger employer will be to be willing to make compensation exceptions to attract top talent. Don't push too hard for a salary exception unless you are at a senior management level with a big company, or know that you have little or no competition for the position.

A strategy that can help you if you're sure that no exceptions will be made to the salary structure and you really want the job is to take it, do a dynamite job, and then hold the employer's feet to the fire. When an employer knows what you can do and doesn't want to go through the recruitment process again, it is often willing to redefine your job in a way that allows the employer to pay you more without violating its guidelines and creating unhappiness in the ranks. If for example, your title is senior manager, you could be given a VP title, which carries a larger compensation package, but doesn't alter your responsibilities. There are many variations on this theme, so when you both want it to work, think about this approach.

Are You Fixed or Variable Overhead?

As I mentioned earlier, any employer sees you as a cost of doing business. You may be best friends with the owner or the boss, but business is business. Salary and benefits packages are seen by employers as fixed overhead. However, almost all jobs can be configured so some of that overhead can be handled in a more financially friendly way for both of you.

You are probably aware that many sales people are compensated based on their sales productivity: they work on commission, or a salary plus commission, or on a draw against future commissions. Not all other jobs offer this flexibility, but many non-sales jobs are based on salaries plus bonuses for achieving certain understood goals.

If you find yourself unable to move your present or prospective employer to provide a better salary, try discussing some sort of bonus compensation. Virtually everything is negotiable with most employers. Bonus and commission plans are well established in most businesses, but the idea of an employer switching some traditionally fixed salary overhead to variable overhead is not all that common. However, I have never known an employer not to think seriously about an employee's suggestion to take a bonus structure rather than a raise.

Remember that whatever you propose to be based on a bonus must be over and above what you employer presently expects from you in your current position. Also keep in mind that bonuses are one-shot events that are also taxed higher than regular salary. Yes you may be able to do it repeatedly and have almost the same effect as a higher salary, but don't count on this.

How Compensation Is Structured

Every company has a different approach to the way it structures its compensation program. The larger and more complex the company, the more complicated the structure will be. Job descriptions, job rankings, and pay scales will differ widely depending on many factors. It really gets complex in conglomerates whose holdings vary within and across fields and industries. This, of course, means that you need to focus quite tightly when you look for salary information on which to make career decisions. Keep in mind that in situations like this, most companies establish salary midpoints for each position. Depending on how badly they want you, their salary offer usually will have some flexibility.

Most discussions with current and prospective employers about salary should include information on where you fit within the compensation structure. Keep in mind that at this point I am talking about only salary. Try to determine where you fit within the range for your job classification. If the offer is on the low end of the range, you know that there should be room for increases as long as you remain in the present classification. If you have been successful in negotiating a figure at the high end, you'll obviously have less room for improvement unless you are promoted or moved to a different job.

Most employers are pretty open about having this kind of discussion, so don't be reticent about raising the issue. In fact, many prefer to lay the cards on the table up front. It's usually easier for all concerned and it seldom leaves the employer open to criticism if there is a misunderstanding later on.

Be sure that you know when you will be eligible for a salary review, and make sure you know what criteria will be used to grant or deny you an increase. It's general practice to do salary reviews once a year, usually on the anniversary date of your employment. Many companies also do performance reviews, but these are often done on a different schedule and are seldom used exclusively for granting or denying a salary increase. But make sure you know exactly when these events take place and what's going to happen as a result of them.

Some companies, especially larger and more complex corporations, put a cap on the number of increases that can be granted over a stipulated period of time. If, for example, the cap is three raises in any given classification, and you got all three early in your tenure, you either have to wait out the period or see whether you can shift to another department or subsidiary of your employer to restart the clock. And make sure its policy allows for restarting the clock!

Who is your compensation gatekeeper? Someone has to be your advocate and that person has to be someone in your reporting chain. Most often, it will be your immediate boss. However, your boss may have to make your case to his boss and his boss may even have to plead your case to someone else. Most companies will tell you this without your having to plug into the grapevine.

So far this sounds pretty cut and dried, and it is, or there would be chaos. However, I have yet to see a company not stretch its compensation policy when a really valued employee is involved. Most will make exceptions when they have to. But don't push the envelope. And if you are fortunate enough to have an exception made on your behalf, keep it to yourself. You can brag and boast about anything else, but not a salary exception made in your favor by a company with a rigid compensation schedule.

Every Manager Pinches Pennies

Remember I said that salaries are typically seen as a cost of doing business? That's only the start of it. The head of your department has a budget, and one cost on that budget is salaries. Whether or not your department actually produces revenue, your department must be profitable in the overall scheme of things. This means that your boss has to produce and has to control costs. He or she must see you in terms of what you contribute to the department's productivity and at what cost.

In departments that are revenue centers, the job of measuring contribution to profit is a lot easier than in service departments. In sales, for example, there are real numbers involved. There are goals to be met. It's relatively easy to decide who produces, who doesn't, who has to go, and who gets raises. But, in the HR or the accounting departments, there are no "real" numbers. There is work to be done, but no income figures on which to make solid evaluations. As a result, these service departments tend to grow when there is an increased need for their services, but they seldom contract when the need is diminished until there is some sort of crisis.

As I write this, we are seeing herd thinning in all companies and especially in departments that do not actually generate revenue. Managers who staffed up as their companies grew are now being asked to slim down their operations. Hardly a day goes by when there isn't an article in the business press about some company, large or small, that is laying off employees. It's unfortunate, but it's nothing new.

The question for you in terms of your career planning and management should not be whether to switch to the sales department, but what you should be doing to bulletproof yourself and continue doing the work you like and were trained for. It's seldom a question of talent or ability. Much of what most service departments do internally can be bought on the outside, so it's a question of juggling staff so that bases are adequately covered as inexpensively as possible. If you have been with the company for long, chances are it is satisfied with your performance. So while working harder and smatter is always appreciated, your best bet is to work harder and smarter *and* provide an additional economic incentive that will help you be one of the survivors.

Doing this may be easier than you think. C. Northcote Parkinson said in an article that appeared in *The Economist* in 1955, "Work expands to fill the time allotted for its completion." If you are honest with yourself, you can see plenty of elements of your job that you dawdle over and that could be done easier and faster. But speed isn't the issue: it's the time you'll have to take on more responsibility in the department. That makes you more valuable when the boss is deciding who goes and who stays.

I realize that what I am saying rubs you across the grain. Why should you work harder to keep your lousy job when the president and CEO just jumped ship swinging from golden parachutes with diamonds in their pockets? Okay, you can be a martyr; you can say that you never caved. Does that put beans on the table? No, it doesn't. And unless you have some ideas on how to correct the situation, you do what you have to do. When conditions change, you will have plenty of time to thumb your nose at the suits. In fact, right now you can drive by most any federal prison, wave, and the chances are pretty good you will be seen by some suit who crossed the line. There, does that make you feel better? Good!

Striking Out on Your Own

If you are entrepreneurially inclined, there are often good opportunities to leave your job and take your employer with you as a paying client. This is common in sales, where salaried salespeople leave to become independent representatives, selling the products or services of their former employer plus other products and services offered by noncompetitive clients. It has also become more common to see staff people leave to provide services as independents to their former employers.

Many companies now look to their "core competencies" and see that they can do away with a lot of fixed overhead by outsourcing engineering, financial, human resources, and other work to independents. You hear a lot about outsourcing because of the jobs lost to overseas companies, but many smaller companies that want to focus on the work they do best have welcomed requests from employees to leave the payroll and become independent contractors. Give this some serious thought. It could be a great way to start your own business with some immediate income.

Remember, if you do think about striking out on your own, do your personal budget planning very carefully. Consider not just the salary you were making but also the cost of the benefits package that you must pick up yourself. You will become an employer as well as an employee, whether you incorporate or just freelance or consult on your own. This is a field worth exploring, but it's way out of the scope of this book to go any further into the details. See the appendix for some books that might be most helpful.

What's in Your Compensation Package?

Prior to the post World War II period, few people took home anything more than a salary, regardless of how well they were paid. The boom years of the late '40s, '50s, and '60s created a demand for people in virtually all fields of work, but demand was especially high in expanding areas of management, finance, science, and technology.

Demand exceeded supply and companies in need of talented people began competing for their services in ways that few would have imagined just a few years earlier. Salaries were high, of course, but you can only go so far with that. No company president would ever stand for anyone lower on the corporate pecking order being paid more than he or she was being paid. So new and imaginative ways had to be found to attract and pay the needed talent.

The benefits packages that are part of most compensation programs today got their start back then. At the time it was mainly company-paid insurance, but as demand changed, so did the ways of compensating people. Some of the packages are quite imaginative—and some went beyond the borders of legality. Whether they are seen as a boon or a pox, they are here to stay, and you might as well make sure that you get your share.

The company that employs you now probably has a compensation package that is mainly insurance centered. However, you may be entitled to other benefits as well. You are legally entitled to a copy of the compensation package that is appropriate for the level at which you work. If you want to know what the top brass gets, buy some company stock and read the annual report carefully and pay attention to all the notices that go out to stockholders during the year.

Remember, salary is only one factor to consider. If, for example, you have a large family, an excellent company-paid insurance program may be a factor that helps you see a lower than expected salary as being practical. One of the ways major universities attract and retain talented faculty is by providing extensive educational benefits for families. Airlines and other transportation companies usually include deep discount fares for families of employees. Take these benefits seriously; most are quite valuable.

This section discusses the most common benefits available ay many companies today. In general these are the elements found in most compensation packages. This is not to say that all programs will have all of these and that all individual benefits are equally beneficial. Yours may have more and it may have fewer. Your chances of changing the structure of the package are nearly nil, but you can usually assume that there will be some variations as you move from one level to another. For example, as an entry-level employee, you may not be in line for a stock-option program, but as you rise this option could become available.

The information the HR department gave you when you joined the company should give you all the information you need. It is up to you to read and understand the package. If you have any questions at all, ask. And keep an eye on the material that is sent to you periodically about these programs. Make sure you are aware of any and all changes that are made to them. Don't assume that the benefit granted to you the day you signed on is going to be the same on the day that you need it.

Insurance

Health insurance is included in most employment compensation packages. Make sure you know exactly what you are getting and whether or not some of the premium will be your responsibility. It's not enough to know that your employer's policy is with a well-known and respected insurance company. You need to know the full extent of the coverage. Make sure your dependents are covered adequately. Make sure that there are no exceptions in the policy that might exclude you or any of your family. And be sure to ask when the coverage starts. Some companies set their health coverage to begin only after a certain period of employment, often six months from your starting date.

Most life insurance in employment benefits packages is term insurance. You may have some latitude in the amounts, higher coverage being paid for by deductions from your salary. Keep in mind that the policy will probably be cancelled if and when you leave the company. These policies can be converted to personal ownership when you leave, but the premium will usually be quite a bit higher. In effect, your employer buys this insurance at a bulk discount by guaranteeing a certain number of employee policy holders.

Pensions

A pension plan is especially important if you are planning long-term work with your employer. These plans, most often structured as defined-benefit programs, provide payments after you retire based on formulas that include length of employment and your salary level at the time you retire.

You were probably given a packet of information on a plan when you joined the firm. Chances are, between the time you joined the company and now, that plan has gone through many changes and modifications. Between now and the time you actually retire, there will probably be more changes. There usually is nothing sinister in all this, but, unless you stay on top of it, you may find that your retirement will different than you planned for. The plan may be even better that you thought it would be when you signed on. But just make sure.

You have very little direct control over most company retirement plans. However 401(k) plans, named for their title in the federal tax code, allow for considerable control, and today are far more popular than the old company-sponsored plans. These plans provide for an individual account for each employee. Employees and employers contribute to the accounts, and the money is placed in an account that is invested and controlled by a trust. These plans are popular with employers mainly because they are aware of exactly what their expenses are.

The real benefit that most employees see in them is portability. If you leave your job, you can take the account with you. Also, you have a fair amount of latitude in the amounts you can contribute. All this sounds great—and it usually is—however, make sure that you have faith in the trust that administers the program. There is usually very little room for the trust to steal, but be sure you understand and approve of the trust's investment strategies. This is not a place to speculate!

Most 401(k) plans invest their accumulated funds in the stock market. As I write this chapter, the stock market is taking a beating, and so are 401(k) trust accounts. But, like mutual funds, the diversification possibilities available to the investing trust should control for these variations. I don't mean to frighten you, but cycle after cycle we see that the free lunch can often be rather expensive. These plans are not get-rich-quick schemes; they are retirement programs. If you feel lucky, buy a lottery ticket.

Stock Purchases and Options

Many public corporations offer stock purchase plans to employees. They are frequently set up so that stock is acquired automatically and the purchase price is deducted from your paycheck. One nice benefit of this is that you get the stock without having to pay a brokerage fee—and, if you're lucky, you might even get an employee discount! Your stock is usually supplied fully registered and it's yours to do with as you see fit. Many of the stories you hear about employees becoming rich through company stock purchase plans are true and awe inspiring. Who really knew back then that Xerox or Microsoft would do the spectacular things that they did? Of course, you could be lucky or you could work for a company whose stock goes south. But then, the stock market is a crap shoot so why not take a little company stock and see what happens.

Stock options are another thing. Options are granted at a value that is above the current market price. They become valuable only when the market price becomes greater than the option price. Many conditions can be applied to a stock option; for example, you may be prohibited from exercising the option for a certain period of time, and there may be a terminal date by which the option has to be exercised. Most stock option plans I have seen state that if an employee leaves prior to his or her option rights becoming available, the options are lost.

Right Move

Stock options are complex and can be very confusing. Don't think that you have mastered the subject when you finally understand the plan offered by your present employer; if you move to another company with a stock-option, you'll have to start all over. Don't be daunted by this! Many of the people you read about who became wealthy did it with options on their employer's stock. But despite their relative naïveté, they did their homework and worked the stock-option system for all it was worth.

It may be too early in your career to think of the tax consequences of making money from options on your employers stock, but remember this: if you exercise your rights in your stock-option agreement and sell your stock immediately at a profit, you will be hit with income taxed based on regular income. That can be disastrous. On the other hand, if you hold your shares for the time specified by the terms of your agreement with your employer, they could be worth less than you paid for them. I'm not a financial person; I'm not even a big gambler. So I have no more to say on this subject other than be careful!

Privately held corporations are permitted by federal law to establish employee stock option plans. Publicly traded corporations can use the plans, but they are most often used by smaller, privately help corporations. These plans can be quite complex and any discussion of them is beyond the scope of this book. However, you should keep in mind that it's a really rare company that allows enough people to own stock so they can outvote major stockholders. Further, since the company's stock is not publicly traded, you are limited in what you can do with it if you decide to sell it. All that having been said, there have been some cases where a privately held company with an ESOP program was acquired by a larger and better financed company. The stock acquired through ESOP programs becomes stock in the acquiring company. But don't bet the farm on this happening to you. If your privately held employer has compensation packages other than ESOP plans, avoid ESOP plans.

Profit Sharing

Many companies have admirable profit sharing plans, but just as many have plans that leave a lot to be desired. What you might get as your share can usually be judged by what the company has done in the past. Once a company establishes a profit-sharing program, it usually becomes public knowledge. Any cutback, even if the company is in great shape, will send the money people into a panic. Short of reading the entrails of a chicken, behavior like this can ripple through the stock price. But then you know all about the stock market, don't you? Just remember that profits are shared are based on the largesse of management and major stockholders. Think of profit sharing as an occasional windfall.

Bonuses

A bonus is nice to get, but like profit sharing, don't count on it for your long-term career and financial planning. Bonuses can be paid based on predetermined amounts for meeting specified goals. And they can be given as a matter of course, such as an annual Christmas bonus. If your terms of employment include a bonus, be sure to ask for the details.

Other Benefits

The issues I've just described deal mainly with the financial elements of your employment. Here are some of the others that could be important to you.

Special leave privileges could include maternity or paternity leaves, leave for health reasons, and leave for family issues. Health issues should be understood clearly. If you are hospitalized for an extended period, your employer may put you on temporary disability rather than carrying you on a short-term leave basis. The insurance issues are beyond the scope of this book, but if you have these concerns make sure you fully understand your employer's special leave provisions.

You will want to know when you might be able to take your first vacation. Ask about any special times or situations when you might not be allowed to take vacations. Accounting firms, for example, seldom let employees take vacation time during the tax season.

If you are going to relocate for your new job, be sure you are familiar with your employer's relocation reimbursement plan.

Education Opportunities

Many of the more enlightened companies offer some sort of educational support. Some will pay all or part of the cost of coursework that leads to better performance of your job. Others have on site training and educational programs. If you are interested in these educational opportunities check out the details with your HR department, or with the person who is interviewing you for a new job. Education is expensive, whether it's some form of skill training, or advanced degrees. A Ph.D. your company pays for could be well worth the smaller salary you are paid in the process. As I keep saying, it boils down to money most of the time!

Termination Conditions

Termination without cause usually includes some form of compensation. The recent waves of downsizing have brought this issue to the public consciousness, and I probably don't have to outline the consequences of losing a job and not having another lined up. It's a difficult issue to bring up at interview time, but when prefaced with your concern about the vagaries and uncertainty of your industry specifically and the economy in general, most interviewers don't take offense.

This was a long chapter. It had to be. Few of us work for the fun of it. Compensation is important in terms of what we need and use money for, and it's also an important measure of our own self worth. Remember, however, that there is more to work than just making money. If you're not happy in your work, the rest of your life will suffer almost as much as it might if you were not able to meet your expenses. I urge you to do what you like, even if you make less money than you might by doing something else. In my work I have met far too many people who, whether by choice or circumstances find themselves in very unhappy work situations. Some are making millions a year, others are getting by. Work satisfaction has no personal boundaries.

The Least You Need to Know

- ◆ Salary is only one element of your compensation.

- ◆ Some benefits programs actually make it worthwhile to consider a smaller salary.

- ◆ Negotiating the top salary in a pay category may make you feel good, but it could put you behind the eight ball for future raises.

- ◆ You think "salary," your employer thinks "cost." Think like your employer and you will have a winning edge.

Part 5

Setting Your Milestones for Success

So far, I have dealt mainly with the nuts and bolts of career planning and management. Now it gets up close and personal. We look at family matters, other personal matters, and the things that really matter to you. And we discuss benchmarks you use to keep your career on track. You will learn how to spot clues you never thought would make any difference in your career. And you will discover how to take a hit, recover, and run for the goal. The only final exam will be what you make of everything that has gone before.

Chapter 23

Your Career Strategies and Tactics

In This Chapter

- ◆ Creating your personal career plan
- ◆ How to strategize in a volatile and unstable job market
- ◆ Identifying the tactics that will keep your plan on track
- ◆ Knowing when you need help and where to get it
- ◆ Making your own decisions

The 22 chapters that preceded this one have focused on getting you ready for this and the next two chapters. Each of the earlier chapters can help you with specific career related issues. However, if you read all the chapters, you should have a pretty good picture of yourself and your career as it stands today. And if you did as I asked, you should have a shoe box full of notes, checklists, and other stuff that will help you do your career planning.

This chapter is about strategy and tactics. The next two are about actual career planning. Don't confuse strategy with planning. Strategies are plans. Plans are blueprints. Blueprints show you how to build a house. The next chapter takes you step-by-step through short-term planning and the chapter that follows that is your guide to long-term planning.

The strategies and tactics I discuss will help keep you focused on your plan. At the same time they will give you the flexibility you need when things take a turn you didn't expect. Without strategies and tactics, you have no flexibility. Given that the world of work changes so rapidly, I'm sure you see that without the underpinning of carefully thought out strategies and tactics, any plan is bound to take you to more than a few dead ends.

Strategic Career Planning

In my estimation, far too much of what passes for career planning today is simply deciding where you want to be in a specified number of years and identifying the steps you have to take along the way. If your goal is to be the advertising manager of the firm that employs you, most career-planning systems simply list and describe the jobs you need to master along the way. A typical career plan to the top ad job would list the stops you have to make along the way in the creative department, the media department, the production department, and some management experience along the way. That's a map—not a plan! A real plan includes strategies and tactics, not just the ports of call on the way to the top.

Everything you have read in this book so far has been presented with the sole purpose of helping you to gather information about yourself and the fields of work that interest you most. I've distinctly avoided suggesting that you start assembling anything that even resembled a career plan. I wanted you to arrive at this point with a good idea of yourself in terms of the work you do or that you envision doing. And I wanted you to arrive with some pretty good information in that shoebox. Now, you and I are going to strategize. We are going to create tactics to help you negotiate the career passage you envision for yourself.

Every successful corporation plans strategically. Why not plan your career the same way? Many people do, without realizing that they are actually using the principles, but most people simply don't think strategically when it comes to their careers. Consider why most people change jobs in the first place: they want more money. Nothing wrong with that. But moving to another job just because it pays more money is not a strategic move, it's a recipe for disaster.

Most people who plan their careers strategically will tell you that they would seriously consider taking another job for *less* money than they're currently making if that job ultimately took them closer to their goal than a job that, for now, offers a big raise. These people are thinking strategically. You should be thinking strategically, too.

A career strategy should tell you in very clear terms who you are, relative to the career you have chosen, and what you have to do to get where you want to be. This is based on extensive information gathering—which you should have been doing as a result of reading the first 22 chapters of this book. A strategic plan includes alternatives for you if you discover that your goals are unreachable for personal reasons as well as reasons that may be out of your control.

By its very nature, strategic planning is long-term planning. This doesn't mean that your strategic plan will be of no short-term—actually, it will probably be of more short-term use than you imagine. Remember, strategic plans include alternatives when short term goals are blocked. This is a subject I address in the next chapter in more detail.

How Can You Stay Competitive?

Every step you have taken in your career so far has probably been done in a competitive environment. Whether you recently moved to a better job at another company or got a promotion within your current company, you had to compete with others who wanted the same job. You were selected over others who might have been seen as less qualified. What did you do to get this competitive edge? Was it happenstance, or was it part of a carefully orchestrated plan on your part?

Most corporations have what they call a mission statement. There's every good reason for you to have one, too. A corporate mission statement a summary of a company's goals and the strategies that it uses to allocate its resources. Your mission statement should be short and to the point and should take no more than one page to write. Ask yourself, "What are my goals in the world of work?" and "What do I have to do to remain competitive for the anticipated life of my career?" and you will have a very powerful tool in your hands. Believe me, the mission statements of many of the biggest and most successful corporations are seldom much more complicated.

Okay, so what do I mean by the anticipated life of your career? It can mean whatever you want it to mean, but I strongly suggest that you set one long-term date, such as the date you would like to retire. Then, set intermediate dates that relate to the steps along the way you will need to negotiate. For example, in the previous example, how long would you anticipate having to spend in the creative department before you are ready to move on to the next step, advertising manager of the firm that employs you?

I mentioned the allocation of resources as an element in corporate career planning. This is also a critical consideration for your career planning, and one that I have never seen discussed in even the better career-planning systems available today. You have two resources to consider, those that are personal and those that are economic.

Your personal resources will vary considerably with your lifestyle. Early in your career, you may be more than willing to take more courses to improve your competitiveness in the workplace. You probably have fewer distractions then than you do as you take on more personal or family responsibilities. Your allocation of finances and time become a critical element in your career plan.

How Often Should You Check Your Course?

Now you have an alpha and an omega, a beginning and an end. And you should have listed the steps you'll take along the way to achieve your ultimate goal. But a strategic plan requires fairly regular attention. Recall that I told you that a strategic plan provides alternatives, not just a connect-the-dots chart to some fantasy. You may think you are on target, but it's a big mistake not to carefully review your progress at regular intervals. Note small as well as large events in your work situation and any changes that have occurred within your company and within your field that could have an impact on your work life. This becomes a reality check for you as well as notes to use when you face an unanticipated shift that might require immediate attention.

Set regular dates for your review based on what is happening within the organization that employs you and on the external events that could have an impact on your career. Given perfect career stability—which never really happens, by the way—I'd say that everyone should do a routine career review every six months and a comprehensive review once a year.

Getting back to your shoebox, you should have notes in it that relate to both variables. Now is the time to extract and use them. The articles you clipped on business in general and your field in particular will be especially helpful. Your personal notes as well as the important interoffice memos you saved will definitely give you an opportunity to spot trends, good and bad, that might affect your career with your present employer. Simply stated, a regular review of your strategic plan gives you the opportunity to take advantage of opportunities and correct for unanticipated problems.

As I write this, we are faced with a very unstable economy. By the time the book is in print, it may be better or it may be worse. Predicting the future is not my strength. However, having spent most of my life in the career planning and management field, I can tell you that what is happening now will happen again…and again. This means that it might be a good idea to adjust your planning to include more frequent reviews, or adapting a continuous mode, rather than one that is done in discrete steps. This is most easily done by selecting the key elements of your personal career and the key elements of your employer's trajectory in the current economy and monitoring them more frequently. Most of us do this more or less intuitively. However, here's one word or warning. Don't let this make you less productive at actual job, or leave you with no time for a personal life.

Creating Your Own Strategic Career Plan

There's a lot more to strategic planning than I have just described, but for most career strategic planning, this is about all you will need. Now it's time to create your plan, geared to your lifestyle, career, career plans, and life goals. Do you have that shoebox handy? You're going to need it.

Your Personal Mission Statement

Corporate mission statements begin with a reason why the organization exists in the first place. Without invoking any of the competing philosophies of why we exist, let's agree that for the purpose of your mission statement, you exist to maximize your human as well as your economic potential. You probably have higher reasons for your existence, and I certainly have no quarrel with that, but let's stick to your real world concerns of maximizing your personal happiness and achieving your definition of economic sustainability in a rapidly changing world.

The clearer your mission statement, the easier it will be for you to create the tactics and strategies I shall describe shortly that will help you achieve your goals.

It may surprise you that many of the mission statements of major world corporations are only a few short sentences long. I believe in brevity, but being that brief with a personal career mission statement is, I feel, a mistake. I suggest that you include in your mission statement an idea of your overarching personal philosophy of work as it relates to you directly and as it might relate to your vision of your future. As concerned as you might be about some of the troubles of the world, stick to yourself for this. Don't get windy and eloquent. Stick to the task at hand. Shoot for a half page, but you will be making a big mistake if you go beyond one page of double-spaced typing.

Set Up Your Own SWOT Team

No, that's not a spelling error. SWOT stands for Strengths, Weaknesses, Opportunities, and Threats. There is a nice formal system for creating an evaluative matrix of these four concepts, but it really isn't necessary. If you're interested, I have listed in the appendix some online sources you can use to create your own personal SWOT analysis. When you begin to examine what you enter about yourself under each of these headings, the key elements for your strategic plan will become fairly obvious. The number you may arrive at by doing a formal SWOT analysis is sort of like knowing your IQ. It just doesn't make all that much difference; you probably already know about how smart you are and where you might come up shot. Let's look at each element individually.

Your strengths are what set you above others. Coming up with these factors requires more than an ego trip. It requires that you face yourself in a way that may not be comfortable for you. For example, one of my coaching clients had told me several times that she felt a major strength of hers was that she was good at math. However, I knew that her co-workers were always leery of accepting any computations she did without carefully checking her work. We all indulge in denial to protect our self image, and my client was sure enough of herself to understand this and look at other positive aspects of her personality and work to include in her list of strengths.

As I said, your strengths are what make you different from others around you. To have any value in your career plan, you must compare apples with apples. You may be way ahead of all those with whom you might competing for a promotion on your ability to do a market analysis. But if your job spec doesn't involve market analysis, it's not a strength in terms of your career planning.

Your weaknesses, like your strengths, must be directly relevant to the work you are doing or would like to do. Think of your weaknesses in terms of where you might be vulnerable in a competitive situation. Keep in mind that this is relative. You may be weak because the person with whom you are competing is much stronger on one aspect of the job in contention. That doesn't mean that you're objectively weak; only that you're weak compared to the other candidate. However it's determined, it's an issue that you must deal with appropriately.

Your opportunities are most readily defined by the need for people with your skills and experience, and the openings that exist for people with your talents. Occupations, professions, and job titles are in constant flux based on any number of factors. The economy in general, the relative strength of your field, the local supply of people who want the same job, and many other factors. As I have pointed out in several of the earlier chapters, you can have most of this information on your fingertips simply by accessing the various government employment data websites.

Remember that obvious opportunities will draw a lot of competitive bidding. If you're smart, you will use the data to which you have access to try to project when there will be a need for your skills before the market catches on. It's a cliché, but planning ahead makes good sense when you plan your career.

The most common threats that will make it more difficult for you to get promoted or to get the job you want could include everything from a general slowdown of the economy to the sudden appearance of something that threatens to make you redundant, or worse, obsolete.

It's been my experience that most people see such things as a slight by a colleague at a meeting as far more important than any real threat such as the arrival of a major competitor in your marketing area. Don't sweat the small stuff. Pay attention only to those elements that are directly and immediately relevant to your career planning. All the other stuff does nothing more than sap your energy and attention.

However you analyze the information you gather from your SWOT analysis, keep in mind that its primary use is to provide a baseline for future improvement in your life and work. By reviewing your plan on a regular basis, you can create benchmarks that will give you a clear picture of your progress. I usually suggest that you benchmark your own progress as well as events in your work life that have both direct and indirect effects on your career.

Set Your Goals

You should establish your strategic goals as tools to help you bridge the gaps that exist between where you currently stand and the objectives you have described in your mission statement. In a very real sense, you should see your goals as action plans that identify the minimum standards that will be acceptable to achieve the progress you are seeking.

Your real problem is whether to set easy or difficult goals for yourself. Accomplishing a bunch of easy goals may give you more positive feedback faster than you could get from having difficulty with a single complex or difficult goal. You have to know yourself and you have to act rationally. In simplest terms, don't baby yourself, and don't overburden yourself.

Most strategic planning at the corporate level involves further structuring all the elements. This can be helpful for career planning, but my observation has been that the effort involved seldom produces results worth the time and effort. So for those who are familiar with the nuances of corporate strategic planning, please bear with me. I'm just trying to save time and get you to where you want to be as quickly and as effectively as possible.

Tactics are the specific steps and actions you will take to move yourself forward. Make sure your tactics are always directly aligned with your mission statement and your long-term career goals. It is extremely easy to be sidetracked by something that seems valid but turns out to take you in a different direction. Office rumors are typically responsible for people allowing themselves to be sidetracked. A rumor of a salary freeze, for example, can be quite intimidating, but don't alter your strategy until you know all the facts.

Right Move

As you should have observed, strategy and tactics are two different but interrelated tools. If however, you still are confused, think in military terms. Some generals in history are credited with being great strategists. Others are remembered for being tacticians. The cooperation of these two has almost always accounted for the greatest military successes. The strategists said, "This is what we must do." The tacticians said, "This is how we must do it."

As long as you keep asking yourself, Am I doing the right thing? you will stay on track. A strategic career plan should regularly put you in positions where you have to make decisions. It should be a burr under your saddle. The world around you moves in unpredictable ways and if your strategic career plan is to be of any real benefit to you, it has to prod you to take action. Your strategic career plan must be adaptive. Its goal is not only to get you where you want to be, but to keep you relevant where you presently are.

What Your Strategic Career Plan Is Not

Your career plan is all about decisions, but it doesn't make the decisions; you do. If you fail to make decisions when they are called for, your plan will be a failure. As much as you plan and hope to make the right decisions, you will always make a few bad ones. That's par for the course and you will be able to change decisions or modify your plan—but you must make decisions!

Your plan is based on anticipating elements of the future. However, you will make most of your decisions before you get to the future. In some cases your collected data will dictate what has to be done, but usually your decisions will be based on your own insight, judgment, fears, excitement, and whatever other emotions might be involved at the moment.

Career Alert

Don't expect your career planning to go flawlessly, no matter how carefully you plan. Your thoughts and feelings may change as you go along. The world in general and your work world in particular is always in a state of flux. You will have insights tomorrow that elude you today. Career planning is both a rigid and a very creative activity. Don't be surprised to discover that the job you thought would be perfect turns out to be all wrong. You may be tempted to say that all the planning was a waste of time, but even though it may show you that you were off track, it will almost always show you how to get on the right track.

Most people I know and coach often choose to share their planning with someone else. A wife, a husband, even a child, close relative, or friend is often involved. I discuss this in some detail in Chapter 26. If you are sharing your planning with someone, or thinking about it, I suggest that you share this book with that person, too. It will help when everyone is, literally, on the same page.

Monitoring Your Strategic Career Plan

Everything I have written so far has been presented in terms of a dynamic career-planning system. That is, it is active, not passive, and you are in touch with your goals and the outside elements that will have an effect on your plan. Whether you have chosen to implement your plan in discrete steps or to manage it seamlessly is up to you. However, you should occasionally step back and look at everything that has happened since you last took a look.

It is tempting to think that any plan is on track when you are aware of the planned steps having taken place and you get a sense of productive forward motion. However successful and productive the small steps may be, you may have overlooked some things that add up to problems or a need to change direction. It's forest-for-the-trees sort of thing. A tree here and a tree there are seldom noticed, but when a grove disappears, you may finally see it from a larger perspective.

If it helps you, set both short- and long-time goals and guidelines. Get feedback from those to whom you have entrusted your plans. You wouldn't take a long road trip without checking the map or your position on your GPS device. Do the same with your career plan.

The Least You Need to Know

- Career planning need not be difficult and time-consuming.

- Your strategies and tactics are tools; you are always in full charge.

- Career planning is not a one-shot activity; you have do regular tune ups.

- Your career plan is not a straitjacket, it's a guide that will take you where you want to go and keep you out of blind alleys.

Chapter 24

Don't Take This Personally, But ...

In This Chapter

- ◆ Why personal considerations often trump reality.
- ◆ Your plan begins today, not tomorrow.
- ◆ Why moving on may be better that sticking it out.
- ◆ How to keep your career plan from becoming a straight jacket.
- ◆ How to analyze corporate culture and subculture.

If there's one phrase that most people hate to hear, it's, "Don't take this personally, but …." This is because it's most often followed with some lame excuse for downsizing or outright termination. How can you not take something like that personally?

You know and I know that these words are used in a feeble attempt to assure someone that what is about to happen to them is not their fault. But however the blow is softened, it is personal! You may have gotten the impression as you read the earlier chapters in this book that the whole career-planning business can be pretty impersonal. Well, it is—and it isn't. If your father owns the business, it can get pretty personal. Otherwise it really is about your economic value to an employer, regardless of whether he or she claims to feel your pain as you leave the building for the last time.

I have saved my discussion of the personal side until now to make absolutely sure that you understand the reality of work and your relation to it. Now, it's time to talk personally.

The Shouldas and Couldas of Career Planning

In that classic movie, *On the Waterfront*, Terry the boxer says to his brother, Charley, "I coulda been a contender." Those five words sum up a life spent in pursuit of an unfulfilled dream. Whether your career is boxing or business, or anything else for that matter, it is personal. How many times have you asked yourself whether or not your present job is secure, or whether it offers the opportunities you dream of? Or suppose you had an opportunity to do the work you really love, but taking it would mean some loss in salary or even prestige. That's pretty personal, isn't it? These and many other uncertainties cross everyone's mind from time to time, even when there are no threats of layoffs. So let's get personal!

Whatever you are doing at the moment, it is probably the result of some planning. You may be working at a job that has excited you since childhood, or you may be working at something that you only recently discovered interested you. It could have taken you years of study, or may have required nothing more than a willingness to sign on when the opportunity presented itself. In short, despite all your best efforts and intentions, there is a lot of randomness involved. Jobs that intrigued you a few years ago may not even exist today. And the job that intrigues you today may not exist in a few years.

As you have probably guessed, I'm making the case for both short-term and long-term planning. The tools and steps I outlined in the previous chapters will help you with both. Suppose your long-term goal is to be a senior executive of a major company that manufactures products that have always interested you. Obviously, you have steps to take before you're ready to be considered for that job, and your long-term planning should give you a pretty clear idea of the steps you have to take to get there. Your short-term planning involves the work you must do to move from step to step, while keeping your focus on your long-term goal.

Throughout your career you will meet people who will tell you what they could have or should have done to improve their careers but never did. Listen carefully to these people, but don't let their negativity get you down. Apart from being the victims of events that might have been out of their control, most of these people continue to make the same mistakes over and over again. More often than not, they are intelligent people who you might think should have known better; their problem is that they don't trust their own judgment. Armed with the best advice, they failed to act on it. Their "couldas" and "shouldas" are lessons for you to learn. Just don't let them wear you down.

> **Career Alert**
>
> A career plan can become a straitjacket. By carefully planning your short-term goals you will find it much easier to cut and run when something goes wrong than you might if you took bigger steps with greater consequences in the balance. Don't be afraid to investigate what the fates may deal you. It could be a whack on the side of the head, or a boost to the executive suite.

What Do You Really Want?

If you are presently working, you probably have a few co-workers doing work similar to yours. What do you think each of them sees for themselves in career terms? You may already have some ideas of their goals and ambitions from informal discussions, but my guess is that each sees his or her career in very different terms. One might see his or her present position as a launching platform for future steps to a much bigger job. Another may be perfectly satisfied to work at his or her current job forever. And another might complain about being in the wrong field altogether. Do any of these people see their jobs in the same way as you do? Maybe, maybe not. My point is that there is no single path that is right for all, even for those who are doing the same kind of work.

The failure of many simpler career-planning strategies is that they try to be all things to all people. That simply isn't possible. Career planning isn't a road map; it's a collection of tactics and strategies. You may have seen other plans laced with lists and checklists, forms and spreadsheets. While I can see advantages to some elements of these systems, I have avoided anything that implies that if you take such-and-such a step, this or that will happen. These systems fail to acknowledge the randomness of the work world and the personal aspects that are, in my estimation, key elements.

> **Right Move**
>
> Any career plan, no matter how simple or complex, should lead you to work that is consistent with your own lifestyle. Only you know what is best for you. Don't settle for something that makes you uncomfortable in the long run. Short term burrs under your saddle may be annoyances, but they are also probably telling you something that you should not ignore.

The Here and Now of Your Present Job

Whether you are working or not working, whether you are just starting out or are well into your career, you are at a starting point. Whatever you have done in the past and whatever has happened to you that was out of your control is over and done with. I really hate this cliché, but here goes anyway: *today is the first day of the rest of your life.* It does make a point, doesn't it?

You really have no alternative but to focus on today. For the moment, let's assume you are employed. Whether you are facing a layoff or planning your next career move, you have to ask yourself if and how your present job affects your career planning strategies. Does your present job offer the opportunities you seek? Do these opportunities lead to the chance to move up? Are there opportunities to move over within the corporate structure that could lead to further and faster moves up? Or is this the time to think about moving to another company altogether?

Do a thorough analysis of all the opportunities that might exist with your present employer. Use all the tools I've given you in the first two sections of the book. Your main interest should center on the stability of your current employer and the opportunities that currently exist. Pretend you are thinking about your present employer as someone you might want to work for, not as the organization that already pays your salary. It helps to shift your point of view when you're considering something as important as a career change. And here's where it does get personal and subjective. Ask yourself how well you like your job and whether or not this is the kind of company you would want to work for the rest of your life.

You may be qualified for greater responsibility, but will you have an opportunity to take advantage of it? Is there someone else who might get the spot you're qualified for? Suppose the way is clear to the next level, and you want to know what the timing is. How long will you have to wait to move up?

At this point, you should thoroughly review your corporate culture. Some companies tend to bring in outsiders above a certain level of responsibility. Never underestimate this "new blood" factor. A little judicious snooping should give you a clear picture of when outsiders tend to be hired and those within the company become plateaued.

Many larger companies with complex levels of management have well-drawn profiles of the people they want for each level of management. If the company is somewhat rigid in its promotion practices, your profile may have taken you as far as you can go. Job level requirements are seldom kept secret, so check out just what's needed to get you to the next level. Perhaps some continuing education credits will do the trick. In fact, the more progressive companies I have known will pay for some or even all of the course work. Check out what's available.

> **Career Alert**
>
> Employee educational benefits are usually in a state of flux. If you are thinking of taking courses you might need to move to the next level, get the latest employee package from the HR department. Even if what you want isn't included, make an appointment to discuss your plans. Many companies are quite flexible and even those that aren't may have some changes in the wind that you can take advantage of in the near future.

Remember, if you work for one of those large conglomerates, opportunities for advancement probably exist in other divisions, owned companies, and subsidiaries, but in most cases, you'll probably have to scout them out. Every company has its own procedures, so be sure you do your research in the prescribed way. You don't want to endanger your present position. Most companies with which I've had experience are usually quite willing to help blocked employees find employment within the family, especially if the employee is valued and it seems that he or she is serious about career advancement.

Maybe It's Time To Move On

For whatever reason, there will be times in your career when the best move is a move out. As much as you like your present job and your co-workers, when it becomes apparent that your growth is limited, you just have to do it. It's not easy to say good-bye to friends and employers who liked you, but, and here comes the personal stuff, it's your life and you have to make the most of it.

My first advice on this subject is to not make a move until you have a place to move to. I have met far too many people who made the decision and were afraid they would change their mind if they didn't to it right away. This is a really big mistake! No matter how highly regarded you are by your present employer, jumping ship without a plan can be a disaster. First, it tells a prospective employer that you are impulsive, a characteristic not held in high regard by most employers. And, second, it usually results in a less than enthusiastic recommendation when you need one.

It's really important to leave your present employer on a high note. Even though you have had serious disagreements with your present employer, mend those fences as best

226   **Part 5:** Setting Your Milestones for Success

as possible. You don't have to leave on a buddy-buddy basis, but you have absolutely nothing to gain by letting off steam.

Case in Point

There is a story told in an industry which shall remain nameless of a highly valued employee who had serious disagreements with his employer. The employee was a highly regarded figure in his industry and could have worked anywhere. One day this fellow reached his tipping point and had it out with the CEO in front of a group of stockholders. He ended his tirade with a dramatic resignation and simply left the building. It was said that he secretly thought the CEO would come crawling to him. That didn't happen. He also assumed that since he had been scouted many times by his former employer's competitors, he could work anywhere. Surprise! No one wanted to touch him. This misguided fellow never worked again in his field. In fact, urban business legend has it that he is now a greeter at a local megastore. Don't let this happen to you.

You should carefully and quietly plan your move. Just go about your work as though nothing else was on your mind. It's probably not a good idea to even tell your closest friends on the job what you are doing. Apart from the occasion malicious person you might run across, even best friends let things slip.

Your first step in planning a move out is to establish a schedule. Believe it or not, this is one of the most important parts of your plan. Without a specific date for leaving, I can assure you that you will probably never do it. Set a date, plan the steps you must take, and adhere to the schedule. Wishful thinking is not careful planning and execution. I would advise that your target date be no longer than six months in advance. Anything longer and you just may lose interest. Shorter is better, since it puts some heat on you, but don't make it so short that you are overwhelmed by everything you have to do.

You not only want to schedule your own move, you want to schedule the work you need to complete for your present employer. Again, whether you are on good terms or not, never give anyone the opportunity to block your career with even a casual negative remark.

All of the earlier chapters should have prepared you for this step. The notes you stored in your shoebox will provide additional guidelines. But, remember, most of what you have read is real-world stuff. At this point, it's time to think of the personal stuff.

What Do You Really Dislike?

Get personal; what bugs you about your present job. We've already talked about such things as salary and a lack of growth potential. What about the people you work with? Do you respect them as individuals? As co-workers? There will always be a few people you work with who can make your life either just unpleasant or downright miserable. The more difficult the people are to deal with, the more important it may be for you to move on. If these people stand in your way for growth and promotion, the reason to move is pretty compelling. But if they are just run-of-the-mill pains, you can probably learn to live with them. After all, you may run into worse in your next job. Better the devil you know than the devil you don't.

What about working conditions? It's not fun to work in unpleasant surroundings. However, I once met a senior executive who shared a very small office with another senior executive. At their level, this was unusual except for the fact that most people, executives as well as staff, worked under similar circumstances. None seemed unhappy about the situation. It turned out that they were all well paid, liked and respected each other, and saw the space as a minor discomfort compared with other factors.

I know of another company with really plush offices, but whose executive turnover rate is off the charts. To put it simply, it's a miserable company to work for and even big offices didn't compensate for all the negatives.

A Moving Experience

We are a mobile society, but just how far would you be willing to move to advance your career? Some people get antsy after they have been in one spot for even a short period of time. Others get serious jitters at the thought of moving just a few miles.

The issue often boils down to where the major opportunities for your work skills and interests are located. Today, most industries can be said to be headquartered in one spot or another. Book publishing, for example, is thought of as being a New York industry. There are many fine publishers scattered all over the country, but would you consider uprooting to work for a company in a distant city with only one publishing company? It may be the job of your dreams, but suppose that company suddenly folds and there are no second acts where you now live. Before you say absolutely no, think about whether you might be able to negotiate with a distant prospective employer. You may be able to negotiate a cost of moving clause to return to square one under certain circumstances. Just remember, although nothing may be mentioned in the employee handbook, just about everything is negotiable.

Many companies headquartered outside of the United States make a habit of transferring employees to the home office for a few years experience. Some do this only with people they have their eye on for future growth and want to confirm their feelings by some up front and personal contact. Others do it because they feel that the only way their employees can get a feel for their real mission is by working at parent company headquarters. Whatever the reasons, an offer for an assignment at headquarters is not a move to turn down, even if the company isn't located in a very pleasant place.

Corporate Culture, a Fuzzy Notion with a Big Impact

Corporate culture is another of those ideas that the more literal among us tend to think of as smoke and mirrors. It's not, and you should get a handle on some of the concepts or you will be in for some unpleasant career surprises. Ask the next three people you see what your company's corporate culture is and you will get three different answers. But ask the same three people if the company puts too much heat on them to perform their job and you will get immediate and real answers. Ask the same three whether the company really cares about its customers and you'll also get some real answers.

These and other areas are all part of what makes up a company's corporate culture. Maybe we can't define it clearly, but we can surely define all the elements that go into making up a corporate culture. Perhaps, then, corporate culture is the sum of that substance.

I talked with several of my HR clients about this and together they agree that the elements that motivate employees, how employees are rewarded and punished, and the unspoken relationships between the various layers of management seem to form the base of what is commonly called corporate culture. They all added, however, that every company has its own bank of unspoken and unwritten rules that seem to guide the company's culture. I guess this is about as close as we are going to get to a definition, so let's get right to the elements of corporate culture that can be important in your career planning.

Since your employer or future employer is highly unlikely to hand you something called the Company Culture Handbook, you are going to have to look elsewhere for clues. Actually, you probably won't have to dig much at all; just listening to your co-workers, especially the long-timers, will give you a crash course. Corporate culture is literally handed down informally from employee to employee. The carefully written company history should give you most of the facts, but it's the stories and corporate folklore behind these stories that have the mother lode. Needless to say, much of the folklore will bear some careful examination. However, when you compare the old stories with those currently circulating, you should begin to see elements that repeat themselves. Look for patterns, key words, and phrases. You'll see them, I know you will.

While the stories themselves can be fascinating, what you must really look for are the conclusions your co-workers draw from them. Are they more inclined to agree with the stories that heap mud on management? Is management considered not only benevolent, but genuinely interested in the welfare of the employees? You should be able to get a pretty good idea of how your co-workers feel about the company from their reactions to the stories on the corporate grapevine.

How Do Outsiders See the Culture?

Your co-workers will be a good start, but for many reasons their impressions may not reflect the real corporate culture. After all, when an employee sets his or her sights on spending some time in the company's employ, it's risky to badmouth the boss.

If possible, try to talk with former employees. Why did they leave? Would they return if given the opportunity? The answers to these and similar questions can tell you a lot. Listen to the first-hand stories they can tell. Ask them what happened to them during their terms of employment. Asking for history with which they were not involved will be a waste of time and effort.

See if you can get input from current suppliers, customers and possibly even competitors. Again, stick with their first-hand experience and skip the ancient history.

> **Right Move**
>
> The stories themselves will be interesting and enlightening, but try to get at the motivations behind them. Look for what might seem to be a smokescreen for some unpleasant truth about the company.

Beyond the corporate folklore, there are many other clues worth checking out. For example, what are people wearing? It's not uncommon to see the CFO of a high-tech company show up for work in jeans and a tatty sport jacket. The same job held by someone with the same qualifications in another field would probably require a suit and tie. Office layout and furnishings can also be very telling. If you're used to working in a designer-planned office, you might be uncomfortable in a tacky place laced with full wastebaskets. However, you would be surprised at how quickly you can adapt when someone doubles your salary but tells you that you have to share an office. Keep an open mind!

Corporate Subcultures Are Important, Too

The overall corporate culture is usually management driven. It may be carefully planned or it may just evolve, but it exists and it exists at the pleasure of those who run things from the top. Management will happily support anything that tends to support their goals. What doesn't support their goals also exists as pockets of subcultures.

Don't assume that every subculture is subversive. I have seen many cases where individuals anxious to move things faster form their own informal groups to get things done with less bureaucratic intervention. There groups are usually tacitly accepted by top management as long as the group's goals are in sync with corporate goals.

On the other hand, the chances are that there are subcultures that have both real and imagined reasons for being. It's one thing to find an occasional cranky person who does nothing but badmouth the company, but when you spot a subculture of more than a few individuals, you have reason to be suspicious. Check out them all, but be wary of making any major decisions based solely on what you hear—good or bad.

Key Elements of Most Corporate Cultures

As tough as it may be to put a label on the notion of a corporate culture, there are the elements that pretty much make it up, at least from your perspective as an employee or a prospective employee.

How Performance Is Rewarded

Think of this apart from the way bonuses and salary increases are rewarded. You should have a pretty good picture of this from the employee handbook, or from discussions you have had with your boss or someone in the HR department. Do small good deeds get regular attaboys from immediate supervisors as well as from those on up the chain of command? Is the acknowledgement of exceptional performance made publicly? In other words, are you made to feel that what you did above and beyond the call of duty was appreciated?

What about those who don't pull their weight or even intentionally work against corporate goals? When discovered, are they held accountable, tolerated, or possibly even dismissed? Are your less motivated co-workers likely to see you as a threat to their lack of initiative? This kind of co-worker animosity can occasionally lead to unpleasant subculture situations that make work quite difficult. How a company treats those who willingly fail to perform often tells you a lot about the personal strengths of those in the chain of command.

The Overall Management Style

Everything you read in the employee handbook may paint a picture of the perfect place to work, but the unwritten and often unspoken things often tell you the most about a job. I don't remember who it was, but a number of years ago the CEO of a major corporation used to visit the employee parking lot at quitting time. Whenever he saw anyone carrying what appeared to be a lot of work home, he would stop and ask them why they were unable to complete their work without taking it home. His goal was not to harass employees, but to make sure they were not overburdened. If they were, he saw to it that they got the help they needed during regular working hours. He was truly an enlightened CEO. And probably a rare one!

Another clue to look for is the willingness of management to listen to questions and to answer them quickly and honestly. Remember that corporate culture norms are usually based on how those in the chain of command see how those above them might respond. If top management is open and cooperative, even the most tight-lipped managers in the chain of command will hew to the corporate line. See if you can spot the bottlenecks, if you think they exist. You may not be able to do anything about them, but at least you will know where the buck has been stopped.

Is Management Thoughtful or Ruled by Crises?

It might surprise you, but even some of the largest companies are run by lurching from one crisis to another. This doesn't necessarily mean that you might not be comfortable working for them. But it does mean that if you are uncomfortable with this style, your office will come with a preinstalled panic button.

Here is where you should carefully differentiate between the overall corporate culture and the subcultures that dominate in the department in which you work or might work. Again, if you are comfortable with this style, go for it, but don't delude yourself into thinking that you might be able to change things. Once a subculture takes hold and functions well, there's very little you or anyone else can do or say to change things.

Finally, beware if you are being hired with the hidden agenda that your job will include turning a crises-managed department into a happy and smooth-running one. You might pull it off, but unless you have been told specifically that this is part of your assignment, avoid making the commitment.

The Least You Need to Know

- Never let your personal needs be pushed aside.

- What you don't want from a job may be even more important than what you want from it.

- Accepting the corporate subculture is as important as accepting the overall corporate culture.

- Outsiders can sometimes tell you more about the company than insiders.

- You can usually adjust to difficult people, but it's seldom possible to adjust to bad management policies.

Chapter 25

Career Planning Is a Family Affair

In This Chapter

- Those near and dear to you will be concerned and helpful in your career planning, but …

- Understand when family members are trying to have too much control over your career planning

- How to talk with your life partner about plans that may affect the relationship

- What to do if your planning comes a-cropper

- Making the most of the dual-career family

It's hard to imagine that there hasn't been more research on this subject until quite recently. After all, how many people have gone into the family business hating it? How many took courses to please a parent, even if there was only a hint or a suggestion made? This subject has been more of a sub-set of research than a subject of prime interest, but some serious research has been done recently.

I use the term *family* here to indicate those people who are or have been close enough to you to have had an effect on your career plans. This would include those we traditionally define as family, but it can also include a stepfamily, a husband, a wife, a partner, or anyone close enough for you to personally consider when you think about your career planning.

If families have so much influence on family members, it's safe to assume that some of that influence is felt in matters of career planning. The more rigid the family rules and traditions, the more influence the family usually has on its member's career decisions. Conversely, those who tend to exert little influence over others in a family can often point to relatives, whether successful or not, who have gone off in diverse directions. The amount and quality of the influence is usually based on such things as national origin, religion, social status, and all the other things that make us who we are.

Families in Flux

Not only is our concept of what makes up a family changing, but the concept of a career is changing. You may think of a career now as you did just a few years ago, but look carefully and you will see that work has become much more project-driven than it ever was. The stigma that used to be attached to those who moved quickly from job to job—job-hopper—is no longer used as a pejorative. However, planning is just as important today as it was when we had a more traditional picture of our life's work. The major difference, however, is that our planning now includes career shifts as well as job shifts. Accountants become architects. Engineers become editors. Some see this as threatening; others see it as an opportunity to be more than we ever thought possible.

The shifts in family structure have been just as dramatic. The two-career family is the norm today, not just because of economic needs, but because of everyone's need for personal fulfillment. Single adults are raising children, and gender relationships are no longer defined by the term *husband and wife*. All this means that career planning is more necessary and more complex than ever.

You really have two issues to consider when your career planning involves those close to you. The first is the influence you will, as a career-planning person, have on your family. The second is the influence your family will have on your planning and ultimate career decisions. Make sure you understand and address both.

What does your family really know about your interests? You have to decide just how much your family knows about the choices you are facing and how much they can actually be helpful. Everyone wants their daughter or son to be a doctor, but is it in the cards? Do *you* want to be a doctor? Your family's fantasies should not be the basis for your lifetime career planning. Depending on the family, this decision can send you in one direction and your family in another. I hope not. But in most cases like this that I have seen, the family comes back together later on.

Right Move _____

Family members mean well when they try to help, but it can often be seen as inter-ference. You can usually turn their objections into support by asking them to research the topics in contention and then discussing the findings openly. Most family objec-tions to career moves are made out of fear that you might be making a mistake. Show them the upside and the downside and convince them that the choice is worth it.

If your family sees your career plans differently than you do, try to get them to listen to what you are saying before they raise objections. Also, it helps if you can work them through a more realistic definition of success than what they may have in mind. This is the point where most families disagree about career planning. It boils down to get-ting them to be less judgmental and more accommodating to your ideas and goals.

Keep Your Family in the Loop

Whether you are single and living thousands of miles from Mom and Dad or have a family of your own that you go home to every night, your career plans and activities are of direct and immediate interest to your family. Whatever you do will have some effect on them. Don't wait for them to call and ask, "How are things going?" Even if nothing is happening, stay in touch. Even a cheerful e-mail, even if you say nothing about your career activities, will be wel-comed. Don't give the family nudge the opportunity to say, "So, how come we never hear from you?"

Your family's support to you is just as important. Family members may help directly by sending resumes, making con-tacts, and typing letters and e-mails, or they may be just passively involved. Either way, you need them, too. Even if it's just some occasional encouragement, it all helps.

Right Move _____

Change does mean stress, even when it's all of the thumbs-up variety. It's stress-ful for you and it's stressful for those closest to you. One way to reduce your own stress is by reducing the stress on your fam-ily. An occasional by-the-way kind of comment, even when there is no substantive news, goes a long way to help.

Most of the older members of your family probably aren't up to speed on the ways of the working world, even if they are still working. Their advice, whether asked for or freely offered, should be acknowledged gratefully and with as little comment as possible. Unless a particular family member is in a position to be of very real help, the well-wishers and family cheerleaders can sometimes bog you down. But don't tick them off! They are on your side and they do want you to succeed, even if they think you should have been a doctor rather than a street musician.

Most of all, avoid dumping surprises on your family. Even if you have news you know they will not be expecting, don't drop it on them all at once. This goes for good news as well as bad. A coaching client of mine reported recently that she had not kept her family as well informed as she should have with her career plans. Then she landed a job that was definitely a big step up. When she called her family to tell them the good news, her father's first response was, "Wow! Are you sure you can handle it?" That's a whack on the side of the head for anyone. She admitted to me that she had been lax in communicating with them, and had she been more forthcoming with news, the response would have been far more positive.

How To Talk to Your Kids About a Career Move

Another client told me that he had even involved his kids in his career planning. He knew that he wanted to make a move and would do so when the he discovered the right opportunity. He said that his kids had overheard him and his wife discussing the plans and this had created some apprehension in them. So he and his wife decided to make it a family affair, like planning a vacation. The kids were in their early teens, so they had an idea of what was going on and why. The big surprise, he explained, was the enthusiasm with which they took part. He said that many of their suggestions and research was really very helpful.

Career News

Recent research has shown that involving kids in family decisions can be beneficial for everyone. In the past, kids were sheltered from "bad" news. The trauma on them when things went wrong was far greater that it was when they were made aware of what was happening. Even when events are positive, kids get scared. Of course, some kids require more gentle involvement than others. If you go this route, test the waters in small steps and see how they respond.

It's best to involve the kids only when your plans are on pretty firm ground. Taking them through the ups and downs of euphoria and dejection can be a big strain on them. Most kids, even those close to maturity, don't react too well to events that have even a minor impact on their lives.

Answer their questions honestly and forthrightly. If you have to give them some bad news, prepare them for it; don't hit them with it all at once. Above all, listen carefully to their comments, concerns, and fears. It goes without saying that you should do everything you can to avoid upsetting them. When you know what concerns them most, you are in a much better position to help them work through any change.

Kids sometimes have difficulty asking questions, especially those that might be emotionally charged. Make sure you fully understand what they are asking before you attempt an answer. Paraphrasing their questions can help you spot a problem, if one exists.

It's best not to avoid answering a child's question. If it's something you would like to think about before answering, respond with something like, "Let's talk about this after we watch TV."

You might also want to double check that the answer you give a child is fully understood. Simply saying, "Does that answer your question?" can usually spot a disconnect.

Questions Your Family Will Ask

Career and job changes evoke all sorts of emotions. As emotional as they may be on you, the career planning or changing person, they can play an even bigger part on the lives of the adults with whom you are close. I've just discussed some of the major issues when children are involved. Adults have the same responses, except that life has already made its mark on them and their responses may either be tempered by experience or loaded with even greater anxiety. Remember, you are probably pretty anxious about all this yourself. It's tough to be the tower of strength when those close to you need support and you could use a little support yourself. Career and job change ranks up there with some of the most frightening of human events. If you have serious concerns, don't hesitate to seek professional advice. It's nothing to be ashamed of.

From my years in the field, I have identified the questions your family are most likely to ask as you plan or initiate your job or career change. I don't have scripts or pat answers for you, but I do have a few suggestions that can help you handle them comfortably.

How Will This Affect Our Home Life?

Depending on how dramatic the change may be, the effect could be profound or go almost without incident. The best way to deal with it is to prepare a few answers in advance. Be honest, but avoid being dramatic, whether the changes are going to be positive or negative. I usually suggest that the person have some examples of what to expect, rather than to talk in abstract terms.

For example, if the change involves a move, gather all the material you can about the place to which you will be moving. Do some research on things that are of specific interest to each member of your family. Brochures on the schools for the kids, entertainment material for the adults. You know what you and your family enjoy; get everything you can on what exists where you might move. You want to do your best to address elements your family might feel disruptive. Have the information at your fingertips and do everything you can to put a happy face on it.

What About Finances?

The kids probably won't be concerned about this, unless they are already on big allowances. However, the adults in your life will probably have real and serious questions to ask. Remember, it's not uncommon to take a job for less money when you know it will lead to faster promotion and eventually more money. Explaining this takes more than just a little hand-holding. Have facts and figures at your fingertips. Better yet, have the answers in black and white on paper.

Anything at all you can bring to the table when this question is asked will help. One client actually invited his accountant to join him and his wife when they discussed a career move that involved a shift from salaried to commission compensation.

Is This Really the Right Move?

This is the big one! You better be confident if the move is a big one and a lot is at stake. Even when little is involved, those close to you want to know—for sure—that you know what you are doing. No matter how eloquent you may be, don't even think about answering this question without some handouts. Do your homework. If you and your significant other are math-inclined, do some confidence level equations, even if they are just meant to lighten the mood.

This is one question you must answer yourself. It's your confidence they want to know about. No amount of facts and figures will help you here. However, be careful not to oversell your confidence. Salespeople in training are told to beat a hasty retreat as soon as they have the order in hand. The same advice applies here, too. Any sign that you are trying to oversell your confidence will sink your case.

What If the Plan Doesn't Work Out?

Always have a back-up plan ready. Not just to comfort those who might need comforting, but to keep your career in motion. However, don't make the mistake of presenting this as any sort of an alternative. An alternative of the same magnitude as the position you are considering opens the decision for further discussion. You don't want that. Even if your back-up plan has fits that description, pitch it as an escape hatch only. You have made up your mind, and if anyone wants to revisit the decision process, your plans will grind to a halt.

Right Move

If you do the kind of work that can be done freelance, such as consulting and writing, try to establish some contacts for regular work well prior to your planned career shift or job change. If the new job doesn't work out, you will have a cushion to carry you over until you can land the next spot. It's surprising how much work is being done on that basis now, even in fields long thought of as being office-bound.

Unless you left your job involuntarily, you might be able to get your old job back. However practical that can be, it's a humiliating experience. If you had worked for a conglomerate with many branches and other companies on its roster, you might think about finding a spot where you wouldn't have to face the music. It's less of an embarrassment to do this today than it was back when people seldom moved from job to job. Don't rule it out.

Will We Need to Relocate?

Relocation is always a possibility. If you get a job with a multi-location company and the job is at a distant location, the company may pick up all or at least some of the moving expenses. The higher you are on the corporate ladder, the more willing most companies are to share larger and larger portions of relocation expenses. The major issue in the relocation issue will probably be your family.

Your employer may be able to help you and your family adjust to a new environment. If this help isn't available, go to the Internet and check out the area. Even the smallest towns have websites that list groups and associations that might help you and your family adjust. Even the smallest towns usually have something like a newcomers club, often sponsored by the local real estate association. If you are unfortunate enough to be moving to a town that has little available to help newcomers, check the public library and what groups and activities it sponsors. You may not be seriously interested in being part of a group that addresses local history, but many people have told me that joining such a group got them up to speed on their new location faster than they might have with any other group.

Church groups, fraternal organizations, and even university alumni associations can provide opportunities to fit in quickly. A coaching client of mine said that she made more friends quickly by going to local city council meetings. She said that the people who usually attend these meetings are seriously interested in the town. They are usually impressed when newcomers are sufficiently interested in their town to go meetings which can, at times, be terribly boring.

The Dual-Career Family

Today, it's more common than not for both partners in a domestic relationship to work. You might think that the major issue centers around whose career is jettisoned if a there's a need for one to stay home. You'd be wrong. The major issues career counselors report are those that involve the adjustments each has to make to accommodate concurrent careers.

Whether you are currently in a dual-career relationship, or are contemplating one, the issues you need to address are pretty much the same. If, however, you are in the planning stages, you and your partner will benefit from the lessons you might have had to learn the hard way—by experience. Either way, be aware that this is a situation that requires constant attention and can often be more demanding that one in which only one partner works.

These are the major issues you and your partner will have to address.

Define Personal and Career Very Carefully

It's one thing to read about all those glamorous dual-career families in the tabs and popular magazines. But who stays home and takes care of the kids when the other is away on business, or out on sick leave? Do either of you see your career as more important than that of the other? Who takes out the garbage?

All the issues, large and small, should be open for discussion. Neither of you should insist that you have an automatic right to or exemption from something that might be wanted or needed by the other. Hundreds of books have been written on working issues of domestic partnerships, and it's a perennial favorite of newspaper columnists all over. There are no magic answers. Yet, all who write on the subject ultimately boil their advice down to suggesting calm and sensible negotiation, up front and before any serious issues threaten the relationship. I'll stick with that.

Is One Career More Important Than Another?

This is a tough question for most dual-career couples. Even though they may agree that one may bring in more money than the other, or one might be more prestigious than the other, when the lid is finally pried off, the issue and the discussions (arguments?) get very personal. This is a game with no rules other than play (fight?) fairly. More often than not, when it becomes really necessary for one person to relinquish a career, it is the one who either brings in less money or has less future career potential than the other.

Needless to say, discussions that lead to this point get very personal. As long as there is no hitting below the belt, problems can get solved. The aftermath is sometimes as difficult to handle as the hostilities these situations create. If you can agree ahead of time not to act stupidly after the resolution, things should go pretty well. However, in case you haven't noticed, life isn't perfect. People harbor grudges and resentment. But doesn't this happen in all other relationships? Yep! No further comment!

What About Career Sharing?

This may seem like the ideal situation. However, it's usually based on what is happening today. Suppose your partner gets promoted and has to move to another location. It's not uncommon for people to have commuter relationships, even at great distances. However, this is not easy for either partner.

I could go on and on, touching on all the different permutations and combinations that are possible when two people plan to or already have careers along with a life together. Some work out very well, others don't. But then, more than half of all conventional marriages end in divorce, and most of those people have probably never thought of or been in a dual-career situation. Perhaps the best advice I can give you is to do it with your eyes wide open and with full and complete respect for your partner's concerns. This applies to both of you!

The Least You Need to Know

- How you plan your career can be influenced by members of your family, just as you can influence your family by the choices you make. Think of both sides of the issue.

- Everyone in your family will have career suggestions for you; listen, try to appreciate and understand, but make your own decisions.

- Keep those in your immediate family in the planning loop and prepare them for any changes you might consider before announcing any cut-in-stone decisions.

- Most family issues center on finances and work location. Give then high priority in your career planning.

- Dual-career families and domestic partnerships are on the rise. Regardless of your and your partner's status on the job, at home you must be equal partners.

Chapter 26

Keeping Your Eye on the Ball

In This Chapter

◆ How to keep your career plan on course with one or two simple reviews a year

◆ Three steps that will assure your career goals adjust to changing employment demand

◆ How to spot career opportunities others are sure to miss

◆ How to create your own personal career "brand"

◆ How simple personal reflection can reveal hidden talents and abilities

As I've been saying all along, career planning is something you do until the day you retire. You might even continue after you retire, whether you want to or not. Conventional wisdom has it that an annual check-up is about all you need to keep your plan on course. I have a little trouble with that notion. Given the changes we have seen in the way companies and the people who work for them now interact, it's my view that an annual check-up might not be enough.

I have two reasons for thinking this way. The first, and most obvious, is the increasing frequency of major shifts in the workplace that are initiated by employers and sometimes kicked off by forces out of your (or anyone's)

control. And the other is that a shorter check-up interval gives you a clearer picture of your own world of work and some of the opportunities you might never encounter if you limit yourself to an annual review. It's like tuning a radio; turn the dial too fast and you will miss some of the weaker signals. And in many cases it's these weak signals that you should listen to.

Since the social contract between employers and employees has changed considerably, there is far less obligation to stick it out when you see an opportunity to advance your career somewhere else. Of course, this doesn't absolve you from doing the best you can for your current employer and from doing whatever you can to be of assistance to the company if you see an opportunity elsewhere that should not be overlooked. Fair is fair. Never forget that.

How often, then, should you take stock of your career? Under most circumstances, I'd say that it makes sense to do a review every six months. If you plan your review, as I outline in this chapter, it should probably take only a few hours each time you do it. When the average American spends more than 30 hours a week plopped in front of the TV set, 3 or 4 hours every 6 months is a walk in the park.

I believe there are three elements to career monitoring. The first is the establishment of a system of networks and personal connections. The second is a formal evaluation you will do once or twice a year. And the third is a list of suggestions you can follow as often as necessary and can become part of your regular routine without stealing any TV time at all. Let's look at networking first.

Networks Are Lifelines

Networks are nothing new. People stayed in touch with each other by smoke signals, letters, and telephone before there ever was an Internet. The Internet did much more than formalize these interconnections; it moved them from passive to real-time activities. This of course, is in keeping up with the speed at which everything else moves in business and life in general today. But of course, nothing beats the sound of a friend's voice on the telephone once in a while.

The Internet, however, lets you keep multiple contacts going. Round tables, blogs, bulletin boards, whatever you want to call them, allow instant contact and multiple comment and response. The Internet can be and is used in many surprising and practical ways, but there are three ways to use it most effectively to monitor your career progress.

Staying in Touch with Your Support System

Support is available from everywhere. Just be sure that the offered support is what you want and what can help you move your career ahead. I occasionally log onto support blogs in fields that interest me and am often impressed with the quality of support and advice I see. But I'm sometimes concerned that people might follow advice that may be well meaning but can be downright harmful. Since anyone can say anything on a blog and anonymity is usually guaranteed, the experience and authority of bloggers can seldom be verified. Just because something is in print doesn't make it right or even true.

Whether you get your support from an impersonal Internet connection or from trusted friends and associates, you must realize that this is a reciprocal relationship. Others will look to you for support and help, and you should always give it, but be honest if you feel you are on shaky ground when offering some advice. It's appealing to think that someone else considers you an authority on a subject that you know is not your strong suit.

Many personal networks simply evolve naturally. Friends from school stay in touch. Workers who move on stay in touch. And, of course, family members stay in touch. This kind of networking really doesn't require a formal website. In fact, if personal issues are involved, you are much better off just setting up an informal network in which each member lists the e-mail addresses of the others in a group file that is part of every e-mail provider's program. It's very much like the old circular letters that people used via-snail mail.

Career Alert

If you contact others while at work about subjects that you would prefer no one else see, never use your company computer. I have never heard of any intentional snooping, although I'm told that it does happen. However, print out a potentially embarrassing message, and chuck it in your company wastebasket and who knows who might see it. Probably the safest way to communicate at work, if you have the opportunity, is to bring your WiFi-enabled laptop to the office. You can check into your personal stuff at break and lunch time and feel perfectly safe.

Staying in touch with people is very much part of career monitoring. You can sometimes judge your progress by the progress made or not made by others. Members of these informal networks, whether they use the Internet or any other means, usually share tips and leads as well as comments on events in the field in which all members have an interest.

Locating Career Opportunities Ahead of the Pack

In case you wondered why the traditional newspaper classifieds are so much smaller than they were a few years ago, this is mainly the result of Internet networking and career sites. Probably even more effective has been the informal grapevine that includes the Internet as well as all the new and older ways of staying in touch. As employment became more project-oriented than career-oriented, most people felt less concern about talking with others about their careers and about opportunities that might benefit friends. This goes for jobs close to the corporate top as well as all others.

Spotting Coming Trends

The real value of all this interconnectivity is that it can give you heads-up information you can use to evaluate your present position and to anticipate events that you can take advantage of before anyone else spots them. Apart from the sites that are directly career relevant, there is more business-related news and information than ever. Good career plans are based on reviewing current trends against past history and making educated guesses as to what might happen that could impact your career. Reviewing trends and news relative to your career plan is the best way to anticipate problems as well as opportunities.

Your Personal Career Check-Up

Still got that shoebox? Some of the stuff I suggested you throw into it will be quite helpful as you do your annual or semiannual career check up. Those items included notes you made to yourself about all aspects of your career as it unfolds and should include performance reviews, interoffice memos that might be relevant, and whatever else you feel is significant. How you choose to assemble the information is up to you, but the one bit of advice I can offer is to throw out anything that you thought might be valuable when you included it, but is now useless. Every garden grows better without weeds, including your career garden.

Cover the following topics and you will be able to see if you are on or off track, and where your career is heading. These are the topics that are most important to consider when you review your career plan. Remember that your career plan is not a road map that you have to follow slavishly. It's a plan based on strategies to get you where you would like to be. Don't stick to it if your review shows you're off track. Of course, keep changing this and that and you might as well not have a plan, but when your review results suggest better directions and you can confirm that this is a good move, go for it. Life and business are full of unexpected surprises. You may have to avoid some, and you may have to embrace others. Be flexible!

Your Current Position

Where are you relative to the last time you did a check-up? Have you been promoted, have new responsibilities been added to your job description, and where do you stand relative to others in your department? Have there been any changes in your compensation package? What about your reporting relationships? Do you have a new boss?

Note and evaluate these and any other questions that may be relevant to your personal situation. Before you decide whether the changes are positive or negative for you, look at everything. All the elements of your present position hang together in some way, do don't just look at the outstanding elements, whether positive or negative, to make decisions. See what is in sync with your career plan and what may not be. Don't automatically assume that any deviation from your plan requires either that you immediately change your plan *or* your situation. Go through the entire evaluation and then you will be on much safer ground to make decisions.

Your Performance and Achievements

What have you done that makes you more valuable to the company? What have you failed to do that might be a black mark on your record? Did you initiate any changes of note? What have you done beyond what is ordinarily expected of you by your job description?

At this point, it's important to see how you shape up relative to the standards you have set for yourself as well how you measure up to the standards expected by your employer. Note your comfort level with your job. If you are still struggling to master it, this is a sign that you have some running to do. If it's becoming boring, this is a sign that you need a greater challenge, more responsibility, or at least some room to grow.

Your Skills and Other Personal Qualifications

What have you learned on the job? What still remains for you to learn and master? If your job description has changed, is there anything new to learn and master?

Just as important as being up to par with the requirements for your present job is a realistic understanding of what you need to learn or master to move on and up in your career. This is often a good time to see what kind of aid and support your company might offer for advanced education and training. Even if nothing exists, this kind of curiosity sends good vibes to those who have some say in your work life.

Your Work Environment

Have you been moved to a better office, or banished to the thirteenth floor? Has your company moved from previously posh offices to the low rent district? Has the company stopped having the windows washed and the floors swept, or have they painted and redecorated everything?

Any sudden changes in the worksite are often a sign that something is in the wind. A fresh coat of paint and some new furniture sends reassuring signs while unemptied wastebaskets and dirty windows send another. However, before you attach any serious meaning to any of these, make sure you know the reasons behind the activities.

Your Own Personal Needs

Have your needs changed since you took your present job? Are new demands being made of you outside of work since you last reviewed your career plan? Are current economic conditions and other things out of your control having an impact on your personal and economic life?

You may love your job, but your life off the job may be making demands that you hadn't anticipated. Family needs frequently collide when the dream job turns out to be a nightmare. Even if you have no family ties, your personal life can come into conflict with your work life. If you have any personal or family issues, discuss them with someone competent enough to give you good advice before you do anything dramatic. Your personal life is paramount. It's often easier and more practical to make changes in your work life than in your personal life. Just make sure you have your priorities straight and are in control of your emotions before you make any major moves.

Keeping Your Plan on Course

Here are some thoughts on what you can do between reviews. This is not a checklist of things you must do; pick and choose what you feel are more important to you. Some of the suggestions will help keep you on track. Some take more time than others. Some may even seem silly, at least in terms of your current situation. But read them all and give each serious consideration.

Put Some Money Aside

Apart from any regular saving or investment program, it's a good idea to have a nest egg. You can use it to tide you over during an unexpected layoff. You can use it to pay for education and training you might need to move up in your career. I'd even suggest that you open a separate bank account and put in a little money on a regular basis. We both know that unless you do this, when the need arises and you open your regular bankbook, the money won't be there. Right?

Admit Your Goofs

A large part of career planning is based on coming to terms with yourself. Whether you do a formal exploration or you stumble onto who you are along the way, a key issue is fitting into your own skin. When you can't admit your mistakes, you will never be comfortable with yourself, the chances are that you will make the same errors over and over again. That's not the best way to build a career or a comfortable life. You will know you are making progress when you feel comfortable talking with friends about the things you have botched.

Keep a list of your goofs *and* your accomplishments. Don't complicate it with a lot of details. State in clear and unambiguous terms what you did that got thumbs up and what you did that you shouldn't have done. The idea is to keep track of your efforts to do more of what worked and less of what didn't. This is not the place to dig into details, much less your subconscious. You just want to make sure that you learn from your mistakes as well as from the things you do right. The lists should be a major part of your regular review.

Don't Get Upset Over Insensitive Comments

Everyone makes too much of what others may say to or about them. Unless you have psychological training and have had these people on the couch, you will never know what makes them do things, and in most cases it really doesn't matter. You don't have to be loved or even liked by everyone. If, however, you can't shed these emotions easily, pay attention to what people do, not what they say. The old kids' taunt of sticks and stones has more than a grain of truth. Just keep an eye out for what your malcontented co-workers do that may affect you and you will be okay. This subject may seem tangential to your career monitoring, but you do have to pay attention to those around you.

On the flip side, don't forget to offer a "well-done" to co-workers when they deserve it. Don't let this become a mutual admiration society, but when credit is due, make sure that the person who deserves it gets it—and make sure that they know that you care about them. Your network is built person by person and when people trust and support each other, the network grows.

Get a Mentor

Everyone needs someone to turn to from time, whether for career advice or just a nonjudgmental ear on things in general. I use the term *mentor* in a loose way here. Find someone you trust, someone who shares your values and can offer wise counsel when needed, and who is farther along on the career trail than you. Try to find someone who might have been through the steps you are going through who can spot the pitfalls and who can tell you when you are taking positive steps. Feedback is important in career planning and management. If possible, ask this person to share your annual or semiannual reviews. Be sure to tell this person that you welcome all comments, whether asked for or not. It's not a good idea to have more than one person in this role. It is a very personal relationship and having more than one person supplying feed back is far too complicating. Trust is an issue here and asking two for help is saying to both that you are not fully sure that either can do the job.

Update Your Resumé

Your resumé should be up-to-date at all times, and it's important to update it whenever you have something to add or remove. You never know when a friend is going to call and tell you to send a resumé immediately to a company that has an immediate opening that you would kill for. If you have to take a day or two to get it together, it may be too late. The word processor has made this one of the easiest tasks you need to do.

Keep a duplicate file of your resumé on another computer or a disc, or wherever you store other important documents. One of my coaching clients keeps a copy of her resumé in one of those little data-storage sticks she keeps on her key chain. She travels a lot for business and she says that you never know when an opportunity will pop up and you are thousands of miles from the home computer. All you need is someone else's machine and a printer and you're in business.

Ask What You Are Doing and Why

A little introspection never hurts; a lot, however, isn't all that good for you. Don't try to figure out the meaning of life, but do try something like, "Do I really enjoy doing what I am doing?" Or, "What would I do if I weren't doing this?"

Questions like this are answerable without the angst that often accompanies the deeper stuff. I wouldn't suggest trying to formalize this exercise with notes and lists. It will take you down an interesting path, but it will probably take time away from the real world effects that you need to address here and now.

Brand and Promote Yourself

Apart from doing the job you have been hired to do, try to create an image of yourself that is recognizable, but not bodacious. Just doing a great job may not be enough unless your accomplishments can be recognized as something you did or had a hand in. The world hates a blowhard, but the world admires people who achieve but are not overbearing about it. It's a narrow path to walk, but it can be done.

The main reason for branding yourself is to ensure that you stand out from the others around you. All of your work colleagues may be star performers, too. This means that you need to establish yourself in ways that get you immediately recognized. Never, never go the clown route. And being overbearing and pompous always sends the wrong messages. Branding is not self-promotion. You simply want to position yourself in the minds of those who make the decisions you count on when it comes time for raises and promotions.

Your personal brand is the image you want others to have of you. Unless you establish that image yourself, it could be established for you in ways you won't appreciate. It's the old story, do great things, but mess up once and that's what you will be remembered for. Perhaps the easiest brand to get for yourself, and the one that seems to count most at promotion time, is that of being the Go-to Guy or Gal. You get this by taking on the projects others avoid and breaking your back to do a spectacular and visible job of it.

Your image, or brand, requires regular attention and special attention when you do your semiannual or annual career plan review. Check on the relationships you have established as the Go-to Guy. Do they need tending? Check on others with whom you should have the reputation. What needs to be done to make the brand click with them. Remember, don't be obnoxious or obsequious. Be yourself, be the Go-to Guy!

Keep Up Your Information Sources

Your career is built in the context of your job, and most of your benchmarks will be based on the strength and quality of your information sources. People come and people go in any work situation. If one of your key sources leaves, you will probably have a hole in your information supply line. It's not a good move to ask the person who replaces your source to pick up where the other left off, unless you know the person very well and trust him or her completely. In any case, it's usually best to establish other sources.

Check on the quality of the information you have been getting. Is it ahead of the curve, or have you been getting stale news? Check to see if there might be other sources to turn to that might be more productive. This applies to sources you have within the company as well as those on the outside you can turn to. Chief among your outside sources will be a headhunter, if you work at a level headhunters serve. If your headhunter hasn't been in touch for awhile, give him or her a call to see what's happening.

Interview Your Boss

Most managers aren't nitpickers. That is, they will come down hard when something really bad happens, but they are usually willing to let the little things go by. The little things, however, can add up in your boss's mind and become real problems for you. I usually urge my coaching clients to schedule at least one informal review session a year with their boss. This is not to be the formal company review; it's to be a person-to-person chat about how things are going in general.

Ask specific questions about things you know you have slipped up on but haven't been mentioned by your boss. Just acknowledging that you are aware of the problems tells your boss that you are conscientious and working at improving. It also takes a load off his or her mind if there have been any niggling thoughts about your performance. Above all, don't take a defensive attitude, and take whatever is told you seriously. And, of course, report on your progress the next time you have your informal chat.

Review Your Job Requirements

Compare the work you were hired to do with the work you are doing today. If you've been with the company for more than a few years, the chances are the differences will be very noticeable. This is an excellent way to get a feel for the progress you have made and the direction you may be going with the company. If you are still doing the job you were hired for, try to determine how your level of responsibility might have changed, even though you might still be doing the same job.

You may be happy doing the same job for as long as you are with the company, or you may want to move up. Moving up often involves a major shift, especially if you have reached the top of some project-defined employment. Being chief accountant might be as far as you can go in your project-based career climb within the company. Becoming the chief financial officer would be a big step that would ordinarily require either greater management experience or more education in the management arts and sciences. These are key issues for you as you do your regular review.

Career Alert

It's often difficult to move from project-oriented work into management within a company that has already come to accept you as a successful player. More progressive employers often send their best project-oriented employees to school for advanced degrees in management subjects to facilitate the jump to senior management. If you are stymied by this, it's often possible to convince another company that you are ready for that jump to VP-level management from the title of senior manager or department head to a VP level job. In fact, that's pretty much how the title of assistant VP came into being many years—as a stepping stone.

Write a New Job Description for Yourself

If your job has changed very much, rewrite your job description to make it more descriptive of the work you are now doing. Include a projection of where you think the job might be headed and the responsibilities that might be required for the redefined job. Explain why you are capable of handling these responsibilities, or why you feel the company should finance the education you will need as the job evolves.

Be careful not to let this turn into a brag-and-boast piece, because I am suggesting that you give it to your boss, whether he or she is new on the job or is an old-timer.

Make Sure a New Boss Knows All About You

If you have a new boss since your last review, it's a good idea to provide him or her with your current resumé. Don't depend on the new boss to go to the files and find out about all the people who report to him or her. And even if that new boss was that ambitious and conscientious, your resumé is probably out of date. It's not out of order to include with that resumé a brief list and description of your accomplishments on the job. Don't brag and boast, just list them in plain and unambiguous language.

A Perspective

An awful lot of what's written today on the subject of careers draws on popular vernacular and imagery. As much fun as it may be to think of yourself as some sort of warrior on a career-enhancing mission, this often appears to be more form than substance to those who might promote you. We all know that the climb to the top has to involve some competition with others who are vying for the same spot. The higher you get in management, the less likely you are to impress those who promote and award VP titles that you are some kind of superhero. Nothing wrong with fantasizing about vanquishing the competition for the VP job, but keep it to yourself.

The higher you get, the more concerned those above you will be about what you can and can't do and how you will fit in with the management team. The best way you can get a handle on what might be the appropriate behavior in your particular company is just to watch and listen to those who now hold the jobs that you aspire to. And don't give me the sellout stuff. If you want the job, be the person most likely to get it.

The Least You Need to Know

- The job you were hired for will always be in a state of change.

- Doing an annual or semiannual career review shouldn't take more than a few hours.

- Your own personal needs and the needs of your family are paramount, but a well-planned career should make it easy to satisfy them.

- It's not bragging to make sure the boss knows what you are doing that is worthy of recognition.

- If you don't have a career plan, you'll flounder. If you do have a career plan and don't follow it, you'd do worse than flounder.

Chapter 27

Overcoming the Obstacles in Your Path

In This Chapter

- How to deal with the age issues, whether you are young or old
- A recession shouldn't mean depression for you
- When talking to yourself is a good sign
- Dealing with those who derail your career plans
- Go back to school, no matter where you live

If there weren't obstacles to career planning and growth, you would only have to plan once. But there are obstacles. Some will be minor inconveniences; others will be important enough for you to make major changes in your plans. Some will be put in your path intentionally, others will arrive at random. Some will be real, others will be imaginary. A career plan, as I've been saying all along, is not a road map, it's a strategy for getting where you want to be. This chapter identifies the boulders and pebbles you will encounter and gives you life-tested strategies to overcome them.

How Old Are You?

Mention age in the context of employment and the first thing most people think of is age discrimination as it applies to older job applicants. Federal law protects people who are 40 years old or older from employment discrimination based on age. However, it only applies to companies with 20 or more employees. This includes state and locals governments.

Age is a real issue, whether you are in your 20s or 70s. Young people face implicit age discrimination when a prospective employer might assume they lack maturity. People middle-aged and older often feel the effects, too—for example, when a prospective employer faces the possibility of having to pay higher health insurance premiums than it would for a younger but less experienced worker. Take your pick, age can be an issue. There is no way around it unless you have real proof, so the best way to deal with it is to simply act your age and make sure that all your other qualities are just what the prospective employer needs. However, if you can prove age discrimination, report it and do all you can to see that the company that broke the law is prosecuted.

The law doesn't prevent employers from asking for a job applicant's age. However, asking for age can be seen as a deterrent to older potential employees and can be interpreted by courts as an intent to discriminate, so you will rarely encounter an application form on which you are asked for your age.

It's unlawful for an employer to deny employee benefits to workers because of age. However, in some circumstances when an employer can prove that reduced benefits based on age can be provided at the same cost to younger workers, the employer may prevail. This can be a tough case to prove, but don't let it deter you from checking it out if you feel you have a case.

Career News

The year 2007 saw 19,103 charges of age discrimination brought before the Equal Opportunities Employment Commission. The commission resolved 16,134 of these charges and recovered $66.8 million in benefits for those who brought the charges. The law does have real teeth!

It's also unlawful for employment advertising to include age-preference references, except in certain circumstances where age is a bona fide requirement. I have never come across any instances of where this has been done. However, I imagine if you are looking for models to appear in ads for clothing being promoted to an older audience, it would be legitimate to state specific age qualifications.

It is possible for an employer to petition the government for a specific waiver of the age discrimination laws and win if they can prove their case. If you find yourself being considered for employment by a company that claims to have gotten a specific waiver, be sure that you get a copy of the waiver and check it out with an attorney.

As a result of some pretty hefty settlements, age discrimination—at least overt discrimination—is much less of a problem than it has been in the past. However, where there's a law, there are plenty of people whose only goal is to figure out ways to subvert it. The law is on your side, but you have to prove your case!

Are You Currently Unemployed?

All career-planning advice used to come with the admonition not to quit your present job until you have landed your next. Generally speaking, this is good advice, but not necessarily for the same reasons it used to be. Until the era of lifetime employment with one company all but vanished, a person without a job, especially in mid-career, was considered damaged goods. It was thought that if you were without work, there must be a good reason and it was more than likely your own fault. Those who were unemployed often had serious identity issues.

Not so any more. Valued as well as marginal employees get the gate these days when the stockholders clamor for cost cuts and enhanced profits. Layoffs and plant closings are so common that it's rare to find anyone who would consider current unemployment as a reason to pass on making a job offer. What does exist, however, is the feeling you might have about yourself if you were one of those chosen to walk the plank. In short, your self-image is bruised.

The only emotion worth attending to when you find yourself without work for reasons other than personal is that which should drive you to look for a better job. Any feelings of self-recrimination are only going to slow you down.

The truth is that sometimes a layoff could be the best thing to happen to you. Changing jobs under the best of circumstances is stressful. You have to make new friends, you have to prove yourself, and you usually need at least five or six months to know whether or not things are going to work out. For these and other reasons, many people avoid taking the step voluntarily, even when offered something better out of the blue.

So when the plug is pulled, your employer may be doing you a favor. It may not seem that way at the time, but if you are like many people I know, you will look back on the event as the kick in the pants you needed to get you off dead center. But when it happens, it hurts a lot.

Economic Downturns

As I write this chapter, the government is still waffling about whether we are really in a recession or not. Yet, despite this lack of a formal declaration, each month shows negative numbers in terms of jobs created and big numbers in terms of layoffs. The Fed can't decide whether to bail out the industries that played a major role in the debacle, and home foreclosures are at an all-time high. People who were making six-figure incomes are selling the family jewels, and people who were just getting by are no longer getting by. It's painful for an awful lot of people, and the blame game is being played wherever it will play well.

To the person who is no longer working because of conditions that bear no relation-ship to skills or job performance, this is a recession, but it's nothing new. I'm not excusing any unethical conduct that leads to or accompanies these situations, but you must remember that economic cycles have always been with us and always will be with us. They can be modulated so that the effects are less disruptive, but all the lessons learned are soon forgotten when the next bubble starts to take on air.

One of the best strategies to use when the economy goes sour and you are sidetracked for reasons out of your control is to assume a very proactive stance and to learn to accept rejection. Being passive when most around you are passive is not the way to go. You need to do what has to be done and do it better than anyone else. This often means rebranding yourself. Become the cost-conscious engineer, the budget-watching marketing manager, the turn-around accountant. Flexibility is always important in career planning and management, but it's especially important when the tide turns against you.

Even in the worst of downturns, people still have jobs. The work still has to be done. Recessions don't last forever and if you can manage to keep your job and have a hand in your employer's recovery, you should be in line for much better things later. Even if your boss has a short memory when payback time arrives, you have a record that should open some better doors.

"We Have Met the Enemy and He Is Us!"

This marvelous line was spoken by a cartoon character named Pogo. Drawn by Walt Kelly, the strip was very popular in the 1950s, and a poster with this line is still sold and posted in offices and cubicles all over the country. As with most well-remembered statements, it never fails to strike a nerve when it is quoted in the right situation. And as you must have guessed, it's just a more amusing way of saying that we are our own worst enemies. But just what does that mean, and how does it relate to your career planning and management? Briefly, it means that we often do more harm to ourselves than others do to us.

The harm we do is more passive than active. Only people with serious problems actually plan and do things they know will hurt themselves. However, the passive hurt we inflict on ourselves is mainly that we fail to act when we know that we should act. We see signs, we're pretty sure what they mean, but we cross our fingers and hope that things will be okay and that we won't have do anything about the problem. Some people fail to respond to signals, positive or negative, because they upset the way they have ordered their lives. Experience has probably reinforced these feelings when doing nothing resulted in no harm done, and possibly some good happening, all serendipitously. This all adds up to a reluctance to take charge of your life. Surprisingly, even many people who have done elaborate career planning fail to respond when it's called for.

If you find yourself behaving this way, you should set some quiet time aside and give serious thought to how you benefit from avoiding risk, what possible harm might come from the risks you might be exposed to, and what you have been missing all along by taking the path of least resistance. Remember that we talked about introspection earlier? Now is another time to put this skill to use. But do more than just the mental activity. Try to see whether you can come up with real answers. Suppose your reluctance to make a move resulted in your not getting a major promotion. Find out how much money and what kind of perks you left on the table when you took a hike. Then do all you can to determine whether you would have succeeded in the job you didn't take.

This is where this exercise gets scary for many people. It can help to involve a close and trusted friend or relative to help you see yourself more clearly. You will probably hear things that are personally unsettling if the person is honest and really wants to be helpful. Don't argue—just listen. Then discuss it. This is usually all it takes to open your eyes. It can be a big step to shift from neutral to overdrive, but remember that there are a few gears in between that can help to get you to speed without a jolt. But just in case you need a little more than this to get you going, here is a plan that works very well.

Visualize Yourself in the Job You Want

Since you already have a career plan and a good handle on the tactics you will use to achieve your goal, you probably have a pretty good idea of what it must be like to be doing what you aspire to do. So let yourself go. Visualize the good stuff as well as the bad. Remember, the career you aspire to will have its problems as well as its benefits.

> **Right Move**
>
> When you do this kind of visualization, you are free to fail and no one is going to stick it to you for goofing. This means that you can be a lot more imaginative in the solutions you come up with. Let yourself go. It's a really liberating experience and one that I'm sure you will continue when you face real problems.

Pick a few of the things you might have to face that are difficult or unpleasant. Then, work through how you would handle them. My guess is that you will see that solving the problems that intimidate you will appear a lot less threatening to you once you have solved a few in the job you envision.

Don't limit yourself to visualization of problem solving; visualize yourself as the capable person you need to be to achieve your goal. And don't think you're weird if you find yourself having an actual dialogue with yourself. Many people report that some of their most productive visualization sessions involve this kind of conversation. Just don't do it in public!

When People Make Life Difficult for You

We've all met unpleasant people and will continue to meet them, no matter how high we climb or how much responsibility we assume. They are the people who are either in your face with negative personal comments, or who say things behind your back. They are unsure of themselves and in order to feel better about themselves, they will try to put you down. It's tempting to feel sorry for people who need to do this, and it's just as tempting to engage them to defend your own self-esteem. However, there is a better way.

Those who put you down can become obstacles in your career path. You really have to determine the level of the threat in terms of your career, as well as to understand what it would take to counter the affront. In most cases, however, the best response is to simply acknowledge the comment with a simple shrug and a comment that doesn't invite further discussion. Never, never let this situation put you in a defensive posture. An I-really-don't-care response is not what they are looking for, and they usually don't know what to do when they see that they haven't provoked you.

On the other hand, the confrontational bully can be something else. Typically, this person makes his or her accusations in front of others. He or she is looking to provoke you and knows that any fumble on your part will be seen as an acknowledgement of the accusation. The confrontational bully has the advantage—temporarily.

You can defuse this situation by remaining calm, offering no defense, and replying something like, "That's interesting, tell me more about it." This is a reply to a taunt that is never expected. You are expected to stammer, try to gather your wits and offer a weak and unconvincing defense. By showing that you are not afraid of what has been said, and by even encouraging more comment, you let your opponent dig his own hole. Continue with content-free comments like, "What do you mean by that?" This is the verbal equivalent of the core of most martial arts; make use of your opponent's force as your own force.

The face-to-face and public confrontation, while often very unpleasant, is usually the best way to put an end to ongoing behind-the-scenes harassment. Any discussing with your tormentor without an audience will have little effect. You really need to have it out in public so that your tormentor is seen for what he or she really is. And the best way to do this is as I have just described. Keep cool. Respond only with factual comments and remain in control of the action. It works every time!

Choose Your Friends Carefully

You may have to work with someone who always sees the glass half full, but it's your choice to be around whoever you want otherwise. I sometimes feel that the super-booster types are as troublesome as those who always choose the gloomy path. However, if you have a choice, avoid the downers. You may feel you have an obligation to a downer who has become a good friend, and that's fine. But it's important that you at least have some people who are up, realistically well adjusted, and just plain fun to be around.

You don't have to be a joiner type to join a group made up of people who have common interests and are upbeat. And unless you live in some really rural location, there is bound to be at least one formal or informal group with which you can associate. Just to prove my point, I just used the Internet to locate groups interested in fishing, chess playing, and cooking in areas of the country that are thinly populated. I had no trouble locating groups, all within several miles of the rural spots I selected based on population size and distance from major metropolitan areas. So there goes your excuse. Get out there and mix it up. It does wonders for your outlook.

Dealing With Disabilities and Handicaps

It has become a lot easier for handicapped people to find work and progress in it than it was a few years ago. The enactment of the American With Disabilities Act has all but removed the most egregious forms of discrimination. If you are unfamiliar with the act, type www.ada.gov in your web browser and the text of the complete act will pop up on your screen.

Quite apart from the act, the Internet has made it possible for many people unable to get to a place of work easily to work from home. It's not only a boon for those with physical disabilities that prevent them from going to a job, it has also provided a source of work for many people whose only handicap is not living close enough to the work they like to do and which can be done at a distance over the Internet. The amount of information on this subject on the Internet is staggering, so start with the ADA site and follow the links. Help is there!

When You Need to Learn More

It's not that difficult to get a spot as a guest lecturer at most colleges and universities with minimum qualifications, but it's impossible to get tenure without a doctorate. Just try moving up to chief welder in a shipyard if the only thing you can do is braze light metals. Education is a key to advancement in almost every job today. And lack of an education certainly qualifies as an obstacle to your career.

When you have topped out because of a lack of skills or education, the only thing holding you back may be a course you could take without ever leaving your home. Again, the Internet to the rescue! We used to call them correspondence schools and the lessons and homework traveled back and forth between teachers and students by snail mail. There still is considerable learning taking place this way, but much more of it is now done via the Internet and it's called distance learning today.

Major and minor colleges and universities offer coursework via the Internet. There are literally thousands of commercial and other schools all over the world that offer distance learning programs. Literally, nothing should hold you back from getting the education you need. Depending on your income, there are also many sources of private and public money to support your learning. Check with your employer, friends, and fraternal, social, and professional groups for information on the courses and the money that might be available to pay for your schooling. Many unions have extensive education programs for members.

If you are lucky enough to live near any colleges and universities, they will probably all have some form of adult continuing education courses on campus. In fact, continuing adult education has become a major source of growth and income for some of the bigger and better colleges and universities. While researching this chapter, I went online and checked out the adult programs available in some of the major universities within about 100 miles of my home. Columbia, New York University, the University of Pennsylvania, and many smaller colleges and universities list extensive programs. In most cases, these courses have few, if any, prerequisites. You may not want to take an adult-ed class in nonparametric statistics unless you have had the intro material, but if you really wanted to do it, you could get in a class. These are not degree-awarding programs, but most provide certificates of successful completion, which is often all you need to get your career on track.

The Least You Need to Know

- Your age may actually be a benefit, not a handicap.

- Being unemployed is not a stigma.

- You can learn what you need to advance your career without leaving your home.

- Disabilities should not prevent you from pursuing the career you want.

- Economic downturns often lead to employment opportunities you may have never considered before.

28

Questions You Should Ask

This is a long chapter made up of questions you need to ask of others and of yourself. The subject matter resists formal organization, so I have skipped the usual list. Each question is followed by a detailed explanation of why the questions should be asked and how you can benefit from the answers.

Your career plan should point you in the direction that is best for you, and your job search should have helped you identify the employers you might like to work for or that might have actually made you an offer. Now what?

Whether you have an employment offer in hand or are evaluating opportunities you or your headhunter have turned up, you must know everything possible about the employers you are considering. A job is more than a good salary and a nice benefits package. It would be nice to know something about the person who will be your immediate boss, for example. Will your family find the location congenial? And why has such a good job been open for so long?

See what I mean? Along with the questions you should ask, I have included tips to help you get the answers and to dig behind the answers if you have any concerns. I urge you to read all, even though you may think they don't apply to you. Accepting a job offer is a lot like buying a car. Before you visit the show-rooms, you read everything you can about the cars that interest you. Then you visit the dealers and your adrenaline starts to flow. The dealer makes an offer you can't resist and you are about to sign the contract when you spot the rust proofing and undercoating charge—which, by the way, the salesman seems to have forgotten to mention ….

If you have questions—any questions—ask. If the answers don't satisfy you ask more questions. Career moves are major events in your life.

The Job Itself

What, exactly, are the tasks and responsibilities of the job?

You've probably either been told what the job is all about or even been given a printed description of the job. Job descriptions can be vague or they can be clear and under-standable. Don't let any vague questions remain unanswered.

You need to make sure that this is the right job for this stage of your career. Are you overqualified or not qualified enough? Is there any possibility that the job may take you in a different direction that you anticipate in your long-term career plan? Remember, you are looking for the perfect job and the employer is looking for the perfect employee. Is there enough room in the middle for both of you to be happy, productive, and successful?

Are you expected to accomplish any special assignments or goals that are not outlined in the job description?

Job descriptions, verbal and written, seldom include anything about ongoing projects that you will be expected to undertake. It's not uncommon to discover that the person who left the job has left a lot of unfinished work that you must pick up. Some of this work may be only tangentially related to what is described in the job description.

The more specific the goals and objectives, the better for you. If for example, you are being employed as a salesperson and were told that your goal is to increase sales by 20 percent, you better know what that 20 percent is based on. Just as important, make sure that any specific goals are stated in terms of the time in which they are expected to be achieved. Also see if you can get a handle on what failure to achieve the goal will mean. Are there second chances?

Are the job objectives reasonable?

Most job descriptions are reasonable, but what can be unreasonable is either the way they are to be accomplished or the time allotted for their accomplishment. If time is a factor, will you be compensated for any time spent beyond normal business hours? Below a certain job level, most jobs require that those putting in the time be paid at a rate higher than the base rate. Above a certain executive level, you are expected to "donate" the time needed to get the job done. Therefore, whether you are applying for a shop-level job or one in the executive suite, make sure that you have a very clear picture of what you are expected to do and the time it takes to get the work done.

The way the work is to be accomplished is another issue. Complex jobs usually involve assistants and assistance. Will that help be forthcoming? Will the help be temporary, based on a specific project, or will you have people assigned to you permanently? Will you share the assistants with others?

What about travel?

Travel can be an issue at any level. The two most important issues here are how much time will be required and how will it be compensated for. If your employer expects you to travel, pick the expenses yourself, and apply for reimbursement, be sure you know the payment cycle. You also want to make sure you know the limits involved. First class or coach? Can you go to a four-star hotel, or is Motel 6 the venue of choice? Is a company car available? What about entertainment—who can you entertain and how much can you spend? Company credit card? Get all the facts on paper if possible.

Corner office, or the thirteenth floor?

If there's ever an issue that arouses status-conscious executives, it's the size and location of the office. A few years back, there was a feeble attempt to do away with this morass by setting up "open offices." In essence, the open office was just a big hall in which everyone at every level worked together. It never caught on, mainly for two reasons. Status really is an important factor in people's desire to climb the ladder, and an open office kicked that idea in the pants. The other was that the open office, no matter how well designed, was noisy and impersonal. They just weren't as productive as expected by those who dreamed them up.

You really should have an opportunity to at least see the general environment in which you will work. I suggest asking to see it early on, at least before the job starts to sound too good to turn down and you then discover that you will be working in the office right above the punch press, where it's advisable not to keep coffee cups too close to the edge of the desk.

Are there opportunities for growth?

A look at the table of organization will give you an idea of where your job might lead in the future. However, this isn't enough to know. See if you can discover how many people, at least in your department, have moved up in the ranks. Try to determine the level at which the company begins to hire more from the outside than promote from within. This is especially important if you see the job in terms of long-range employment and personal growth.

Are there any educational opportunities available?

Typically, companies that prefer to promote from within will take a serious interest in training and educating employees. Although most companies that see education as a key element of their overall plans usually provide employees with literature describing what is available, don't hesitate to ask about other opportunities, especially when you can prove that the education or training will help you do a better job. Better yet, bring a plan to the HR department that includes the school and the classes you want to take and the benefits you envision for the company. You will be surprised at how flexible some companies can be.

If you have people reporting to you, how much discretion will you have in selecting them and directing them?

The larger the company, the more the HR department usually takes over the screening and hiring process. This can take a burden off your shoulders, but it can also saddle you with subordinates with whom you just cannot work. I suggest that you get specific answers to this question before you accept a job in which you will have others reporting to you.

Suppose you take a job that a current employee was hoping to get as a promotion, and now that person will report to you. This can be a very uncomfortable spot to be in. And horror of horrors, how would you like to find yourself in charge of the boss's incompetent nephew? Ask before it's too late!

How sensitive is the job to possible downsizing or consolidation?

This is a question that is really hard to answer, except that some jobs, in general, are more vulnerable to this kind of thinking. About the best way to get a handle is to see what they have done in the past. I wish I could give you more help with this one, but the answer really depends on who is running the show and what the investors expect him or her to do to ensure profits. And this is a scene that is usually so fluid that it's difficult to nail things down.

Company Management

Who is the top dog and would you want to work for him or her?

I'm talking about the Big Guy, not your immediate boss. The CEO, whoever he or she may be, is ultimately responsible for a lot of what may or may not happen to you. The snide remarks from your co-workers and inattention from your immediate boss pale when compared with the havoc that can be wreaked by people you may never even meet.

Fortunately there's usually a lot of information available about those who run the huge companies so many people now work for. A lot of it is public information available on the Internet. I would be unwise to mention any of those currently being lampooned on the late night TV shows, so let me refer you to a really interesting example of the kind of guy you would never want to work for. His name is Al Dunlap, and a few years ago the press began referring to him as Chainsaw Al. Chainsaw fired thousands of employees of a company he headed in a profit-enhancing move. It was later discovered that he had padded the company's revenue numbers by what can only be charitably called creative accounting. If you never heard of Chainsaw, read about him. He's the subject of several books and millions of words that are available on the Internet.

The point is this: the Big Guy may be more of a problem for your career than your immediate boss. He or she could also be the best thing to ever happen to you.

How is the company structured?

The smaller the company, the more obvious and direct the structure will be. But if you work for one of the monster conglomerates, you may have some difficulty getting a clear picture of how the company is actually structured.

Most companies are usually organized along traditional corporate lines, but some companies do things differently and it makes sense to understand any unusual structures. Just knowing who plays the lead in various departmental meetings will help you know where the power is and where it isn't, but that's just the beginning.

Some companies are highly centralized and others operate like sprawling fiefdoms. Again, it is important to know where the power is. If nothing else, you will probably have a good idea of where the layoffs will be centered if they come.

See if you can discover how well your boss stands with the chain of command. Is he or she in a position to give you a promotion or a raise, or must your request have to go through the routine channels?

What seems to be the average tenure of your co-workers and the hierarchy of your department?

Your company may be stable and profitable, but your department may be thought of as either superfluous or a major contributor to company profitability. One way to get an early handle on this is to check out the comings and goings of those in your department. As you might guess, rapid and frequent turnover at any level in the department is not a good sign. If you get unpleasant signs, first see if it's just your department or a company-wide problem.

How does management rate on the toady scale?

No, that's not a spelling error, it is toady. A chain of command made up of sycophantic toads in not a good sign. Sooner or later, yes-men and yes-women are unable to do the jobs they were hired to do and things begin to fall apart. It's also not a good sign when close relatives of the Big Guy have important jobs with the company that they seem to do by way of occasional cell calls from the golf club.

It's not always easy to spot relatives of the boss just by seeing if the names are the same. Sons-in-law and daughters-in-law can be just as disruptive as junior. Don't make fun of the Big Guy in public until you know where all the relatives are planted.

How many people will you report to?

You may be told that you have only one boss, but that you will be expected to report to someone else as well. This is not a good sign. Taking direction from two people puts you in a very difficult position. Try to arrange to have only one person to report to.

Does the company make use of a lot of outside consultants?

If the consultants are hired to provide services that are not available from the paid staff, don't worry too much. Most of these consultants are well paid for their specialty work, and it's usually done on a project basis. However, when the company has suits running all over the place talking management babble relative to strategic and long-term planning, think carefully about making the move. I'm not knocking consultants, but it's not a good sign for you as a new guy on the block. It's not the kind of stability that lets you go home sure that you will have a job in the morning.

Is the company in the midst of the "management method du jour" syndrome?

Management fads come and go, but when they are in the ascendancy, some companies seem to jump on board almost blindly. The open-office thing I mentioned earlier is a typical example. If you are expected to jump into a position based on management theories totally unfamiliar to you, try to get up to speed as quickly as possible.

How experienced are the people you will be working with?

The more experienced, the better for you. Inexperienced bosses and co-workers can be a real warning sign. You will never know when a clueless boss will blame his or her mess-up on you. Paranoid? Maybe, but stuff happens.

Generally speaking, the larger the company, the more often your boss and his or her boss and bosses will be reviewed. Smaller companies can seldom afford that luxury. Small companies that have been around for a while have generally survived their shake-down cruise and have capable management in place. Rapidly growing smaller companies usually find themselves at one time or another with people hired quickly who are not all that experienced. It's not easy to tell how experienced a person might be, but when you are to work in a department made up mostly of recently hired people, it's not a really good sign. A department is a team. And a team is built over time.

Competition

Who are the company's major competitors?

Run, do not walk, when the interviewer tells you that the company has no competitors. Every company has competitors and every company can be graded relative to its position to the others and whether it's gaining market share or losing out. Even if a company is losing position or market share doesn't mean that you should not take the job. A loss may be the result of a tactical decision that has focused finances and efforts in a project that will put it ahead in the long run. Also a company on a slide may be an opportunity for a person with your particular skills to turn it around. Turnaround specialists are needed and usually highly rewarded by companies of any size when they can do what has to be done.

It's not unfair to ask a prospective employer what plans they have for specific competitive activity. Every good job seeker knows enough about the companies he or she discusses jobs with, right? However, don't be surprised if they are reluctant to discuss it. You could be a spy! Don't press if this becomes an issue.

If the company has been in business for a long time, it can be a lot easier to see their competitive position just by reviewing what trade and professional magazines say about them. Not every company wants or needs to be number one. In fact, it's often better to be number two and stable than number one and running on high-interest borrowed money. Let number one spend the developmental money!

Are you in a sunrise or a sunset industry?

The industry in general can be a key issue in making employment decisions. This is especially true today in the electronics and communications fields. Where are the software companies that dominated 10 years ago (other than Microsoft, of course)? Would you think it wise to stake your career with a company whose competitors have left the field to do other things?

On the other hand, is it safe to cast your lot with a start-up company that is doing things no one else is doing? You might want to talk with the people who took jobs with Xerox Corporation for peanuts when it first started up. Also talk with some of the people who started with Polaroid and left a few years later as very, very wealthy people.

Is globalization a factor?

I may be wrong, but I think globalization will be a factor in just about every industry and in every job field within the next few years. Right now, we only hear about the giants in terms of globalization. Whether you are comfortable with the idea or not, globalization is a critical economic issue for businesses and individuals. My guess is that while a lot of work has been exported recently, before too long someone will discover that the same can be done here in the good old United States.

We have a huge and willing workforce. All it takes is some smarty pants to figure out how to put it to work via the Internet. Frankly, I think the only reason it hasn't been done is that most people prefer to complain more than think of ways to make a buck. So what are you waiting for! In the meantime, if you are working in a field that could be decimated by globalization, CYA—I think you know what that means.

Are consolidations a factor in your field?

In the absence of other more telling things, consolidations are not necessarily bad for you and your career. Competitors often prefer to merge rather than to wage economic wars that are costly to both. However, watch out for any companies that do this in violation of the antitrust laws.

In general, consolidations are based either on financial or strategic issues. When small companies with big ideas need capital to exploit their ideas, consolidation with a big and well-financed company is often a great way to go. The same applies to strategic consolidations. A small company in need of a sales force can often acquire it by consolidation rather than growing their own force. Consolidations can be risky for you or the best thing that could happen. Just make sure you know where you will stand after the consolidation.

How Is The Company Owned?

Is the company privately owned?

A privately owned company could be in the hands of one individual or a group of people, some of whom might be related. These relationships can be tricky; bet on the wrong cousin and no matter how well you do your job, it may not last as long as you might like. One bit of advice; stay out of family fights!

If the company is incorporated, how is it owned?

Conglomerates come in all sizes and shapes. You should be able to get a clear picture of the ownership structure if your employer is owned by one of the larger conglomerates from the public records. The one thing to look for is whether the owner(s) see the company you will work for as a significant contributor to overall profits. If it costs more to maintain your company than it might cost to buy the products or services offered, think carefully about any long-term career plans.

Would a change in ownership have an impact on your job?

It might be a problem if a company that acquires your employer sees any duplication or "redundancies" in the combined staff. The only advice I can give here is to avoid working for a company that is or has been a takeover target, unless you can be seen as too important for the acquiring company to lose. You might even be in a position to feather your nest with some better twigs if you really have the goods. A change in ownership may be a positive, too.

Have the owners been taking profits heavily recently?

Sudden and significant profit-taking, whether from a privately or publicly held company, is not a good sign. Significant profit-taking is usually based on well-educated guesses about the company—or on activity that might get some people a free vacation in a federal prison. Watch your step.

Do the owners take an active part in company management?

Keep in mind that some may see active participation as meddling and others may see it as what's needed to keep the business running. When you know something about the health of the company, you will be in a better position to determine whether micromanagement or hands-off is what is needed, and what is done. Neither style is good or bad in absolute terms; each is a problem only when you see the style as being inappropriate for current and anticipated operations.

Do any of the owners have compensation packages that are out of proportion to profits, or industry standards?

If you work for a larger, publicly traded corporation, this information floats freely in the stock market, but when you work for a small, privately held company, you will never know, unless you are hired as the comptroller. Generally speaking, when the owner of the small, privately held company you work for has homes in London, Paris, Rome, and Hackensack, you want to be careful. What he or she is doing is probably legal, but it's not too comforting when you do your job and barely meet the mortgage payments, and the owner is skiing in Switzerland for a month.

How old is the owner and how capable are his or her heirs?

This doesn't take a lot of thought, but many people tend to put the question aside because the present owner is such a nice guy. Then, when junior takes over, it hits the fan. You might want to see if the owner has an exit strategy, whether the exit is planned or unplanned as the result of taking up skydiving at age 95.

Financial Stability

If the company is publicly owned, have you seen a recent financial statement?

Even owning just one share of the company's stock will qualify you as a stockholder, and this entitles you to a copy of all the publicly distributed financial statements. Learn to read a financial statement and be able to interpret the information in terms of the economic and other factors that are not reported in the statement. Your goal, of course, is to try to spot any numbers or activity that could impact your employment. I can't give you the crash course in reading and understanding a financial statement here, but what you should be most concerned with is whether or not the company has sufficient operating capital to at least stay in business and, at best, to grow. If the funds are insufficient, check to see if they have the ability and capacity to attract the funds that might be needed.

Can you get financial information from a privately held corporation?

It's seldom easy to get the kind of information that would be really helpful unless you are seeking a job that has major profit or fiscal responsibility. Even then, management of some privately held businesses can be really close-mouthed about the finances.

If you are really getting stonewalled and you're generally uneasy about the company, you can often get some idea of what's going on by looking carefully at the facilities. Simple things like window cleaning, office cleaning, and landscaping can give you some clues. When things look bad, the management of most privately held companies first try to save money on the things that don't cost all that much, but when added together can make a difference. Better not to cut the grass than to fire the sales manager. See if you can determine how promptly they pay their bills. If you know that they have a charge account for company vehicles at a local gas station, get your tank filled there and probe the owner a bit. Questions like, "What's happening over at Zilch Industries these days?" may be enough to get some answers.

It can often be as difficult to get financial information on an incorporated company that is owned by another company. Given the merger and acquisition activities we have been seeing in the past few years, many companies are in this category. A PR friend told me that a good way to get a handle on subsidiaries of larger company is to see how the subs are treated in the annual reports and in the general corporate promotional literature. The subsidiaries in good standing get top billing; the others are generally treated in descending order of importance to the parent company.

Are the company's fiscal and financial years in sync? Some are not. Be aware that the glowing report you are shown may be many months old and, as you seek the job, the company may be on the brink of some kind of disaster.

The statements issued by publicly held corporations must be subjected to an independent auditor's review. If the auditor's statement is conditional, it will be issued as a "subject to" report. This means that, subject to things that may or may not happen in the future, the business might be in serious trouble. Reports issued by auditors on privately held companies are far less reliable.

Is the company making or losing money?

The last line on a profit and loss statement is labeled Net Income or Loss. Watch for the minus sign! Even if you see a profit in the millions, you might be advised to think carefully about taking the job until you know the accounting procedures used and how the profits were calculated. Further, unless you know the standards for other companies, a number that knocks your socks off may send more financially savvy applicants heading for the hills. See if the numbers, whether profit or loss, show any changes over the past few years. Also see whether you can determine how much of the reported profit you are shown is based on one dynamite contract that will be tough to do the next year, or is it par for the course.

A company balance sheet showing a loss may not necessarily be in a bad position. The loss could be due in part to heavy capital investment. However, the best way to make sure is to look at the company's financial history if you can get your hands on the information. If you see a history of losses, be sure to ask about the company's plan to turn things around. If all they can say is that they are hoping for the best, wish them luck and move on.

How imaginative are their accountants?

I can't tell you everything you need to know about how major losses are turned into staggering profits by accounting magic, but I can suggest that you read some of the books about the companies whose former execs are currently guests of the government in places like Danbury. I think you will learn more and enjoy the reading far more than a course in accounting.

Keep in mind that most executive bonuses are based on the production of profits. Those clever enough to create real profits are occasionally driven to use their skills in less socially acceptable ways. In other words, they lie and they cheat. I know, you're shocked, *shocked!* But forewarned is forearmed.

When your company publicly announces that they are restating earnings after recently publishing some good news, take cover. Someone caught them with their hands in the cookie jar and there's probably more bad news to come.

What is the debt equity ratio?

I realize that this question and some of the others in this section may be beyond what you know about finance. However, to be as helpful as I can, I am including it and a few others. Please bear with me. In simplest terms, a debt equity ratio is a picture of the company's capitalization with the shareholder's equity. It's a figure that security analysts pay a lot of attention to and so should you—if you can get your hands on the numbers. In general terms, the higher the company's capitalization relative to the amount of the stockholder's equity, the better the economic shape of the company.

What does the cash-flow picture show?

Believe it or not, a company's balance sheet may show impressive profits but the company may actually be approaching the red line, or the red numbers. Again this is complicated, so I'll use an example to explain it. Suppose that the company has very slow-paying customers and has built up a significant amount of money reported as receivables. However the company is making the payments on time to keep its business running. That's a cash-flow problem! Income is slow in arriving; payments go out faster than income. The company may draw on cash reserves or borrowed money, but it's not a healthy situation to be in. A line-by-line analysis of the cash flow will help you get a clearer picture, but that's not easy to get.

It's not uncommon to read about some recent start-up that has huge sales booked being acquired by some organization that can supply the capital needed to maintain the momentum. This, too, gets a lot more complicated, but you should be aware that a company with huge sales booked for its products or services may not be in financial position to deliver. This is seldom a problem for well-established large or small companies, but it does show up with start-ups.

Why are there so many footnotes on the company's financial statement?

From a career-planner's point of view, the more the footnotes, the more cautious you should be about the company. Footnotes are used to explain information that slows the reading down, but more to the point, they explain information that those who write reports know must be included, but prefer that you avoid seeing. How often do you read footnotes on anything? Most people skip over them and hope to deduce the total meaning from the material that follows.

Footnotes on financial reports can tell you a lot if you know what to look for and how to interpret them. Again, this is way beyond the scope of this book. However, if you have financial statements from a company you might want to work for that is dappled with footnotes, ask someone you trust to help you interpret their meaning. As they so often say, the devil is in the details.

Should I read the entire business plan?

A formal business plan is a creative blend of fact and fiction. The fiction part is made of the dreams of the owners. The factual portion should describe everything an investor needs to know to make a reasoned investment. In general, they are created before a business actually exists, although it's not uncommon for existing companies planning expansions and diversification to do a similar report. Read them carefully, but pay more attention to the facts than the fiction. Those who write these reports seldom lie, but good writers of fiction can often have you believing in anything. Caveat emptor! Also let the prospective employee beware!

Compensation and Benefits

How does the company arrive at its compensation package?

When you negotiate for a job, you tend to think mainly of salary. You will probably make your decision based heavily on what others in similar companies are being paid for similar work. This is not unusual, but it means that you can often leave a lot on the table if you don't look beyond the actual salary. You're seen as a cost that includes salary and a lot of other things. Some companies even do their compensation by apportioning part of some of overhead factor to each employee. You really don't need to know this kind of detail, but I mention it to punctuate the point that you better think beyond salary alone.

Think about the entire benefits package and the company's attitude toward expense compensation, overtime, and whatever else they may think is important. Let me stress that while you see the job as something that will pay you $90,000 a year, the company sees you as a much more complex cost, and when that cost/benefit ratio gets out of whack, you should have your resumé ready.

Is there room in the salary for you to get a raise, or would you have to be promoted to a higher position to make more money?

Most companies have a salary range for each job level. If you took the first offer, you will probably start at the lower end of the range for your job. However, if you negotiated aggressively, you may be paid at the top end of the range for the job. This leaves you little room to negotiate for more later, and if a promotion is not possible, you may have to make other plans.

This obviously doesn't mean that you should start low so you have room for a raise. It does argue for shooting for the median. You will be paid fairly, and you will have time to see if this where you want to stay for a while. Raises can be easier to get than promotions, so start in the middle, get your raise, and then decide whether it's worth bucking for a promotion or if it's time to take a hike.

How does the employer define its salary-increase procedure?

Some companies base their salary increase policy on performance, others have rigid plans, and others use a combination of both approaches and usually throw in a few ideas of their own. Be sure you know exactly how it's done and how you are being treated in your pay grade. Ask whether the raises vary in amount based on some review factor, or whether the raises are based on numbers cut in stone. Ask about how often you can expect to be in a position to get a raise and what the denial of a raise means in terms of your performance and future with the company.

Despite what may appear to be very rigid rules governing the granting of raises, most companies will make exceptions when pushed hard by someone they are afraid may quit. It's not uncommon in these situations for the additional compensation to be given some way other than in salary, especially if the company makes a real point to all employees that "rules are rules." The concession may be added in terms of enhanced benefits.

Who do you have to petition for a raise?

You may be subject to a formal performance review in which the raise is approved or disapproved. In a loosely structured company, it may simply be up to your supervisor to petition the Big Guy on your behalf. The process and the people involved are seldom kept secret, so find out early and make sure you go the right person. Always adhere to the chain of command when it comes to asking for more money. It's not a good idea to skip anyone.

Should you count on bonuses when managing your income?

The only time you can count on a bonus is if it is in print in your employment contract. The exact terms must be stated. That is, how often and when will bonuses be calculated and given? You should have a clear understanding of the calculations and rationale for the amount of the bonus.

Is working on commission a good move?

There is nothing wrong with working on commission, but most jobs that involve commission income also include either a draw against commission, or a base salary plus commission. An entire book could be and probably has been written on this subject, but I will leave you with one thought: most people who are successful commission salespeople don't want to work any other way. They know what they can do and the money they make is totally under their control. It may surprise you to know that some commission salespeople are so good at what they do that they can sell more than the company can deliver. When that happens, their income is limited because commissions are usually paid either when orders are shipped or when the customer pays for the shipment.

If you are really interested in working on a commission income alone, I'd suggest that you become an independent manufacturers' representative. When you do this, you can represent more than one company, though never companies that compete with each other. For information on this very interesting field, contact the Manufacturers' Agents National Association. Check its website at www.MANAonline.org.

What about pay for work above and beyond the call of duty?

Depending on your level within the company, you may be paid time-and-a-half or possibly more for work required beyond the regular work week. At higher job levels, there is seldom any direct extra compensation, but bonuses may be based on the work accomplished beyond regular work hours but not compensated in any planned way. Some companies assume that their executives will simply put in the time when it is needed. Others—a very few—prefer that their executives go home on time and without briefcases so that they can return refreshed and ready to go the next day. These companies are in the minority, but most that have this policy are considered some of the best and most enlightened companies.

Are pensions worth considering, since most people will probably work for many companies during a working lifetime?

Absolutely! However, the traditionally defined benefit pension plan is less popular than the much more flexible 401(k) plan. One of the main benefits of a retirement plan based on a 401(k) plan is that it is portable. You can take it with you when you change jobs, where more of the defined benefit pension plans lack that flexibility. Also under the rules of a 401(k) plan you have control over the amount of money you put in and where the money might be invested. Most 401(k) plans are based on pooled income stock investments. Just keep in mind that your retirement money is subject to the same stock variations that you would have as an individual investor.

The Least You Need to Know

The answers you get to the questions in this chapter that apply to your individual situation will help you see yourself in a clearer light and see your career plans in very practical terms.

Chapter 29

Moving On—Literally!

In This Chapter

- Discover why you may be asked to move to a different area, or even another country
- Learn why a transfer offer is usually made only to special people
- Understand why certain locations should be avoided
- See why lifestyle changes can be as important as career moves
- Learn why it may really be best to turn down a move that includes a raise and a promotion

Not too long ago, those who worked for IBM often quipped that IBM stood for "I've Been Moved." It wasn't just IBM that shuffled people from place to place; most of the other giants of the time saw moving employees regularly as part of their training. The theory had it that this varied exposure broadened employees' experience and overall view of the companies and the markets they served. I can't comment on whether it did or didn't serve those purposes, but it did result in a fair amount of unhappiness in the families of those who had been moved. Today, employees are moved to distant locations mainly because they are needed there and the company would rather take on the expense of a move than take a chance with a local hire.

While companies have pretty much abandoned this experiment in management development, individuals have taken it up as a way to attain career goals a lot faster than waiting for a spot to open in the chain of command within their present employer's ranks. And in times of economic uncertainty, it is often the best way to maintain a certain amount of career trajectory. It's not uncommon today to see articles in the business press referring to those who move to grow as "gypsy managers." Sometimes the term is used as a pejorative and sometimes it is used admiringly. Let's look at in this chapter from the perspective of an admirer.

Going Where the Opportunities Are

In general, most businesses cluster in fairly well defined areas. New York City is headquarters for more book publishers than exist in all the other states combined. New Jersey has more pharmaceutical companies than any other state. When a promising biochemist announces that he or she is moving from New Jersey to Flat Mattress, Nebraska, for a better job, the goodbye party is usually more like a wake than a bon voyage bash. If the job doesn't pan out, there is no place to go but back home, and that's an expensive and often embarrassing move.

It's tempting to quote Willy Sutton here and agree that you should go where the money is. But there are limits to this kind of thinking. The raise in income and other benefits should be big enough to cover any and all career disasters that could possibly befall you. The company that hires you will probably pick up your initial relocation costs, but surely won't pay your costs back if things don't work out. And think about the problems this creates for the family. Spouses often have to give up promising careers, and if kids are involved there can be real problems.

Right Move

Most careers are improved these days by moving from job to job. If no other companies in the area can provide you with the potential for some growth, it's probably time to move. But get everything in writing first! Or think about starting a new career right where you are.

Unless your work is so specialized, it's often possible to take other jobs in different fields if your move doesn't work out. People who are in general management and most of the support services can usually weather a disappointing move by doing similar work in totally different fields. An accountant, for example, doesn't have to be able to do a chemical analysis if he or she moves from an electronics firm to one that manufactures chemicals. Good sales and marketing people can usually shift gears pretty easily. In fact, one of the ways of presenting yourself to a new industry is by explaining that you bring a fresh view to the company that may have been blinkered for too many years.

Taking a Transfer

Many companies transfer people to other locations when the move benefits both the company and the employee. The days of mass moves that IBM and others did are long gone. So if your present employer offers you a spot in another state, or even in another country, you can pretty much take this as a sign that you are on your way up to something better.

Offshore companies operating in the United States often offer stints at the overseas home office to people they want to keep and grow. This is an excellent sign and an opportunity that you should consider very seriously. These companies certainly won't tell you so, but a turn-down is often a shut-down in their serious interest in you as an employee to consider for promotion and growth.

The move to "Siberia" is pretty much a thing of the past. When companies were hesitant to fire people, they used to transfer marginal employees to the dead-end offices that the company often maintained. Companies seldom keep remote and unproductive places any more. So if you are offered a transfer, it's probably because your company thinks highly of you.

In general, the larger the employer, the more likely you might be moved, and the more help you will be offered in the process. Large firms that move people regularly usually have staff devoted the job of helping you move. Most will help with the basics—finding the right mover and the best places to live—and many will go to great lengths to see that you are welcomed not only by the office, but by some members of the general community as well.

Moving to a Brand New Job

You've had it with your present job and there are no good jobs where you live. I don't think I have to tell you that, with a few clicks on the Internet, you can locate good jobs anywhere in a matter of minutes. As easy as it is to find good jobs, it's still a royal pain to pack up and move a great distance to take a better job.

A survey recently reported in *Fortune Magazine* done by CareerBuilder.com showed that out of 5,272 employees interviewed, 42 percent said that they had moved to another city at least once for a better job. Thirty-two percent had moved even farther, to a different state or region. Of these movers, 31 percent claimed that their employers picked up the moving costs. So if costs are holding you back from looking for work that would require a move, you have a 30 percent chance of getting a potential employer to pick up the tab. Not the best odds, but at you least you know that it can be done.

Many of my coaching clients have moved several times, and all for better jobs. This is a small sample. But most told me that when a company agreed to pick up the moving tab they frequently also offered to pay for short-term accommodations until permanent housing had been found. All of this is, of course, negotiable and I'd suggest that you don't discuss it until you have the job offer in hand.

Moving Overseas

I'm sure it hasn't escaped your notice that more than a few of the larger international companies have major presences here in the United States. Most of these companies employ a mix of American citizens and their own nationals from the home office. As I already mentioned, it's not uncommon for these companies to offer transfers to the home office or specialized locations outside the United States to U.S. citizens they want to keep and promote. This is a very good career sign and one which should be taken seriously. Most will relocate an employee's entire family for the period of the assignment and they will usually pick up all associated costs. Some even pick up school expenses for kids to attend English-language schools in the host country.

Take these offers seriously. In fact, if you are on the track that generally leads to an assignment like this, it usually pays to lobby for it. Be subtle, but let the powers that be know that you are willing to suffer all the problems and privations associated with living in London, or even Paris!

> **Career News**
>
> You can learn a foreign language a lot more easily with one of the better audio training programs. Most are on DVD. Learn the basics from one of these self-teaching programs and it will be a lot easier to go the distance either by taking a regular course, or just picking it up on the fly.

Don't be held back by not being able to speak the language of the company that employs you. Most offshore companies take it for granted that while their citizens may speak several languages, most Americans are monolinguistic. One of the other languages that most people in the world speak other than their own is English. But why not take the time to learn your company's language? It would make points with your employer and make you more employable in the long run. In fact, many companies I know will pick up the cost of language training for employees they hope will stick with them for the long haul.

Cost of Living in Your New Location

No two places are alike when it comes to cost of living. Contiguous towns can be miles apart in economic terms. A small town in Montana is going to be a lot less expensive to live in than an apartment in the middle of Manhattan (New York, not Kansas). Most progressive employers take this into consideration, but remember that this cuts two ways.

If the place you are moving to costs more to live in than the place where you currently live, there will probably be an upward adjustment. But the same equation will also point up that a place you are being sent to costs less to live in than your present location. Just so you aren't fantasizing about a McMansion somewhere!

Check out local property tax rates and be sure to see if there's any local legislation pending that will raise those taxes significantly. Check on utility costs. You can't do much about them except to know what to expect when you keep your thermostat set at 90 degrees all winter.

What About the Neighbors?

If it looks like this will be a long-term assignment, think carefully about where you move and what kind of real estate you invest in. I'd suggest that you put all your stuff in storage for a while at the new location and rent first. There is no way to get a feel for neighborhoods on a Sunday drive with an enthusiastic real estate agent.

One of my clients bought a house immediately on arrival in what looked like a very charming neighborhood. And it really was charming. But she had strong political convictions and when she and her furniture arrived, a local election was in progress and every one of her new neighbors had signs on their lawns for the "other" party. She learned to live with it, but never really felt at home in what, to her eye, had been a very attractive neighborhood.

Very few towns don't have a chamber of commerce or at least a couple of local merchants who act like one. Stop in and introduce yourself and have a couple of specific questions for which you would like answers, such as the property tax rate or what the schools are like. You will get the answers to these and many unanswered questions as well. Local businesspeople are anxious to promote their town, so be prepared for the pitch. Remember, the greeters are sizing you up, too.

The Tax Costs in Your New Neighborhood

You should have a pretty clear picture of what it currently costs to support your lifestyle where you currently live. Don't make the mistake of thinking that the same numbers will work in your new location. Most of the variations to check out will be pretty obvious, but most people never think to see if there is a tax increase pending, or if local utilities are about to hike rates significantly. Check the public records of all the organizations that need government approval for raising rates before you commit to anything.

You could find an area which seems to be all in one town, but it might indeed be within the borders of two towns, each with a different tax rate. The services you need must be funded by law. Don't be fooled by a spot with very low local taxes. The difference will surely be picked up by what you pay in tax money to the state. There might even be some county taxes to pay, too.

As a matter of fact, low local taxes should ring a large and noisy bell if you have kids. A town that votes down its school budget regularly as a matter of principle will probably have a very attractive tax rate. But you can bet that the school system probably stinks. Or you may find that you have to haul your own garbage to the dump. These and other surprises are not what a new arrival wants to hear after signing for a mortgage on a cottage in Wistful Vista by the Sea.

Some states seem to have done miracles by having very low or no income taxes at all. Their secret is in the use of a sales tax. Few who live in states that have gone this route ever take the time to see just how much money they pay in sales taxes each year. They are hidden and often called stealth taxes. Buy a loaf of bread for two bucks and don't be surprised to find that 25 cents of that amounts to a 12.5 percent tax. I can't say this for sure, but from what I have read on the subject, most people would be better off with a state income tax at a graduated rate than with the typical sales tax. But when you see "No State Income Tax" on the real estate pitch it can be pretty alluring.

Local town taxes go mostly to support schools and other local services. If you see a high base rate, be sure to see whether there is a correspondingly high rate of kids going on to better colleges and universities. Don't be fooled by the sports trophies the school teams win. Be afraid, very afraid, if the tax-to-successful-grad ratio is very much out of whack.

Every state taxes its residents differently. This means that moving from your present location to another state might make a difference up or down for you. Just keep in mind that state taxes can be used to reduce the taxes you pay to the Federal government.

What You Will Live In

Move to a big city and you will probably live in an apartment. Move to the burbs, or a city with easy access to them and you just might have a house. Where you live within a suburban area and where you live within a metropolitan area will largely be determined by your present lifestyle, the cost to maintain the lifestyle you presently enjoy and your current income. But you already knew that, didn't you?

As I write this, however, the housing market is in the dumps. I can't verify this, but a colleague told me the other day that a major development in one of the big western sates just made a two-for-one offer to anyone with cash. Buy one house, get one free.

Most people who relocate have to sell or rent their present home in order to afford buying another house or apartment. Carrying two mortgages if you can't unload your present home will not be easy. In fact, the absence of a wad of cash from the sale of your present home may severely hinder you from buying another at your new location. But a rental income stream that exceeds your expense to maintain your present home helps some when the numbers are crunched.

As I mentioned earlier, the smart thing to do is rent first. Get a feel for the territory and the housing market. Get to know people who can help you. If your employer is one of the biggies, it may even have a relocation department that can take a large load off your shoulders.

Getting to and from Your New Job

Transportation in your new area should be considered very carefully. Move from Des Moines to the middle of New York City and bring your car and you are asking for trouble. None but the very wealthy and the very pretentious of Gotham keep their own cars. On the other hand, move from the Big Apple to Des Moines without a car, and people will think you are pretty naïve.

Unfortunately, most areas of the United States are not all that well served by public transportation. And in many places that are, people still insist on spending hours driving bumper-to-bumper each way rather than catching a bus. Go figure!

Where public transportation exists and it's convenient for you to use, check out the discounts available for regular commutation. Unfortunately, most plans I have seen involve buying monthly commutation tickets. Take a two-week vacation and work the other two weeks and you'll accumulate some pretty worthless paper.

Quality of Life Concerns

This is a big country with many regional difference and some pretty intense feelings between some of the regions. It's a lot better than it used to be, but it's sometimes difficult for someone transferred to a really different culture to be comfortable. It's easy to say, "get over it," but that just won't do.

A friend moved to a small rural town a number of years ago. He was a consulting engineer and worked from home, traveling all over the world at times. After living in this town for nearly 15 years, he decided to go to one of the local town council meetings with a simple and unthreatening question about the woods near his home. When he rose and asked his question, the council president asked him how long he had lived in the town. My friend told him, and the council president replied, "You haven't lived here long enough to ask that question." And he wasn't kidding. Extreme? Possibly, but you could get lucky.

You will want to know about the churches in the area, the schools, the recreation possibilities, the climate, and anything else that might be important to you.

And even if your spouse and kids are happy about the move, you may have other relatives who will really miss you. Think about it.

The Least You Need to Know

- Offers of distant transfers usually send very good career signals.
- Moving to a very different part of the country can be a jarring experience for your family.
- Moving on your own should be considered only if there are enough employment opportunities in the area you plan to move to.
- The costs of company sponsored moves are usually paid for fully by your employer.
- Think as carefully about the quality of life where you might move as you would about the career opportunities the move offers.

30

The Self-Employment Wild Card

In This Chapter

- ◆ Why going it alone is no more risky than working for someone else
- ◆ How to test your readiness for self-employment
- ◆ You don't have to start a business to be self-employed
- ◆ You can even skip working for someone altogether

This book is about employment and how you can plan and manage your career as a company employee. So far, I have stressed three alternatives; moving up in your present job, moving laterally in your present job, and moving out of your present job to become an employee of another organization.

There is, however, one more alternative, and that is moving out—altogether. I have not given it the attention I have given the three other options, simply because it is seldom very high on most people's lists. However, I would be remiss if I didn't tell you something about this alternative.

What follows is a broad outline of what is involved in self-employment, mainly from a personal perspective. If, after reading this chapter, you feel this is a possible alternative for you, there is a wealth of information on how to do it successfully in dozens of books and on more than a few internet sites. As intimidating as it may seem, if you really know yourself well and fully understand the risks and possibilities, self-employment may be the way for you to go.

Self-Employment and Starting Your Own Business

When most people think about working for themselves, their thoughts usually center on starting a business. They look at franchises, dream of what kind of store they could put in the vacant shop next to the candy store, or seriously consider offering one of the many professional services that are frequently contracted for by larger companies.

You don't have to start a typical business to be self-employed. Depending on what you do, your only investment might be the registration fee your state requires for you to open the door and get a commercial bank account. So, if you have ruled out self-employment because of the heavy investment needed for franchises, or the expense of inventory of some sort, press the clear key on your mental computer and read on.

More than a few people who have experienced downsizing in which their employers have put them on a part-time status have discovered that they could use their new situation as a springboard for self-employment. The major impact of most downsizing is the loss of company-paid benefits such as health insurance. However, just about every field has organizations that have used their collective buying power to help members get insurance at reasonable rates.

Historically, the number of self-employed people tends to decline as the economy gains strength. Conversely, the number grows as overall economic activity slows down. This is easy to understand and it points out that it often takes a kick in the pants to get people to do things they might have wanted to do all along. So let's see if you have what it takes.

Career News

According to statistics released in April 2008, 78 percent of all business in the United States is classified as small business. Their combined revenue for the current reporting year was $951 billion. Most of these are classified as businesses with no employees. In other words, they are self-employed individuals. Impressive? Yes, it is!

Do You Have the Temperament to Go It Alone?

Make no mistake; it's lonely at the top. That goes for being the CEO of a major international corporation as well as being the YCY (You-in-Charge of You) of whatever you do when you go it alone. Most people who have done it will tell you that they were amazed to discover that they really had the emotional resources they needed, even when they were really fearful about it. It's like jumping into a lake without doing the toe-test first. Once you're in, whether it's warm or cold, you do whatever you have to do.

Most of the research I have seen on the characteristics of successful self-employed people focuses on similar elements. Again, I'm avoiding the usual check-list type of quiz. You just can't judge yourself by anything as simple as a collection of pop-test scores. Making the decision to go it alone requires a lot of thought and you can begin by thinking carefully about the following issues.

How Well Do You Handle Uncertainty?

In general, most people tend to handle uncertainty in direct proportion to their current obligations. That is, if you have a big family and heavy financial commitments, you are going to be a lot more concerned about the outcome of your move. Uncertainty, however, is a given in everything you do, whether it's taking a job with a different company, or setting off on your own.

Uncertainty is an emotional issue that should be handled by dealing mainly with the reality issues. Stewing about whether or not the money will be there or whether or not you will be able to get insurance on your own can be resolved by doing whatever is necessary to get the facts you need. It may turn out that the facts are against you and that you have to head in a different direction. But at least you will have taken real action. Or you might still be willing to make the move if most of the other elements I describe below fall into place.

> **Case in Point**
>
> "It seems that the right thing to do is not to fear mistakes, to plunge in, to do the best that one can, hoping to learn enough from blunders to correct them eventually." —Abraham Maslow, American psychologist

How Well Organized Are You?

Being well organized is, I think, overrated. However, it seems to be on the lists of most who write on the subject, and it's my opinion that the better organized you are, the easier your work life will be. I just won't go as far as most and say that if you are not well organized you are doomed to failure. In fact, I might even go as far as to say that if you are overly organized, you might have more problems than those whose filing system is just piles of paper here and there.

I'm on good ground here because a lot of research has shown that extremely well organized people often miss the critical point that organization is not an end in itself. Don't let this throw you, but give it some thought.

How Well Do You Deal with All Kinds of People?

This is a very important factor. We all have our own opinions about how well we deal with others. And often we are very surprised to learn that our opinions are way off-base. You may think that you handled that cranky client perfectly, and then get surprised when the cranky client tells you he is taking his business elsewhere.

Without taking a battery of tests, I'd suggest that you just ask a few people you work with how they feel about your dealings with people. Always ask this question in the context of a specific situation. Avoid generalities. People, even those who may not care for you, will usually say something nice in response to a softball question. For example, if you just came out of a meeting with a difficult client, ask some of those who were also at the meeting what they thought of something specific you did or said. "Was I right when I told Joe to go back and do the numbers again?" That elicits information you can use. "How do you think I handled Joe?" usually gets you the noncommittal, "Not bad." No help there.

Working on your own, you are free to dump cranky clients any time you want—if you can afford the loss of business. As an employee, you don't have much choice. You can be canned just as easily for offending a major customer.

> **Career Alert**
>
> As important as it is to be and be seen as people-friendly, it's just as important to realize that not everyone will be your friend. Being consistently fair not only solidifies friendships, it can go a long way to disarming those who might seek to undermine you.

Are You a Self-Starter?

Sadly, too much of the work most people do when they work for others is based on someone else's direction. This is sad, because it builds up expectations that aren't all that helpful when independence is declared. To be successfully self-employed, you have to be both boss and employee. This may seem like something out of a corny self-help manual, but actually having conversations (in your head, of course) with yourself can help put you on the right track. A simple virtual dialogue often helps you see the work from both positions a lot more clearly. It allows you to view the experience of the boss/employee situation in real time and from both perspectives.

You will discover that in both roles you see the situation as mini dramas and the situations become comic. However, you have to be able to laugh at yourself uncritically to really get it. But don't let anyone catch you actually talking to yourself—keep it in your head. Sooner or later you will drop the head talk and be the self-starter you (the boss) thinks you (the employee) should be.

How Good Are You at Planning?

Planning means thinking ahead. And thinking ahead means anticipating more than just the end of the day. The truth is that you get ahead as an employee in good part by planning ahead, by anticipating events that might and might not happen. So you are probably pretty good at planning right now, even though you might think otherwise.

Good planning is based on anticipation of events and on having your responses to these events ready to use. Notice that I said responses, not response. Good planning is based on being ready with several alternatives to situations that may or may not happen. Telling a client that the report you will produce for him will cost $10,000, but being prepared to settle for less by diminishing the scope of the report proportionately is good planning. Good planning is having the answers ready before the questions are asked. Good planning is knowing how much operating capital you need to keep going. Good planning is knowing that your competitor is going to underbid you and being ready with an alternative proposal that will eat the competitor's lunch.

No tests I know of will tell you whether or not you are good at planning. However, it's easy enough to look back and see whether you anticipated problems well enough in advance to solve them quickly, or whether you are frequently caught flatfooted. Fortunately, just working at planning is often enough to correct all but the worst of problems.

How Easily Do You Make Decisions?

Making good decisions easily is a good sign. Making bad decisions just as easily is a bad sign. So is procrastination. This is really an issue of trusting your judgment. Make a bunch of bad decisions and you get gun-shy. Make a bunch of good decisions and you can get cocky.

Decision making is a complex subject, but in simple terms the best decisions are usually made when you first define the problem clearly and then identify all the possible alternatives and probable outcomes. Of course, the closer the alternatives are to each other, the more difficult it is to make a decision. But you have to start somewhere.

This chapter isn't about how to do it, it's about whether you see yourself as a good or a bad decision maker. Look back and see what worked for you and what didn't. This should give you some idea of yourself as decision maker. If you see yourself as somewhat weak in this area, don't worry. There's plenty of good material in any library on the subject, and it is a subject that is learnable.

The key issue, however, is your ability to make decisions independently. As an employee, you probably had plenty of people to work with and to help you. Working on your own, it's all up to you. If this seems like a heavy burden think of it this way. Make a good decision when you are on your own and you get all the credit. Make a bad one and you get the blame. However, you have a better opportunity to correct your mistakes when you are on your own than when you work for someone else. Foul-ups are usually handed to someone else for the fix.

Are You Willing To Work Long Hours?

Long hours are a fact of life, whether you work for yourself or for someone else. Your current job description may say that office hours are 9 to 5, but how often do you stay after closing and work until the cleaning crew shows up? How often do you take work home on nights and weekends? You may work even longer hours initially, but chances are, once you get settled in your self-employment routine, you will not put in any more hours for yourself than you did as an employee toting a briefcase full of work home each night.

Just for fun, if you are currently employed and take work home from time to time, and occasionally work late at the office, keep a record of those hours. I'm assuming that you are off the clock, but if you punch a clock you already know how many extra hours you put in. Do this for a couple of months and then average it out. I think you will be surprised at how many hours you work over and above your nine-to-five requirement.

Most self-employed people I know tell me that the long hours do get shorter, but the extra time they spend on their own work is far more enjoyable than doing it for someone else.

How Well Do You Handle Setbacks?

I don't have to tell you that life is often two steps forward and one step back. When you're first starting out on your own, that ratio may be reversed more than a few times. It isn't easy to find yourself in a totally new and often threatening situation in which a cherished client moves his business somewhere, or you discover that work that has been outsourced to you and been outsourced overseas.

The subject of dealing with adversity, or the plain old stuff-happens situations, is well worked over from every conceivable perspective. The truth is that no one approach works best for everyone, despite all the claims to the contrary. You may be the kind of person who needs some comforting words and a little hand-holding from time to time. That's fine. On the other hand, you may be the kind of person who pushes offers of help aside and plunges right into the fray. That, too, is fine.

You have to know yourself in terms of your approach to handling adversity. Look back at difficult situations you faced in the past and you will probably see a pattern emerge. In short, whatever has worked well for you before should work well for you in your new situation.

Don't spend a lot of time avoiding situations that you think might be difficult to handle. Spend that time learning how to deal with the problems and you will be a happier, and probably wealthier, self-employed person in the long run.

What About Your Quality of Life?

Whether you're on your own or have major family obligations, you need to think about quality of life if you are considering going the self-employed route. Obviously, those without major obligations have a lot more maneuvering room, but you still have to think about yourself very seriously.

Surprisingly, most people I've known who have left the ranks of the regularly employed did so after they had acquired some pretty heavy commitments. And most did it voluntarily. As you climb the corporate ladder, the job-growth funnel gets narrower and narrower. Opportunity constriction is often enough to send people out on their own, where they have far more control over their work life. Not everyone becomes self-employed under duress.

Skipping the Job Route Altogether

So far, I have been talking about self-employment as just another alternative for those who are already employed. Probably more than a few of you reading this are just starting out and may have never had a job other than lifeguard at the local beach during summer vacation. Would you think I was nuts if I told you that, if you are seriously interested in working for yourself, skipping the paid job is definitely a possibility?

Almost everyone who writes on this subject claims that it's best to work at a traditional job before thinking about being self-employed. Yes, I know: more than a few jobs are almost impossible to do unless you learned them as someone else's employee, but let me tell you a few reasons why you might be better off skipping the traditional route if conditions are right.

What Do You Really Learn Working for Someone Else?

Most jobs involve doing the same thing over and over, with very little exposure to anything else. And I'm not just talking about typical factory work, I'm talking about a lot of the jobs done by many middle and upper management people. You may learn and hone some specific skills, but have you learned anything that will help you start and manage a small business? Not likely. And this is why so many small-business start-ups fail. You learned the ins and outs of bookkeeping on the job, so you think it's a simple jump from doing it for an employer to doing it for clients of your own small business. Perhaps—but if that's all you bring to the table, you're in for trouble.

Doing the same thing over and over for an employer keeps the paycheck coming, but it also prevents you from learning what you'll need to learn to run your own small business. It could be easier and quicker to take a few basic business courses and jump into the fray directly. It takes guts and a willingness to fail and keep picking yourself up, but I have met a few over the years who have done exactly this and who are very successful and happy people who have never had a "real" job.

What About the Risk?

What about it? How much more risky is going it alone from the start than doing a great job for someone else and suddenly being told that your job is now being moved 10,000 miles away? Most reports claim that the average person starting out in the workforce today will have at least six different jobs in a lifetime. Many will have a lot more. Talk about risk—and you have virtually no control over it!

How About Explaining the Lack of Experience?

Most work today, other than brain surgery and the other sciences, can usually be learned and mastered easily with some concentrated effort. I met a woman a number of years ago who had just received a degree in interior design and, without ever working for anyone else, started out on her own. She was up front about the lack of experience and told potential clients that if they were dissatisfied with her work, she would refund the fee.

This is a tough offer to turn down. After all, how subjective is satisfaction in a field like interior design? She told me that she only had one client who asked for his money back. But, she claimed that she learned more from this experience than from most of her other early forays. You just have to be imaginative, take some risks, and go for it.

What About a Social Life?

Most people build their personal life around some major aspect of their business life. Nothing wrong with that, except that you can become too attached to people who may not have the same drives and motivation as you. Those who have chosen the corporate route usually get very defensive when told there might be other ways of making a living. We are all defensive of our attitudes and beliefs, so get used to it. Just don't let anyone's defense of a personal view cloud the view you have of the same situation.

Self-Employment Can Lead to More Than Just Current Income

Any business, whether it's capital intensive or one in which the principal asset locks the door at the end of each day, can become more than just a source of current income. In fact, many businesses are started specifically to be sold later.

The typical self-employed individual, however, usually provides a personal service of some kind and seldom thinks of his or her business surviving after retirement. This can be a big mistake. More than a few solo consultants I have met over the years have "merged" their solo practice with larger consultancies when they were ready to call it quits. The merger avoids the problem of the consultancy's clients fearing they will not get the same service from someone who might just buy out the business. Over time, the founder of the merged solo practice gradually withdraws from active duty. By that time his or her clients have become accustomed to the new people. So keep this in mind if going it alone has any appeal to you.

The Least You Need To Know

- Self-employment is no more risky than working for someone else.

- You can often meet more interesting people on your own than you probably could working for someone else.

- Being self-employed, you have better control over your destiny than you might by working for someone else.

- Many small businesses take on value themselves and can be sold to others.

Chapter 31

The Perfect Job

In This Chapter

- ◆ There is a perfect job for you, but there are strings attached.
- ◆ Discover why the perfect job should also be fun.
- ◆ Learn why the best companies to work for are well respected, even by their most aggressive competitors.
- ◆ The opportunities for personal growth often outweigh money issues.

The perfect job does exist. Surprised? You shouldn't be. However, you shouldn't expect that it will last forever. It may last for years, but you change, the job changes, the economy changes, and what may seem perfect to you today may not be all that perfect somewhere down the road. So we are back to what I have been telling you all along: career planning is a lifetime activity. Do it well early on and all it takes is tweaks and some adjustments now and then. Do it once and forget it and it will whack you in the back of the head when you aren't looking.

But what really is a perfect job? Are there any objective standards that most people agree on? There are, but keep in mind that I am talking about the overall notion of a job—not a job description. I am talking about what you and your employer bring to the table, not the details of the job itself. Over the years I have made notes of what my coaching clients have told me and what some employers have told me about how they see the perfect job. Not surprisingly, both employers and employees pretty much agree on what the perfect job should be. Most would have it that way, if they could. But all sorts of things happen to both parties along the way.

So what really is a perfect job? Here, in summary, is what most people have told me about their vision of the perfect job. See if you agree.

The Job Is Interesting, Challenging, and Fun

Although I am not listing these topics in any particular order, it's interesting to note that a job that is interesting, challenging, and fun to do is often mentioned ahead of money and compensation. In fact, some of the most interesting people I have coached over the years have been willing to work for less money when they saw the job meeting these criteria.

I have always been intrigued by what people think about when they tell me what they look for in a challenging job. I often suspected that this was a cliché that most people thought would impress others, but it turns out that it really isn't. If you think about a job the same way you think about sports, the picture becomes a lot clearer. Learning to hit a baseball requires practice, strength, and skill. Learning to hit a baseball out of the ballpark requires something more, and it's a challenge. You may never aspire to play for the Yankees, but if you could only hit the ball out of the sandlot in town, you know you would have accomplished something. It's personal.

> **Career News**
>
> Have you ever wondered why meeting planners like to open a session with humor? A few years back John Cleese of Monty Python fame did a series of business training films that were, as you might guess, hilarious. However, each one made serious points. Fun is important in your life!

It's no different with a job. You may never be paid more for taking on a challenge, but you go home at night feeling good about yourself. The perfect job offers challenges for you to go beyond the humdrum of daily work. And it can also offer big challenges that lead you to a lot more than what you might have expected when you first took the job.

But what about fun? Why shouldn't a job be fun? Fun is pleasure and pleasure provides positive reinforcement. Just because you are doing serious work, doesn't mean that you can't have fun. You are going to work for a long time, so you might as well have some fun along the way.

A job must be interesting or it will drive you up the wall. Some very interesting studies have shown the ways that employees themselves go about making a dull job interesting. But if you can find a job that captures and holds your interest, you will be a lot happier and your employer will benefit from your best efforts. It's a win-win situation.

The Company Has Your Respect and the Respect of Others

We all like to be associated with winners. When you work for a company whose CEO is under indictment for mail fraud and the CFO was caught watering the stock, life gets a bit antsy. It may seem that chicanery is more the common mode of doing business these days, but it really isn't. While the devious exploits of some of the Big Guys keep making the headlines, far more companies are run by good people you would be proud to say you worked for.

Pride is more than just working for honest people, it's working for people whose standards are high in everything they do. The company has a social conscience, it cares for the people who work for them, and it cares about the world it operates in. I think you will find that the companies that are sincere about these attitudes walk the walk and they don't spend a lot of time and money tooting their horn about it.

The Company Is Financially Stable

Business cycles will always be with us. It's nice to know that the company you work for can weather the inevitable economic storms without having to cut staff. As I write this chapter, we are in a business downturn and nobody seems to agree whether it's a correction or a recession. It will only be accurately defined after the fact, but in the meantime the papers keep reporting on the downsizing of one company after another. I have discussed this at some length already, but for the purpose of defining the perfect company, you want to work for one that is well enough capitalized so that it doesn't have to raid the cookie jar or cut staff to stay afloat.

Fortunately there is plenty of good financial information available on most publicly held

Right Move

Even if your publicly held employer doesn't have a stock purchase plan, buy a few shares on the open market. This will legally entitle you to all the financial reports published by the company. Read them carefully and see how your employer shapes up relative to competitors and your industry in general.

companies and even on some privately held organizations for you to know whether a blip on the stock exchange will eat your job.

Opportunities for Growth and Promotion

Even small companies can offer potential for growth. In fact, many small companies can often provide better growth opportunities than their larger counterparts. Small companies on the move are generally more attractive to those with an entrepreneurial streak. The risks might be greater than the risks involved in working with a bigger company, but careful risk-taking should really be part of your plan.

Larger companies, however, often have more appeal to those for whom risk might be a problem. At least you know when you start with a larger company what the career path looks like. By their very nature, larger companies must be better structured than smaller companies.

You have to think of growth from several perspectives. First of course, it's important to see what the economic growth potential may be. As you assume more responsibility will you be properly compensated for your efforts? Then you must consider growth from a personal perspective. Will you continue to get more and more responsibility? Are there opportunities to learn within the company structure as well as from company sponsored education and training programs?

Remember that titles are not always indicative of growth or responsibility. Some industries have more vice presidents than others who do the actual work. And moving to a VP managerial spot may not really be what you want. I have coached more than a few people who discovered that managing was not what they really wanted to do for the rest of their lives. These people generally are those with special skills and talents who discover that being in management takes them away from what they really like to do and quite often excel at doing. This seems to be especially true in the scientific and creative fields. There are, of course, exceptions; but I mention this only to make sure that you really know yourself. You did read the chapter on this subject, didn't you?

The Organization Is in a Growth Field

Yesterday's wild idea is today's growth field. Before I started writing this morning, I read an article about how the Dutch are converting their quaint old windmills to wind-driven generators. Just a few years ago many thought those who pushed wind power also believed in flying saucers. If you're looking for a growth area to work in, whether you are a scientist or not, this is it. Who knows where it will be a few years hence, but I'd say this is an area with minimum risk.

Then, of course, there are the more traditional areas that will continue to expand, but probably at a slower rate. And there are those that will wither. It has always been this way in the industrialized world and it will probably continue to be the same for as long as we inhabit Earth. I guess the popular line would be to hitch your wagon to a star. And it is good advice.

Management Is Competent and Well Respected

Sadly, we have seen more than few Big Guys doing the perp walk in handcuffs lately. The casual reader of the business pages of most newspapers could easily draw the conclusion that most of American management cheats, steals, and lies. I think it's fair to say that most people from the top brass down are good, devoted and competent people. I am not trying to whitewash reality. We have seen some pretty egregious behavior in the boardrooms recently.

Anyone who has spent more than a few years working, whether it's at the corporate or shop floor level, knows how good it feels to work for someone you admire and can learn from.

The Employer Is Located in Comfortable Surroundings

A few years ago the cost-cutting and profit-boosting gimmick du jour was to move out of pleasant surroundings to places where costs were a lot lower. Some of these places were really nice, and others showed that the planners had nothing more in mind than to save a buck. Fortunately, this movement didn't gain much headway other than with companies that really had location cost problems.

Quite apart from the comfort factor, many fields are concentrated in specific areas. Book publishing, for example, is in New York. Sure there are good publishers scattered all over the country, but their HR people will readily admit how difficult it is to attract some of the specialized talent they need to move away from New York.

Pleasant surroundings are far more important that most people think. As well they should be.

The Least You Need to Know

- You can find the perfect job, but you must work at keeping it perfect.

- Perfect jobs are most often found in organizations that are growing and that welcome people who think outside the box.

- If you don't respect your management, you will never respect the company you work for.

- Comfortable working conditions can be as important as salary and some of the other more tangible elements.

Index